ANTHONY EDWARDS

PAID TO LIVE THE DREAM

A SEAFARER'S TALE OF LIFE AFLOAT

WITH 30 ILLUSTRATIONS, INCLUDING

5 PAINTINGS BY THE ARTIST IAN BOYD

PAID TO LIVE THE DREAM

ISBN-10: 154722102X
ISBN-13: 978-1547221028

www.anthonyedwards.fr

DEDICATION

For my deceased parents who suffered so much in life and who involuntarily passed on the genes that enabled me to live such a wonderful, unconventional life of triumphs and mishaps.

.

AUTHOR'S NOTE

The original idea for this book was to write about one particular substandard and disaster prone motor yacht that I joined in Belgium and delivered to Cannes via the Belgium and French canals. The mishaps that we endured are almost unbelievable for a brand new vessel. It all began on the first day we left the safety of the port and both rudders snapped off in the North Sea. As I was writing this book, it was suggested to me that I include tales of my errant childhood on a council estate and my years working on Thames steam tugs in my native Gravesend. I was 15 years old when I joined Ship Towage Ltd as cook. In this account I have endeavoured to capture the essence of life aboard with the tough, hardworking tugmen, the ever present potential dangers and the long hours worked, as well as the joys of living through the swinging sixties when the mind-set of "make love not war" predominated. The book also tells of how a chance viewing of a short film clip changed my life and inspired me to seek employment on an ocean racing yacht. This eventually led to me skippering private yachts in the Mediterranean. The events described in this book took place between 1958 and 1971 and with the exception of some names, nothing has been changed. The names of the Thames tugs are factual as are the names of the majority of the tugmen. The name Passing Fancy has replaced the true name of the motor yacht on which I travelled from Belgium to the Mediterranean and the names of some people have been changed.

By the same author

Moving On, which is the sequel to this book.

CONTENTS

CONTENTS i

   LIST OF ILLUSTRATIONS i

   Part 1: STEAM TUGS...1

CHAPTER 1 SERENDIPITY 1

CHAPTER 2 GALLEY DUTIES 9

CHAPTER 3 DEATH AND SEX.......................................21

CHAPTER 4 THE WAY IT WAS 33

CHAPTER 5 ON STANDBY 49

CHAPTER 6 FAREWELL TO STEAM 63

CHAPTER 7 THE TRAVEL BUG BITES 75

   Part 2: PLEASURE YACHTS 91

CHAPTER 1 THE BLOODHOUND EFFECT.........................93

CHAPTER 2 GIVING A FINGER TO THE SEA 101

CHAPTER 3 GETTING SPLICED 109

CHAPTER 4 TIME TO REFLECT 125

CHAPTER 5 FOR BETTER AND FOR WORSE 139

CHAPTER 6 THE PASSING FANCY................................161

CHAPTER 7 A BRIDGE TOO LOW 179

CHAPTER 8 THE HEADBANGER 197

CHAPTER 9 JIGGLY BITS 217

CHAPTER 10 WHOSE BOAT IS IT ANYWAY? 243

CHAPTER 11 CORSICA AND SARDINIA 251

CHAPTER 12 ASCENDING TO THE LIGHT 267

CHAPTER 13 IT'S SUPPOSED TO BE SUNNY 275

CHAPTER 14 THE DAY THE LIGHT WENT OUT 299

CHAPTER 15 AS GOOD AS IT GETS 307

SO, WHAT HAPPENED NEXT? 327

ABOUT THE AUTHOR 331

LIST OF ILLUSTRATIONS

1. An old poster for Watkins tugs 1

2. Map of the Thames Estuary 1

3. The Cervia 10

4. Smokey 11

5. The Challenge 19

6. The Gondia...23

7. The Watercock...27

8. The Atlantic Cock 34

9. The towing hook on Cervia 41

10. Roy 54

11. The Moorcock..68

12. The Ocean Racer 105

13. Managing to stand upright! 120

14. The Iberian Peninsular 138

15. Charlie and me 142

16. The cutter anchored in Majorca 148

17. Belgium 169

18. The French canals 175

19. Motoring through the canals 180

20. The Briare aqueduct. 183

21. Coaxing us through one of the locks..............................187

22. On the slip at Chalon. 198

23. Italy and Corsica..201

24. At anchor off Corsica. 226

25. Struggling to look at a chart! 277

26. In Porto Chervo...284

27. With my instructor at G.M. Motors. 308

28. Twinkle relaxing...316

29. The ketch in Menton harbour.....................................319

30. Making the most of the sun.....................................321

I WOULD LIKE TO THANK THE FOLLOWING:

MARJIE EDWARDS, for her understanding, her patience and her invaluable assistance in the preparation for this book's publication. Without her contribution the book may never have been published.

JILL WALTER, for encouraging me to write this book in the first place and for the valuable assistance she gave me.

MIKE HOUCKHAM, for giving me a guided tour of the Cervia in Ramsgate, the generous amount of time he spent with me afterwards and for his additional valued contributions.

BOB MCKECKNIE, for allowing me to access his amazing memory, for verifying the facts as I remembered them and for supplying me with facts that I had forgotten.

KATHRYN PRESTON, for her research into the archives at G. L. Watson in Liverpool, and for supplying me with information of my old commands.

IAN BOYD, for kindly allowing me to use his paintings of the tugs.

1. An old poster for Watkins tugs

Part 1: STEAM TUGS

There are many points in the history of an invention which the inventor himself is apt to overlook as trifling, but in which posterity never fails to take a deep interest. The progress of the human mind is never traced with such a lively interest as through the steps by which it perfects a great invention; and there is certainly no invention respecting which this minute information will be more sought after, than in the case of the steam-engine. – Sir David Brewster.

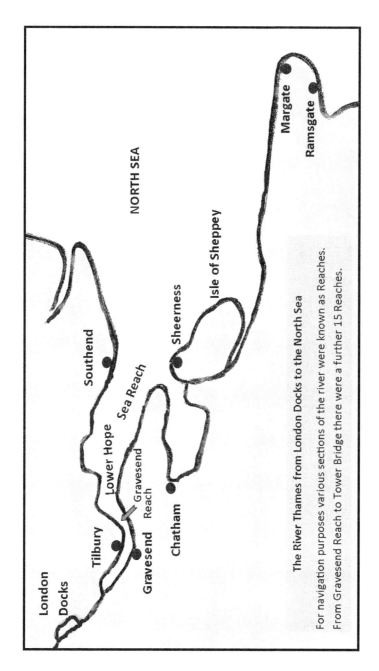

The River Thames from London Docks to the North Sea

For navigation purposes various sections of the river were known as Reaches. From Gravesend Reach to Tower Bridge there were a further 15 Reaches.

2. Map of the Thames Estuary

CHAPTER 1
SERENDIPITY

He had a gun and was heading towards us. He'd already almost shot and killed one of my crew members and he was angry with us because we'd foiled his plan to disappear with thousands of French francs of other people's money. I swung the steering wheel over hard to starboard at the same time as I pushed the throttle lever to maximum. The 40 hp. Johnson outboard motor roared and the speedboat heeled over alarmingly so that the rubbing strake was almost at water level as we spun around in a tight 180° turn. It was another blisteringly hot day on the Cote d'Azur. The sun was shining in a cloudless blue sky and there was a gentle south westerly breeze. The blue-hued Esterel Mountains lined the western coast of the bay of Cannes, the tourists and locals were stretched out on the golden sand beaches and yachts were anchored in sheltered places. But none of that interested us. The only thing on our minds was to reach the safety of Port Pierre-Canto as quickly as possible. How had I ended up in this situation? I'd better go back to where it all began 11 years earlier on a cold, grey winter's day in England.

And so it begins

The design of Gravesend's Clock Tower was based on the Elizabeth Tower that houses Big Ben in the Palace of Westminster. It was dedicated to Queen Victoria to commemorate her 50th year of reign and was a focal point in the town. I was 15 years old, not long left school and wandering aimlessly early one afternoon when I stopped beneath it. I paused there momentarily as a thought flashed into my otherwise unoccupied mind. It's intriguing how an inner voice seems to sometimes communicate with a certainty that is hard to ignore. I hesitated a while, should I or shouldn't I? Oh go for it I decided, as Mahatma Gandhi once said, "The future depends on what you do today". Without further ado, I turned and strutted down Harmer Street. Although work was plentiful for school leavers in the '50s, I was looking for an exciting outdoor activity. I crossed into Royal Pier Road and at the end reached The Royal Terrace Pier. I faltered momentarily as a doubt crossed my mind, then plucked up the courage to continue. I entered and walked along the wooden corridor, glancing at the doors on either side. At the end on the right-hand side, I saw what I was looking for: a door with "Ship Towage Ltd" etched onto a wooden plaque. I tapped nervously on the door and went in. It was a spacious, untidy room with a window overlooking the lower reaches of the Thames and obviously a place of constant activity. A well-built, grey haired man was seated behind a large wooden desk shuffling through some papers spread in front of him. Behind him was a small, slim, dark haired man flitting from one side of the office to the other receiving and relaying messages on VHF radios in a nasally, whining voice. Tug Skippers were calling in to report their current situations and awaiting new orders and the two office agents discussed and made decisions quickly and easily despite the constant cacophony in the background.

Not being sure what to do, I stood motionless and when the grey-haired one, who had the air of being in command, glanced up at me I shyly asked him if they had any job prospects for me. There was no discussion whatsoever. He had barely raised his head as he occupied himself with more important issues and barked,

"Be back here at six o'clock tonight with your kit, you can join as cook." Then he turned to his colleague and gave out further instructions and that was it.

I was taken aback and then excitement took over. Oh, my God. I really wasn't expecting that! Not just a positive response but an instant job offer. I didn't know what kit I would need and didn't like to ask. I exited and rushed back up Harmer Street to the clock tower, turned left for the bus stop and could barely contain my excitement as I waited for the number 46 on the Maidstone and District line to get me home. The bus seemed to take an age to arrive and there were only a few hours remaining until six o'clock. Finally, it appeared in the distance and rolled to a stop where I waited. The queue started shuffling on and I felt like barging past them in my impatience to get home as quickly as possible.

The main economy of Gravesend was from the River Thames and maritime trade. Seventy-five million tonnes of shipping each year would pass through during the 1950's and 60's, importing and exporting around two thousand four hundred million tonnes of meat, sugar, grain, wool, tea, timber and other goods. The Port of London Authority has had a base on the Royal Terrace Pier since the 19th century and it is operational twenty-four hours a day. The pier was built in 1844 and was given the prefix "Royal" in honour of Princess Alexandra of Denmark who arrived there in 1865 on her way to marry the Prince of Wales, later King Edward VII. It had been and still is a departure point for pilot cutters carrying river and sea pilots to the ships sailing in and out of the Thames. The tug control centre was also based there and steam tugs had been operating from there since the mid-19th century. Gravesend also had a sea cadet training college, which was referred to as the Peanut Factory by locals and for some unknown reason, the trainee cadets were known as peanuts.

On the journey home, I was able to reflect on what had just happened. I knew that jobs on the tugs were highly sought after and stayed pretty much within families. Although I had a cousin who worked on them as Mate I had never thought to ask him to help me join the tugs since he was much older than me and for that reason, we weren't close. I also knew that the wages could be exceptionally good.

I was glad when the bus eventually turned into Old Road East where I got off and rushed home. I couldn't wait to tell my parents and start packing my kit. As soon as I arrived home, I immediately blurted out the good news as I rushed through the door.

"Guess what?" I spluttered, "I've got a job on the tugs. I've got to be back there tonight at six o'clock."

Dad was seated in his usual chair beside the fire and in front of the television. He was an Eastender, born in West Ham and spoke in cockney rhyming slang, a language that originated in London's East End around 1840. The reason for its development is not known for certain and many of its expressions are used in everyday parlance although most people are unaware of their origin. For example "Take a butchers" related to butchers hook, meaning look. Rhyming slang uses two or more words from a phrase, an event, a place name or a person's name where the last word rhymes with the commonly used word and then the last word is dropped. Dad, for instance, would always talk of his "titfa" meaning his hat, (tit for tat = hat). I never heard him say the word hat. He wore a whistle (whistle and flute = suit) and I had a skin (skin and blister = sister). I wonder how many people realise that when they refer to somebody as a berk that this is in fact from rhyming slang, the origin of which is Berkely Hunt, a famous fox hunt, which rhymes with a well-known four letter expletive. Blowing a raspberry is another commonly used phrase which is again rhyming slang, raspberry tart = fart. I grew up with this intriguing language, which wasn't widely used in Gravesend but was used by Dad.

Dad had spent years at sea down in the boiler room (stokehold) shovelling coal into the furnaces. When he settled down and took a shore based job, he ended up shovelling more coal into the furnaces at the local gas works. All those years breathing in the coal dust and fumes had left him with emphysema and on top of that, a terrible accident occurred at the gas works that had rendered him disabled. He was shovelling coal into one of the furnaces when it exploded and he took the full force of it. The powerful blast propelled the contents of the furnace straight onto him. Subsequently, he'd spent a prolonged period in hospital throughout much of my earlier years. I was never allowed to go to see him, his wounds were so terrible. He'd needed numerous skin grafts and suffered the loss of one eye, so hadn't worked in years. His movement was restricted due to his breathing difficulties so he didn't do much except bet on the horse races and watch on TV each afternoon to see if he'd struck lucky. How lamentable that after having lived through two world wars and survived two separate torpedo attacks that he should end his days thus. Overcoming challenges can make us stronger but it was not easy watching Dad end his days in that way. "Out of suffering have emerged the strongest souls; the most massive characters are seared with scars," said Kahlil Gibran.

"Well done, son," Dad congratulated me, rising from his chair. He was genuinely pleased for me and straight away offered to rescue his old kit bag from where he kept it upstairs.

"I've got me old kit bag up the apples, I'll go and dig it out for ya," he said as he turned and went to get it.

Since he'd been discharged from the merchant navy a long time ago there was no chance of him ever needing it again himself. He soon came back carrying the soiled, white canvas bag. I went up to my room and brought down some clothes and when we'd finished piling them into the kit bag with some toiletries and food it was only one quarter full and looked a bit ridiculous. A smaller bag would have sufficed but I didn't want to disappoint Dad. Mum hovered in the background with a worried look on her face, not quite knowing how to react.

"Do you want something to eat before you go?" she said, wishing to contribute somehow and be a part of Dad's and my enthusiasm.

"No, I'm OK," I assured her as I rummaged around collecting any other items I considered necessary as six o'clock seemed to be approaching fast.

"You must have something," she insisted. "You must be hungry."

"No thanks, maybe later," I said. I was far too excited and anxious not to miss my deadline to think about stopping to eat.

"Shall I put the kettle on then?"

Mum's life was pretty boring so she didn't have a great deal else to think about. She'd spent most of her youth in hospital in her home town of Liverpool for reasons that were never discussed. I do know that for a long time she was confined to a Bath chair; consequently she'd had very little education. She could be belligerent and stubborn, which was difficult to accept and it was only very much later, almost sixty years on in my life

5

that I understood what a cruel hand she'd been dealt in her own life. In addition to the extended hospitalisation and having an evil mother, she'd also had a child out of wedlock when she was twenty, something that was a disgrace in those days. The child was taken from her, never to be seen or heard of again, so she was basically an unhappy person. Because of her limited education, she lacked the knowledge and confidence to pursue any interests other than occupying herself with looking after the family and the home, but she was a loving mother. It must have been heart-wrenching for Mum to have lived all her life not knowing the whereabouts of her daughter and never daring to speak about her. I have been told that towards the end of her life when she was lying on her hospital bed, with tears in her eyes she said to the nurse "Who is looking after my baby?" At that time nobody understood what she meant. So throughout her life, she never forgot about her baby. I didn't learn of the illegitimate child until 2014, by which time her baby had grown into a 76-year-old woman who tracked me down and finally found her only blood relatives. If, when Mum left this three-dimensional world, her spirit made a transition to another dimension, maybe in that new dimension she is aware that the child she never knew has now discovered who her mother was and has made contact with the children of the mother she never knew. Maybe Mum is now at peace and smiling on us. That's a comforting thought and I have gained a sister. It pains me how much my parents suffered in their lives and to think that they may be reliving it all over again. Over the centuries, many brilliant philosophers in their search for an explanation of the universe came to believe that we return to live the exact same lives over and over again in an endless cycle known as the Eternal Return. This belief can be found in Indian philosophy, Ancient Egypt, Mayans, Aztecs, Pythagoreans and more recently Frederich Nietzsche. It is also implied by modern day quantum cosmology. A similar theme was used in the 1993 film Groundhog Day starring Bill Murray and Andie McDowell.

Mum met Dad when he was in Liverpool during the war as part of HMS Mersey, which was not a ship but the Royal Navy's depot where men of the merchant fleet agreed to serve aboard ships under the Navy to make up for the lack of manpower. They married in 1941 and later Mum moved to Gravesend, staying with one of Dad's six sisters whilst he was away at sea. I was born in 1943 and was two years old before Dad returned home and saw me. It was at that time that they moved in to the top floor of a two bedroomed semi-detached council house nearby, which they shared with another family who occupied the sitting room and kitchen downstairs. After that, the only other child they had was my sister who was born in 1948, by which time the other family had long since moved out.

After Dad and I had put together what we thought I'd need to be properly kitted out, I was ready for my adventure and thus began my seafaring days.

"Shall I make you some sandwiches to take with you?" said Mum as she stood by optimistically in her floral pinafore.

"OK," I eventually agreed. It seemed the kindest thing to do and off she went to the kitchen, happy in the knowledge that at least I wouldn't go hungry.

As Dad was such an experienced seaman it made sense for me to profit from his abundance of knowledge.

"Any advice for me, Dad?" I asked as I was leaving.

He stood before me and looked me in the eye as he searched his memory for the most pragmatic counsel that he could offer, then, in a serious voice, his words of wisdom came forth.

"If yer git seasick," he said, "and yer find a little red lump in yer mowf as yer 'eaving yer guts out over the side, whadever yer do don' spit it aht."

"Why not?" I questioned.

"'Cause it'll be the roof of yer arse," he said.

There is an English proverb that says, "Write down the advice of him who loves you, though you like it not at present" but I doubt that the author of that proverb had anything like Dad's words in mind when he said it.

So with Dad's philosophical offering I left, not forgetting, of course, Mum's sandwiches. On many future occasions, however, Dad's words of advice, although of no comfort or practical use, would echo in my mind as I hung vomiting over the ship's side wishing I could die.

.

CHAPTER 2
GALLEY DUTIES

Relief Crew No. 4

Feeling nervous and excited, with Dad's kit bag slung over my shoulder, I set off and took the bus back to the clock tower. My only previous knowledge of anything maritime was hiring a rowing boat on a nearby lake with my best friend Tommy for half an hour on Sunday afternoons. As for cooking, apart from helping Mum to shell peas in the kitchen sometimes, I was a complete novice. Mum cooked excellent meals for us, always using fresh ingredients and I'd enjoyed eating whatever she'd prepared. I was then and still am an enthusiastic eater and there was very little that I didn't consume with relish. I just loved food. Unusually, as a child, I'd enjoyed reading an old copy of Mrs Beaton's cookery book but that was probably due to the fact that it was the only book that I can ever recall seeing at home. Dad started working as a very young boy, so like Mum had little education and consequently little interest in reading anything other than the News of the World and the Herald for his horse racing form.

I trundled down Harmer Street for the second time that day, feeling self-conscious as I lugged the kit bag that was almost as big as I was. It must have been an unusual sight because very few people used wartime kit bags anymore but it was dark by then and there were few people around to notice. At 18.00 hrs exactly I was back in the Ship Towage office on the Royal Terrace Pier. The same two people were still involved in the same hustle and bustle of the office, issuing orders over the radios to the tugs. My excitement was so great that it overpowered my feelings of unease. Once again, there was very little communication from either of them, just a brief instruction from the grey haired one sat behind his desk. When the radio conversations fell silent for a second or two, he looked up and said,

"Go down to the pontoon and go aboard the Cervia, she's waiting for you."

3. The Cervia

Off I went down the brow, a sloping wooden walkway with iron railings either side, to the floating pontoon. I became aware of how much colder it was in the breeze the nearer I got to the river. Lights shone through the port holes of the Cervia as she lay moored alongside. I looked at the prominent black funnel with its red band a third of the way down, silhouetted against the backdrop of the night sky and the lights on the opposite shore. There was a solitary figure standing on deck by an open door. Lights were visible on the various craft making their way up and down river, with the occasional steam whistles screeching the intentions of each vessel to avoid collisions. The smells were a mixture of the sea and smoke. When I reached the tug she was moored facing up river against the tide, held alongside by creaking sisal ropes as they took the strain of the water rushing past at six knots. Strung around the black painted bulwarks were large rubber tyres to provide protection whenever she came alongside other craft and I could hear the throbbing of the engine. The man standing on deck was smiling; he greeted me and took my bag as I clambered over the side onto the steel deck.

4.Smokey

He was well built, balding and wore glasses. He introduced himself to me as Smokey. The smell of diesel accompanied by the rumbling and hissing of the steam engine became more prominent. As soon as I was aboard I heard the ring of the brass telegraph alerting the engine room to stand by. A Deckhand appeared through the open door.

"Let go," the Skipper shouted from the bridge and he leant over to watch the deck hand flick the mooring rope expertly from the mooring post.

"All gone Skip," the Deckhand said.

The telegraph rang once more indicating slow ahead and a corresponding needle on the engine room telegraph did the same. The Engineer opened up the wheel sending more steam into the cylinder heads and the engine thumped into life, turning the giant propeller and we steamed away from the pontoon heading out to the middle of the river. Smokey told me that

11

we were going to the King George V docks in London and then he led me down the ladder to show me the cabin that I would be sharing with him. Only a few hours previously I had been strolling through town without a care in the world, never imagining for one moment that I would find myself in such a situation. I was jubilant.

The tugs in the fleet at that time were steam driven and mostly coal-fired. The Cervia was a relatively recent addition and was oil fired. She was built towards the end of the Second World War having been commissioned by the Navy but was never required, so became part of the Watkins tug fleet in 1946. Her gross tonnage was 233 and she was 34.4 metres in length. She was the first tug that I had ever been on and was one of the most modern of the fleet. In 1954, four years before I joined her, at eleven o'clock in the evening of 25 October, she was towing the P & O liner Arcadia stern first out of Tilbury docks. There were two other tugs in attendance on the bow. As the Cervia crossed the Arcadia's stern with a slack towrope, the ship put her engines into ahead to avoid a collision with another liner waiting to enter the docks. The towrope was pulled tight and the Cervia was girted (pulled over and sank) as a result of the towrope being unable to be released quickly enough. Five crew members, including the Captain, were drowned and the search for the bodies continued until dawn the next day. My cousin Billy was one of only three who survived. Two days later she was re-floated and taken to Ramsgate shipyard for repairs. Today, the Cervia is one of just two of the steam tugs remaining from the original fleet and was, in fact, the very last steam tug ever to operate in the UK. She is currently moored in Ramsgate Royal Harbour where she is being lovingly restored by a dedicated and enthusiastic team of volunteers led by Mike Houckham. Mike is an ex tugman himself, like his father and grandfather before him. He had also served on the Cervia whilst he was a member of relief crew No. 7. She is now one of the very few steamships still in existence and is open to the public.

Once we were under way, Smokey, the caterer and Leading Hand, began outlining my duties.

"This is your bunk." He pointed to the upper berth.

"You can sleep from ten o'clock each night until six in the morning," he told me.

The cabin was small, comfortable, deliciously warm and permeated with the smell of diesel, hemp and a mixture of other unrecognised odours. After Smokey left for the engine room, there wasn't much for me to do except unpack a few bits and pieces and wander around before getting into my bunk. I didn't sleep at all that night. As I lay in the darkened cabin, fully clothed, covered with a rough blanket, I could hear the deck crew running along the decks, tow ropes being hauled aboard, bumps and a slight roll each time we steamed alongside ships and lock sides. Steam whistles blew, communicating signals between ships and tugs and other ships. The telegraph rang over and over again; the Engineer increased or decreased the engine revolutions accordingly and the 1000 hp. triple expansion steam engine thumped and hissed. Occasionally the anchor chain rattled and banged as it shot out of the chain locker when the heavy anchor was dropped, and we heeled over at a steep angle each time the weight was taken on the tow ropes. Smokey came into the cabin to sleep for a few hours when the Chief Engineer relieved him, then left again when he was next on watch. I found the whole experience exhilarating and couldn't resist climbing out of my bunk from time to time to peek out on deck and soak in the atmosphere.

The next day at 06.00 hrs prompt, reality checked in. I was shown around the tug and my duties were outlined in more detail by the Mate, Ken.

"You can start by scrubbing the cabin floors and the table, then collect and wash up all the mugs and plates that are hanging around. We do our own breakfast and afterwards, you can clear away and wash up again. Smokey will see you later and explain what he wants you to cook for the midday meal." he said.

I was shown where to find a galvanised bucket, hot water, and scrubbing brushes etc. and told to get on with it - and I did exactly that. As I scrubbed the wooden floor and table, members of the crew came in and out of the cabin and chatted to me and I learned that I was now a member of Relief Crew No. 4. Nobody asked me my name. I was referred to only as "Cook" or "Cookie."

The total crew consisted of Skipper and Chief Engineer who had their own cabins apart from the rest of the crew. The Leading Hand and two Firemen completed the below deck crew and the Mate, Deckhand and Third Hand were in charge of above decks. Along with other relief crews, our role was to go aboard and take over the running of any of the fleet of tugs where the permanent crew were due time off. Time off, in those days, was sometimes three nights a week if we were lucky. We were supposed to work no more than 48 continuous hours without a spell ashore but this was flexible and always to the advantage of the company. What was referred to as a weekend off once a month could sometimes be from late Saturday evening until 06.00 hrs on Monday morning. Working hours had to be flexible to fit in with the tides and shipping arrivals and departures. As Cook though, I could at least curl up in my bunk every night from 22.00 hrs till 06.00 hrs and even if I didn't sleep too well because of the constant activity, at least I was resting.

The layout and accommodation on each tug varied. Very few had the luxury of the enclosed wheelhouse that was fitted to the Cervia. The other, older tugs had an open, exposed bridge with a small canvas dodger providing limited shelter from the elements but that wasn't to affect me until later when I was transferred to the deck department. My area of interest as Cook was the galley and each one had its own peculiarities. Some galleys were small with hardly any real work surfaces and just about enough room to turn around. The meals for the crew of eight strong, muscular tug men were mostly prepared on cast iron, coal burning stoves in a small, hot galley. Some crews would have a rota with each crew member taking turns as caterer. Sometimes one person would hold the position permanently and sometimes it would be the Cook himself who collected the money from all crew members and decided what would be on each menu. Everybody on board began on the tugs at a young age as Cook. I was fortunate to receive my initial training from Smokey, a keen caterer. He had an extraordinary interest in providing wholesome food and was a gifted and enthusiastic cook. Everything was bought fresh and prepared with no fancy gadgets. I learned a great deal from him and developed a real interest in cooking that has continued throughout my life. It still gives me great pleasure to prepare food of all descriptions and I enjoy devouring the results.

I only had to prepare the main meal at midday but other crews might expect the Cook to prepare more. Typical English fare of main course and desert was served; continental cuisine hadn't yet taken off in the U.K. in 1958, and even if it had it's hard for me to imagine the eight hungry, hardworking tuggies tucking into sole à la bonne femme in preference to a good meat duff. The main meal in the middle of the day had to be ready on time to facilitate the engine room crew's change of watch. Deck crew ate as and when they could relieve each other if towing or steaming up or down river. I was always expected to prepare lots of fresh vegetables and meat and standard desserts of that era. There was no thermostat on the stoves of coal burning tugs so controlling the heat wasn't always easy. I had to control the amount of coal I put in the firebox, adjust the airflow and lift and replace the hotplates. With the inevitable kettle of boiling water on the stove, plus a number of pots of cooking vegetables and maybe a roast or pie in the oven, it could get very hot indeed in the confined space.

To keep the fire burning, I shovelled coal from a coal bucket, a modified oil drum with a rope handle, into the fire box. Water was pumped up by hand to keep the kettle topped up as fast as the crew were emptying it for the endless pint mugs of tea and the saucepans were shuttled to different sections of the stove to try and get them either boiling or simmering. My body dripped with perspiration. The only respite from the heat was to stick my head out of the door and enjoy the cool outside air for a few minutes as I watched the towing process in operation. Working under the expert tuition of Smokey the caterer though, I became quite an accomplished cook and was then mostly left to my own devices. Much to my discomfort, the rest of the crew would occasionally tell me and members of other crews how good they thought I was. I would be overcome with red-cheeked embarrassment but secretly pleased and flattered and knowing how much my efforts were appreciated, I was encouraged to improve even more. I am so grateful to Smokey for his guidance and infectious enthusiasm. There is an Irish proverb that says, "Laughter is the brightest in the place where the food is." and when we were moored to the buoy between towing operations and sat around the table together for the meals, there was always an abundance of laughter and good humoured banter.

Washing up the mountain of crockery, cutlery and pots after meals was done in one of the all-purpose galvanised buckets using lots of soda. The bucket was filled with water using the hand pump and then I would plunge one of the cast iron hot plates directly from the stove into the bucket. The water sizzled and bubbled like crazy as it was instantly heated. An effective way of removing any obstinate or burnt areas from the pans was to scour them with ashes from the fire. To keep the stove hot, the coal bucket needed constant replenishing. I'd take it from the galley along the deck to the fiddley door, lower it on a rope down into the stokehold in the bowels of the tug for the Fireman to fill with coal and then I'd haul it back up and take it into the galley. If the Fireman was disinclined or if he was too busy feeding the furnaces, he'd refuse to cooperate, which meant that I had to descend the hot, metal ladder into the very hot stokehold and fill the bucket myself, then climb the ladder to haul it back up. This was exasperating when it happened in the middle of cooking a meal.

Traipsing the docks

Shopping was time-consuming and tiring. Since I was only required to cook the main meal at midday, the caterer would give me the list of what was needed to feed the nine of us for the next couple of days and each individual crew member would add his own requirements for preparing the additional meals. When the list was completed I'd disembark with a hessian sack or two and set off in search of everything. We always needed lots of potatoes, fresh vegetables, meat, bread, cans, prepared food, bottles of drinks, newspapers, cigarettes and so on. The weight of the sack increased considerably as I continued on my way until finally, it was sometimes as much as I could do to carry it back.

Mostly the shopping would be done in our home port of Gravesend, where we had our own known suppliers. At other times, since we were constantly steaming up and down the Thames and locking into different docks, I would be sent ashore with my sacks in a place I didn't know at all.

There were many working docks on the Thames in the 1950s and 60s covering a total of 2000 acres. They were originally built to accommodate the increasing amount of trade in the 19th century and locking into and steaming through them on the tug, passing through the various cuttings, looked complicated to me. I found out just how complicated when I had to find my way around on foot to do the shopping. I would steel myself for a long, perplexing, circuitous walk in search of the way out through the dock gates. When I eventually arrived at the exit, I would often be in a remote area nowhere near a town or shops, so that involved yet more walking or even bus rides. Sometimes, it would take so long that when I ultimately returned, tired, fed up and exhausted from carrying the heavy sacks on my back, I would discover that the tug was no longer where I had left her or where I thought she might be. She could have been ordered to another area in the same dock, or sometimes to a completely different dock. So off I'd go again, utterly disheartened, in search of her. I often didn't know where to begin looking. The worst case scenario, which was rare, would be that she had been ordered to return to the home port of Gravesend. Then I would have to find a means of getting from London to Gravesend before she left again for somewhere else.

On a dry or reasonable day it was bad enough trudging around loaded down with the weight of the shopping, trying to find my way through the gigantic concrete maze with my visibility virtually blocked by the huge ships moored to the quays and no way to contact the crew. When it was raining, windy, snowing, cold or any combination of the aforementioned, with my vision impaired, it was utterly wretched. I would walk what to me seemed like miles, getting soaking wet and cold, bent double with the weight of the sacks cutting into my shoulders. As the search continued, my fingers would get cramped from holding on tightly to the sacks, which got heavier by the minute and pressed me down. I often needed to stop and put the sacks on the ground to allow the blood to circulate through my fingers and shoulders before swapping to the other shoulder and continuing on what ostensibly could be a long haul. Sometimes I would be able to hitch a ride on another tug and even occasionally, a lighter, if the distance was too great to walk, such as when going to another dock. It was the task of the Lightermen to transport their cargos to their destination by any means appropriate, either using the current itself or getting a tow from a tug, so it wasn't a choice of preference for me, but rather one of desperation. With imagination and determination I'd eventually reach the elusive vessel. As soon as I'd boarded it would be straight to work unpacking and probably preparing mugs of tea for the crew. If I had been gone too long and meal time was imminent, there would be a ravenous crew to feed, so there would be no time to rest. The stove would need stoking, maybe coal to be got from the stokehold and inevitably a mess to clear away if the crew had been too busy to occupy themselves with galley chores during my absence.

No sympathy

I very soon realised that my youth and inexperience didn't entitle me to any special privileges or sympathy. The bare wood mess tables were worn and grooved from years of being scrubbed. One morning whilst scrubbing rather too vigorously, the lateral edge of my thumb slid along the grooved surface and I winced from a stabbing pain as a splinter shot in underneath the nail. As the day wore on and the discomfort increased, the thumb throbbed, reddened and started to swell. That evening when we were moored up to the buoy, I was lying in my bunk nursing the painful thumb and stupidly made the mistake of mentioning it to the crew. I was immediately grabbed, pulled out of the bunk, stretched out and pinned down on the table while two of the crew took turns at trying to dig out the splinter, which was well and truly embedded. They had no possibility of removing it as it had penetrated too deeply. No matter how hard I struggled and yelled they kept me firmly on the table. I had no alternative other than to suffer and wait whilst they prodded and poked, which just made the pain even worse, much to their amusement. I learned very quickly to suffer in silence after that.

Fortunately, the next day we received orders to take the rest of the day off when the permanent crew boarded. The thumb was not looking good - it was terribly swollen and looking a strange colour. When I arrived home my worried mother decided that I should go to the hospital so off she trotted with me in tow. A lovely, gentle mannered nurse took me to a trolley, brought me a hot, sweet cup of tea then bathed my thumb for a while in disinfectant before removing the splinter. She was surprised at the length of it and so was I. It had travelled all the way to the knuckle and presumably broke off there because my thumb was bent over the scrubbing brush, preventing it from travelling any further. She placed it on a pad of cotton wool and gave it to me as a memento. In my ignorance, I took it with me the following day to show it to my fellow crew buddies. Nobody was the least bit interested. The general attitude was of complete indifference. All things considered, life aboard a Thames steam tug in the 1950's and 60's was hard work for a 15-year-old boy but I absolutely loved it! And as Benjamin Franklin once said, "It is the working man who is the happy man. It is the idle man who is the miserable man."

5. The Challenge

CHAPTER 3
DEATH AND SEX

Man overboard

We were moored to the buoy aboard the Challenge, which I knew well, having relieved the permanent crew many times. She was one of the Dick and Page tugs, built in 1931, and is the second vessel from the Ship Towage fleet that is still afloat and able to be visited by the public today. She is listed on the National Register of Historic Vessels and known for the role she played in Operation Dynamo, evacuating the Allied troops from Dunkirk in May/June 1940. She was converted from coal to oil burner at Sheerness in 1964, was laid up in 1971 and was the last steam tug to serve on the Thames. She has since been restored, is operational once more and has been exhibited in London, Liverpool, Southampton, Bristol, and other locations in the UK and abroad and is now owned and cared for by the Dunkirk Little Ships Restoration Trust. The most memorable thing about the Challenge was that she was inundated with cockroaches, more so it seemed than the other tugs. I made the mistake once of swigging from a can of Coca-Cola that I'd left lying around open and was rewarded with a mouthful of hard, lumpy cockroaches. Cockroaches were an annoyance generally, on another occasion at a later date when I was working on deck, I was in a hurry to put on my rubber gloves to manhandle a steel cable, this was necessary because any stray metal strands could rip your hands open as the cable slid rapidly through them. I'd left them in a warm place and a small colony of cockroaches had decided to make them home. When I shoved my hands in, the disgusting little creatures scrambled up my arms and I couldn't get the gloves off quick enough. Both occasions produced howls of laughter from the rest of the crew.

I was resting from my cook duties in the cabin of the Challenge when I heard the radio speaker crackle and was thrilled to hear the announcement that I was to join the Gondia temporarily as Junior Deckhand, commonly referred to as Third Hand. It was customary after a couple of years in the galley for Cooks to be promoted to Third Hand either in the same crew, or almost always a different one. The Gondia was a coal burning steam tug, older than the Cervia by twenty years and had been part of the Watkins fleet, which had amalgamated with Gamecock tugs and Dick and Page tugs to form Ship Towage Ltd. In total there were twelve Watkins tugs, five of them based at Woolwich, and the remaining seven moored onto a buoy upriver from the Royal Terrace Pier. The rest of the fleet, four gamecock tugs and four Dick and page tugs moored on two buoys downriver. The Gondia ended her days in 1966 when she was laid up and scrapped shortly after I left the service of Ship Towage Ltd. to seek a different lifestyle. My time on the Gondia was enjoyable as I learned the deck routine in the company of a fine bunch of men and working as part of a team I began to feel more like one of them. I did miss my old crew mates of Relief Crew No. 4 though. After having worked for almost two years in close confinement with such colourful men, it's inevitable that a rich sense of camaraderie would develop.

One particularly appreciated aspect of this move was that I would have my own bunk and a locker where I could leave my personal items whenever I went home for time off. Most permanent crew members would keep their lockers securely locked so the relief crews had to make do as best they could, carrying their gear with them wherever they went. All relief crews had access to a store on the pier where their basic food supplies - flour, sugar, tea etc., plus working clothes and wet weather gear were kept in a large communal box that had to be carried by two crew members to wherever they were sent. If they were ordered to London to relieve one of the London-based tugs, this large, heavy box had to be carried to Gravesend railway station to take the train to Woolwich and finally the ferry to Woolwich pier where the London-based tugs moored.

6. The Gondia

If the vessel being relieved was in a dock, things became more complicated. For example, perhaps it would be necessary to get off the train at Greenwich, carry the box down the spiral staircase into the Greenwich foot tunnel and cart it all the way along to the next lot of steps going upwards and then on to wherever the tug happened to be.

It was on the Gondia that I had my first personal encounter with the danger involved in towing. This happened very late one night whilst towing a ship into the King George V dock. The blackness of the night was broken by an array of lights from the docks and passing shipping. The pilot on the ship's bridge blew his whistle to direct the tugs, that responded by blasting the same signal on their steam whistles. The Skippers swung the steering wheels over to take up their appropriate positions and rang the brass telegraphs to the engine rooms for the desired engine power. The propellers of the vessels churned up the water as the tow ropes were stretched to take the weight. Deck crews were in position on the aft decks wrapped in warm winter clothing and the Skippers were shouting out orders to them. The Gondia was positioned on the ship's port bow, one of the two bow tugs that were helping swing the ship around to starboard to enter the lock. Two other tugs were attached to her stern. Another ship was anchored just down river from us with tugs in attendance waiting to enter the same dock. Next thing we knew was that the open channel 16 on the VHF sets all around burst into life reporting man overboard. The towing cable on one of the stern tugs had snapped and like a demented snake, whiplashed back along the side deck at an unimaginable speed, snatching up a Deckhand and flicking him over the side before anybody had had time to take stock of the situation. All available tugs in the vicinity scrambled to the scene communicating with each other on the VHF radios. It was pitch black apart from the navigation lights visible on dozens of craft navigating their way up and down river and the water was in turmoil from the wash of propellers and the six-knot tide ebbing out to sea. The search went on and on in vain. The Deckhand was never found. A hush persisted among us for some time after that as we worked throughout the night each in our own thoughts. As the river water ebbed away it took our colleague with it. "Disappearances happen. Pain goes phantom. Blood stops running. And people, people fade away." Anon.

In flagrante delicto

The refitting of our fleet of tugs was carried out at Ramsgate until 1961, after which time it took place at Sheerness. My first visit to the Ramsgate slipway was aboard the Gondia and I had the most wonderful time. We set off from Gravesend on a warm, cloudy day to navigate the confusing passage through the Thames Estuary where many buoys are used to mark the numerous, constantly shifting sandbanks. These buoys are regularly re-sited to correspond with the movement of the sandbanks and the channels between them are shallow. The tides are fickle and there are very few reliable landmarks because of the low lying land. By the time we'd cleared the estuary and entered into the gentle rolling of the North Sea swell, the sky had cleared. It was a beautiful, warm sunny day and when Ramsgate Harbour entrance appeared, we steamed to a safe distance and dropped anchor with the town in view. We sat on the aft deck sunning ourselves as we rolled gently,l waiting for the tide to turn in our favour so that we could proceed to the slipway. The town looked inviting from the sea and I contemplated the pleasures that may be awaiting me. Ramsgate has the United Kingdom's only Royal Harbour, that title being bestowed upon it by King George IV during a visit in 1821, as recognition of the kindness of Ramsgate's inhabitants. It served as a major departure point during both the Napoleonic wars and the Dunkirk evacuation and for many years has been a base for cross channel ferries. Ramsgate is well-known for its Ramsgate Main Sands that has attracted tourists since the 19th century when it gained a reputation as one of England's best-known seaside towns.

When the tide was right for us, we steamed into the harbour, heading towards the Clock House where we slowly nudged our way onto the waiting cradle. We were securely roped into position and hauled up onto the slipway. A number of spectators gathered to watch the operation. I was on the foredeck whilst we were being winched into position and noticed two attractive girls taking an interest in me. Before the winching was finished I'd already arranged a date with them for that evening, which impressed my fellow crew members. I knew straight away that I was going to enjoy Ramsgate. The Gondia was winched up to dry land; wooden posts were placed against the hull on each side and secured in position by hammering in wooden wedges. A ladder was placed in position and securely lashed. There wasn't a lot for the crew to do during the refit so they packed their bags and took the train back home to Gravesend until the refit had been finished. I, however, had no reason to leave. I didn't know the town and it beckoned me to come and explore. The slipway was ideally situated at the edge of the town, with pubs and shops directly opposite. My evening with the two girls was fun but that's all it was, one fun-filled evening. I was 17 years old, a young, virile teenager and it wasn't long at all before I'd met a young, pretty brunette called Sally. She was slightly smaller than me and had a well-developed body. She showed me around and shared with me my all too short stay. I had the time of my life.

The crew accommodation on the Gondia was in the fore part of the vessel. A door on each side deck opened into a passageway with the wood panelled Chief Engineer's cabin on the starboard side and the wood panelled Skipper's cabin on the port side. (The Skipper's and Chief Engineer's cabins throughout the fleet were opulent in comparison to the very basic crew's cabins.) The galley was amidships. Opposite the galley, a ladder descended forward into the crew cabin. My bunk was the top forward one on the port side and it was there that Sally and I would lie, enjoying passionate nights together in complete privacy. One night we were startled by banging and raucous shouting outside. Footsteps clunked on the rungs of the ladder, then on the steel deck. We had invaders. The steel entrance door clanged open and a gang of noisy men spilled into the passageway above. We both shot bolt upright, horrified at what might be happening. Whoever they were, they were not only already aboard but were inside and descending the ladder into the cabin. I have never been the bravest person and the thought of having to defend the lovely Sally filled me with dread. Or had her father discovered our affair and sent in the heavies to deal with me? I quaked at the vision of them all snarling at me as I stood before them, a scrawny, naked teenager attempting to look threatening. I looked directly in the eyes of the first one.

"You dirty, lucky little fucker," said Fred the Fireman when he saw Sally and me in the bunk clutching the blanket around ourselves. The rest of the crew came down one by one. Feeling like a very naughty boy caught misbehaving, I gave them a nervous grin and they immediately erupted into a chorus of ribald comments, albeit in very good humour. Unbeknown to me the crew had decided to return in expectation of the Gondia's refit soon being finalised. The atmosphere became relaxed and light hearted from then on and the poor hapless Sally had little choice but to endure the ribald comments for another hour or so until they'd fallen asleep. The second Fireman, Reg, had the bunk below mine and thankfully he had the decency to pass us our clothes that we'd left on his bunk. With a combined effort, Sally and I, using a little ingenuity and contortion, struggled into our clothes beneath the blanket. It wasn't practical for Sally to make her way home alone so she stayed with me until morning when sadly I had to bid her farewell, as we were due to leave for Gravesend the following day. She was a lovely girl, and we'd had some good times together. We quietly crept out of the cabin and descended the ladder to the quay. We hugged and kissed one more time and then she turned and walked away, turning briefly to wave goodbye. I never saw her again. The American writer Henry Miller said "Sex is one of the nine reasons for reincarnation. The other eight are unimportant." From the deck, the Skipper, Cyril, saw us on the ground below and kept his council but I was later to find just how wary he was of me when I was in the vicinity of females he knew. Sadly, the next day, we rolled down the slipway and set course for Gravesend. From that moment on my reputation as a good cook faded into the distance of time and was replaced for the duration of my final years on the Thames steam tugs as a smooth operating lothario.

Silly buggers

My next temporary posting as Third Hand was on the steam tug Water Cock. The Water Cock was originally part of the Gamecock fleet. She was built in 1923 so was even older than the Gondia, slightly smaller, and equally relied on coal to power her boilers. She was also scrapped in 1966. I didn't spend long aboard this vessel but long enough to get to know and befriend John, one of the two Firemen aboard.

7. The Watercock

27

We socialised and sometimes holidayed together. We were two young men, who did crazy things. We had many laughs on our escapades ashore but what happened on board one evening could have had serious consequences. We were moored on the buoy in the Gravesend Reach awaiting the arrival of a ship that we were to accompany to the London docks and tow into position. Part of my duties as Third Hand was to act as lookout and signal to the Skipper when the ship was in sight. This allowed the Deckhand and Skipper to rest before they accompanied the ship on the upriver run whilst the Mate and I slept.

It was a flood tide so we were bows on to the wide stretch of river from which the ship would approach. I was standing around shivering, wandering up to the foredeck from time to time to see if I could see the approaching lights. John was on his four-hour shift. To keep warm, we decided to hide away in the fore part of the vessel that was reserved normally for the Skipper and Chief Engineer. There were two entrances, one on the port side and one on the starboard side, with a central ladder leading down to the cabins below. There were no lights because we didn't want to spoil my night vision. We started blabbering away about mindless things, chuckling like a couple of silly little children and feeling mischievous. John disappeared to the crew cabin aft and came back with a large, grotesque rubber glove covered in hairs and warts and made up to resemble something out of a horror movie. If you were alone on a dark, tranquil night and you found that unexpectedly clamping down on your shoulder you could well be in need of a clean pair of pants afterwards. When we heard the Skipper coming up from his cabin below, we nipped out to the starboard side deck. The Skipper leant out of the port side to see if there was any sign of the ship approaching, obviously getting a bit agitated as the arrival time drew near. Seeing no sign of the ship, he turned to quietly disappear back down to his cabin.

Our focus on the hand and things supernatural must have opened up a channel invoking an impish demon to possess John because as the Skipper put his foot on the first step, John crept up behind him on tiptoes and clamped the repulsive looking glove on the Skipper's shoulder. In the security of his personal area, the unsuspecting Skipper stopped dead in his tracks, turned and saw the monstrous hand gripping him. He squealed and leapt sideways in horror banging into the support at the side of the steps. A little whimper was audible as his legs momentarily buckled under him from fright and he grasped the handrail to arrest his flight to the bottom of the steps. When he'd recovered from the shock and his face returned to its normal shade of pink, he composed himself remarkably rapidly and looked at John towering over him, his arm outstretched, wiggling the rubber glove with a triumphant grin on his face. I was expecting a vitriolic outburst with the threat of instant dismissal but the Skipper was surprisingly forgiving, no doubt a wee bit embarrassed. The only reaction was a feeble,

"Oh, you frightened me," then he descended to his cabin.

John came back out on deck and we both sidled off tittering childishly. He was the classic, tall, dark, handsome man who girls found hard to resist and he was great fun to be around. I can say, immodestly, that I was considered a good looking young man myself so got along well with the opposite sex. With other friends, we decided one time to take a holiday at Butlins Holiday Camp which, in the early 60s, bore no resemblance to today's Butlins. John had dated one of the Bluecoats almost before we'd finished unpacking. In fact, we all did rather well with the opposite sex that week. One of our friends convinced a waitress to move in with him. When we called by to check out what had been going on, we noticed that she'd left some clothes on the bed in her absence. As the conversation progressed, we began the inevitable chuckling and managed to coerce our friend to dress up in the female attire. The end result was a complete transformation. We encouraged him to parade around in an effeminate manner and as he reached the door, one of us quickly opened it and the rest of us shoved him outside, then slammed and locked the door. It was bad enough that he was standing around in a woman's clothes in full view of everybody but it didn't help his situation when he began banging on the door, shouting and pleading to be let in. That was a foolish thing to have done because it only attracted the attention of everybody who happened to be in their chalets. Well, I call them chalets but in reality, they more resembled prison cells. There were two rows of them, one on either side of the central recreational area and two tiers high. The resulting shouts, jeers and wolf-whistles only brought even more campers to the area to find out what the fuss was about. He had no other choice at that stage but to accept the adulation and put on a show for the enthusiastic observers. I don't know if he ever forgave us.

....

One time when we were moored up at the Royal Terrace Pier, we were the outside tug; the innermost tug was the Contest, with the Gondia between us. The Gondia had received orders over the VHF set to steam to Tilbury docks on the opposite side of the river to Gravesend. I heard her telegraph ring alerting the Engineer to stand by, followed by the answering ring from the engine room. Our Skipper went to the bridge and rang our telegraph for standby so that we could cast off allowing the Gondia to leave. I went to the foredeck to flick our rope off the Gondia's mooring post.

"Let go aft," the Gondia's Skipper, Cyril, ordered the Deckhand, then

"Let go Fo'rad," to the Third Hand. He leant over from the bridge to verify that we had cast off from him and saw me on the Water Cock's foredeck.

"Hello, you dirty little bugger," he said good-naturedly, remembering our time in Ramsgate.

"Hello Skip," I replied, smiling.

As he turned back to take the steering wheel and ring for slow ahead I happened to mention that I'd seen his daughter in town the week previously.

"Oh, I met your daughter last week," I said.

"Hold that rope, don't let go," he yelled to his foredeck hand. "DON'T LET THAT FUCKING ROPE GO!" he repeated even louder than before. He shot back to the side of the bridge and glared down at me.

"What did you say?" he demanded.

"I met your daughter in town last week," I said.

"Where, when, what did you say to her?"

"Nothing really, I just chatted with her for a while, that's all," I said.

"Are you sure?"

"Yes, I just spent a few minutes chatting with her, then she carried on down the street," I told him.

"Well, that's all right then and you make sure you stay away from her. I don't want you anywhere near her you dirty little sod."

By that time a few crew members from both tugs had wandered up to see what the holdup was and when they heard the conversation they looked at me with knowing smiles on their faces. Cyril, reassured that I hadn't tried to bed his delightful daughter, relaxed and smiled at me again before giving the orders to finally cast off.

CHAPTER 4
THE WAY IT WAS

Carry on regardless

After a few months, the time came for me to be transferred to another tug on a permanent basis and I was ordered to join the Atlantic Cock. Some of my most memorable times were aboard this vessel and the next tug that I would join, the Moorcock. Once again, more aged than the Cervia but rather more recent than the previous two vessels, the Atlantic Cock was built in 1932 and continued to operate until she was scrapped in 1970. She was also coal fired. As much as I loved the deck work, there were many times during the cold, sleepless days and nights when I envied the cook, snuggled up in a warm bunk or preparing meals in a nice warm galley. I often envied the engine room crew too as they had a shift of four hours on duty, then four hours off, whereas us Deckhands had to grab time off and sleep as and when we could, day or night. At that stage in my career, I could have chosen to either continue with deck work or join the engine room personnel as a Fireman. The advantages of the latter were the aforementioned four hours on duty and an assured four hours rest before going back down into the stokehold.

The wages were also higher but neither of those perquisites, as appealing as they were, were enough to make me want to head in that direction. Deck work in the open air was always what had attracted me despite being forever tired due to the long hours and lack of sleep.

8. The Atlantic Cock

I had been a small, weedy teenager when I'd started on the tugs but as Third Hand, I started to develop muscles that I never knew I had and with that came an accompanying increase of strength and toughness. The outdoor life suited me well and has done ever since. My principle duties as Third Hand were on the foredeck operating the steam driven windlass and anchor. It was a very physical job, throwing and hauling hawsers, mooring ropes and heaving lines, especially when they were heavy with water, which they often were, either from the rain or because we'd failed to lasso a mooring post and the rope had fallen in the river. We had to then smash them on the decks to try and get rid of the excess water. One night, I threw a mooring rope and felt a sudden, sharp pain in my back. I froze solid, unable to move. I'd missed the mooring post and the rope had fallen in the water.

"Hurry up and get the rope out and take a turn" yelled Roy from the bridge. He needed me to make fast to control the bow so that he could manoeuvre the tug alongside. It's the stern of a vessel that moves, the bow has to be held fast with anchors or ropes to prevent it from swinging around. I don't know how I managed it because I was in pain but I quickly hauled the soggy, heavy rope in and threw it again. The eye fell neatly onto the other tugs mooring post, I quickly made it fast and Roy completed the manoeuvre. Safely moored, I walked with difficulty to the aft cabin, climbed into my bunk and tried to rest. I knew there would be no point in complaining. The rest of that night was agonising. Getting in and out of my bunk each time I was called was difficult and painful but when I threw and hauled in ropes it was infinitely worse. When morning came, mercifully, we were told that a relief crew would be boarding and we could go home until six o'clock the following morning. Later that day I went to see a doctor and when he asked me to bend forward to test my mobility, I found that I couldn't move at all. It took six weeks for it to heal and I've been troubled with it ever since, but fortunately not too often. If only osteopaths or chiropractors had been around in those days, I could have been back at work in no time. The only treatment the doctor was capable of offering me was rest and painkillers, in other words, not very much and nothing seems to have changed today.

When we were navigating up and down the river on the open bridge, the only protection we had to shield us from whatever the weather threw at us was a small canvas dodger. I can't say that it achieved very much. We worked day and night, mostly with very little sleep. It was considered a real bonus If we managed to get four hours sleep during a night. During daylight hours when we weren't towing, we were required to maintain the vessels, chipping, painting and polishing etc. and ropes needed splicing, so we often had very little spare time to ourselves. There were plenty of brass fittings that had to be highly polished once a week. The steam whistle at the top of the funnel, the bell, the portholes, the paraffin lamps, the binnacle and the voice pipe were all brass. Electricity was supplied by a generator but some cabin lamps and navigation lights worked on paraffin as an emergency backup. They had to be kept full, the glasses cleaned and the wicks trimmed regularly so that they worked well when needed. Each crew member had his own set of chores but when it came to bunkering, a filthy job, most of them joined in. When the coal bunker needed replenishing, we'd tie up alongside the coal barge,

Artemis, moored in Gravesend Reach, make sure all the hatches, portholes and doors were closed to keep out the coal dust and remove the wooden hatches from the top of the coal bunker amidships. The crane would pick up and empty tonnes of filthy coal into the bunkers sending coal dust all over the place, which had to be washed away afterwards from every part of the vessel. It could be fun though and like most activities there was always plenty of joking and larking around.

The pendulous Skipper

The Thames was considered difficult for navigation so pilots were compulsory. Part of our duties from time to time, when the pilot cutters were unavailable, was to collect the pilot from the Royal Terrace Pier and take him to the ship that was making its way up or down river. Once he was on board, we'd steam out to the ship and go alongside, matching our speed to that of the ship. The pilot could then grab hold of the Jacob's ladder and make his way up to the decks and onto the bridge. One day, as the pilot was clawing his way up the rope ladder, Tony, the Fireman on duty, for some inexplicable reason known only to himself, decided to throw a bucket of paraffin into the furnace. The Mate, the Deckhand and I were standing on the aft deck chatting when we heard a powerful booming whoosh accompanied by a scream at the same time as we were hit by a blast of hot air. We spun round in the direction of the whoosh in time to see a gigantic column of flames exploding out of the funnel. The pilot, halfway up the ladder, had let out the terrified shriek. He was spinning around clutching onto the ladder for all he was worth as the flames roared from the funnel and shot up in the air past his back. When the searing heat scorched his back, he instinctively spun around on the ladder to turn his back away from the flames. That just exposed his front to the heat so he tried to spin back again. We were gobsmacked, wondering what on earth could have happened as the pilot hung there scared witless with his eyes popping out of his head in terror. When the Skipper questioned the Fireman afterwards, he explained it away by saying that there was a compacted mass of coal dust in the furnace, which he broke up with his rake releasing the pent up gases that ignited and burst into flame. His doubtful explanation seemed to appease everybody, although whether anybody actually believed him is another matter. He later confided in us Deckhands about the paraffin, although he didn't tell us why he did it and we never found out how the pilot fared after his surprise roasting. He must have arrived on the ship's bridge blistered and in a state of shock.

With the pilot installed, we would accompany the ship to Tilbury or London Docks then steam up to the bows where a heaving line had to be thrown up to waiting seamen so that they could attach it to the towing hawser. Tossing the line wasn't always my finest accomplishment. I had the strength and determination but not always the ability and it would sometimes go wildly off course. I could see where it needed to go and the waiting seamen were eager to catch it. I would gather up enough coils of rope in my throwing hand, give a few very impressive swings back and forth to get a good rhythm and momentum, then let it fly upwards to the ship's bow or stern as the case may be, with as much strength as I could muster. The waiting seamen would have no chance of catching it. I'd heave the line and it would take on a life of its own snaking its way towards any unsuspecting sailor who happened to be anywhere other than the target area. There was every likelihood that he could be rendered unconscious by the Turks head that had been weighted with a piece of metal to give the line momentum. On the occasions when my line did land at the spot I'd aimed for I was elated at my accomplishment, discounting the fact that that was exactly what was supposed to happen every time. I would often delay reaching for the line in the hope that the Deckhand, Arthur, would get there first, which he almost always did and would send the line expertly to its intended target with a dexterity that I greatly admired. Over a period of time I became expert myself out of necessity.

With the heaving line tied to the hawser, the Skipper would increase speed to clear the bows of the ship as the tow rope was lowered to us. As the distance between us and the ship increased we'd haul like crazy to try to prevent the hawser from becoming submerged and made even heavier. The speed of the vessels through the water and the strong tide, which could be as much as 8 knots, would add to the weight. As many hands as possible would be needed, the Mate, Deckhands, Firemen and even sometimes, the Cook, to haul the tow rope aboard and manhandle it over the engine room casing to the towing hook. It would then be placed on the hook and a clamp pulled down to hold the rope in place, which was then locked in position with a pin.

"On the hook," Roy, the Mate, would call out to the Skipper on the bridge to let him know that he could increase speed.

The telegraph would ring and the engineer would open up the wheel to increase speed gently until the slack had been taken up on the tow rope.

"Coming up," Roy would cry out, as the towrope cleared the water, followed by "All tight."

That was the signal for the Skipper to ring down to the engine room once more to increase speed and keep the rope tight to start the towing operation.

When the ship entered the lock, the tugs on her stern would slacken the tow rope temporarily, allowing the deck crew to loop a stop rope over it, pulling it down and making it fast to the bits on the aft deck. This kept the main purchase on the towrope well aft so that as the ship's propellers thrashed when she moved ahead, the tug wouldn't be pulled over as had happened to the Cervia. Whenever the tow rope or stop rope were released all hands had to stand well clear to avoid getting hit or caught in any coils, the consequences of which could be dire. The grey haired office agent, Jack, who told me to be back at six with my gear, was a victim himself, which is how he came to be seated behind a desk and not on the deck of a tug. He was serving on the Gondia and made the drastic mistake of getting his foot caught in a bight of the stop rope as it flew through the bits, taking his leg with it and severing it below the knee. His father was one of those who perished when the Cervia was girted and his grandson later fell overboard and drowned in the King George V dock. You may wonder why I was so enamoured with such a dangerous lifestyle, but looking back on it 60 years later I would still do it all again. I have never since worked with such a tough, loyal, generous and fun loving bunch of men.

Deck crew stayed on watch during the towing operation which could last for hours, and the River Thames could be bitterly cold in winter, especially at night. During the big freeze of 1963, the river froze in places and the ice made it difficult getting alongside the ships. Dressed in thick sweaters, duffel coats, pilot boots and anything else we thought might keep us warm, we blew into our hands and stamped our feet to keep the circulation going and comforted ourselves by drinking endless pint mugs of hot tea sweetened with Fussell's condensed milk. It was always a relief to be able to go into the warm galley to make a brew. The Skipper didn't have that luxury because he was committed to staying on the bridge whilst towing, relieved only occasionally by the Mate and he had to rely on one of us taking a piping hot tea to him when he called down for one.

The Skipper was the only crew member supplied with a uniform and peaked cap. He would also have the benefit of a thick warm overcoat, which was very smart with a little half belt at the back. When towing, the Skipper had to turn and face aft sometimes to keep his eye on the towrope, reaching behind him to spin the small steering wheel. There were two steering wheels, a large one for sea voyages and a smaller, steam driven one attached to it for towing purposes. The Atlantic Cock's Skipper, Fred, was rather vertically challenged so stood on tip toes a lot of the time to get a clear view aft. Sometimes he even had to jump up in the air to see what was happening and assess the situation in a split second before landing back down. The Mate, Roy, Deckhand Arthur and I were standing by on the aft deck when we heard howls for help coming from the bridge. The cries were getting hysterical.

"Roy, Roy, Roy," he wailed in panic.

Roy charged up to the bridge and found the Skipper suspended in mid-air, swinging from side to side trying to free himself from the small steering wheel that he'd become attached to. He'd jumped so high that on the way back down, the belt at the back of his overcoat had hooked onto the uppermost spoke of the steering wheel, abruptly breaking his descent. He hung above the flybridge deck gyrating as he frantically tried to unhook himself. The pilot was blowing his whistle giving instructions to the tugs, and our Skipper, firmly hooked to the steering wheel, with his little arms and legs making useless movements at his sides, was unable to carry out the commands. The Mate took hold of him and lifted the little fellow off, placing him back in front of the wheel where he could carry on with his duties. Very shortly after that little fiasco, which was entirely unrelated, Fred was posted to another tug. Another Skipper, also named Fred, was ordered to join us as his replacement. The two of them couldn't have been more different. Little Fred who left us was a fun loving character who mixed with the rest of us at every opportunity. Our new replacement had the most fearsome reputation of the entire fleet and when the radio crackled and we heard that he would be joining us, nobody was happy, and we spoke of hardly anything else that day.

The towing hook was sited amidships, aft of the main casing and over the coal bunker. The upper section consisted of a hinged clamp with an eye that dropped onto the hook, which was held in an upright position by a locking pin. To release the towrope, the locking pin was removed and the vertical spindle on the clamp would be struck with a mighty blow from a sledgehammer. This released the clamp enabling the hook to drop down and the towrope to disengage and disappear over the stern in a flash. Everybody needed to be well clear of the rope when this happened to avoid being whipped overboard. The towrope had to be freed very quickly to avoid the tug being girted and sunk when the ship increased speed. Sometimes there would be so much weight on the taught towrope that it took more than a few hefty swings of the sledgehammer, called the knockaway, to free it, with the Skipper screaming "Let go," "LET GO!"

If during towing, the situation looked so dangerous that the tow rope needed to be released quickly, the Skipper or Mate would order the senior Deckhand to stand by ready to strike the hook with the knockaway to prevent the tug being girted. It wasn't an order that the Deckhand welcomed and it would be with considerable trepidation that he jumped up beside the hook with the sledgehammer at the ready. With the tug heeled over and the tow rope bar tight, it could be difficult, if not impossible to release it with the knockaway, so an axe was kept nearby for such an emergency and such an emergency happened once on the Ocean Cock. The ship she was towing was steaming ahead and the Skipper called to the Deckhand to let go the tow rope. There was so much weight on the hook that it couldn't be released with blows from the knockaway. The order was given to cut through the towrope. The Ocean Cock was being pulled over by the ship. The Deckhand, Bill, took the axe and struck the towrope. It didn't part. The Ocean Cock was heeled way over, almost onto her beam ends, with water gushing through the fiddley doors flooding the engine room and boiler room.

9. The towing hook on Cervia

The cook at the time was Mike Houckham, who is now responsible for restoring the aged Cervia to her former glory at Ramsgate. He was just fifteen years old and was trapped in the galley with water up to his chest. Bill slashed away at the tow rope as if possessed. Eventually the yarns started splitting and finally parted. The tug shot back to the upright position. It was singularly nerve wracking for the Skipper, Billy, my cousin, who'd already survived the girting of the Cervia. He had to be treated for shock afterwards. The water from the flooded engine room, boiler room and fore and aft sections was pumped out after it had found its way into the bilges. Danger was always present and in one particularly disastrous year, three tug hands were lost on three separate occasions. "You gentlemen of England, who live at home at ease, how little do you think on the dangers of the seas." - "The Valiant Sailors" – Martin Parker.

Rum and Grapefruit

On a lighter note, there were occasions when we could profit from unexpected perks during our trips up and down the river. It once became known among the tug hands that moored to a buoy, was a barge loaded with barrels of rum, and that one of the barrels had been opened. It's intriguing how rapidly news of that nature becomes common knowledge. We felt it our duty as honourable citizens to stop off alongside said barge just to verify the facts. It was true, the barrel was open. Our next duty was to verify that it did, in fact, contain rum. We syphoned off some of the contents and tasted it and it was indeed rum. We decided that others may be tempted to over indulge and become inebriated if so much rum was available, so, being caring people we decided to remove some of the contents and therefore the temptation. It was comforting to learn that every other tug crew who called by carried out the same charitable act and that between us, over a short period of time, we'd removed temptation from the weak willed. The barrel was empty and the contents were safely stored at our homes where it somehow seemed to evaporate over time.

On another occasion, we were moored alongside a jetty at night and went off to check that the cargo that had been offloaded from the ship hadn't been tampered with. We came across opened crates of grapefruits and decided that they would probably attract vermin if they were left there and there were all sorts of other reasons why they should be removed. So again, being caring citizens, we set about the responsible task of lessening the attraction to the vermin. We couldn't hold many in our hands; the haul would be limited, so we stuffed our trousers into our socks and sea boots, undid our belts and filled our trouser legs up with the fruit. That was a good idea that enabled us to carry as many as possible but not such a good idea when we tried walking back to the waiting tug. As we set off, one of our number, the Deckhand, Arthur, stepped out a little too eagerly and the weight of the grapefruits lifted his trouser bottoms out of his sea boots. The grapefruits rolled in all directions and he scrambled around trying to recover them and at the same time keep the others in his trouser legs. We realised that more caution was required. It was a painfully slow progress as we made our way back to the tug, walking with stiff legged movements like robots, trying to keep the fruit in place. We looked utterly ridiculous moving along in slow motion, with our trouser legs bulging out and wobbling.

The goods we bought from the foreign and British seamen when we went alongside a ship were varied and cheap. We'd be offered or would ask for all manner of things, clothing, fishing equipment, crockery, alcohol and cigarettes, all at duty-free prices. Almost every tugman smoked. We were always so tired it was something to do to help keep us awake when we worked through the nights. The cigarettes would be sold to us in packs of two hundred, which encouraged us to smoke more than usual. Because of the tearaways I'd mixed with when I was at school, I'd started smoking at an early age and by the time I'd reached nineteen was smoking twenty Senior Service a day. It wasn't until my increasing coughing spells, the disgusting smell of the smoke on my clothes and the phlegm in the mornings that I realised the utter stupidity of swallowing mouthfuls of smoke, so I stopped, never to smoke again.

Some like it hot

As a teenager I was already earning considerably more than most mature, married men with shore based jobs. It's true that our take home pay packets were well padded but we worked long, hard hours to earn them and it definitely wasn't a job for the weak and fearful. To put it into perspective, a 40 hour week was the accepted standard for an average shore based job, and we tugmen could be working an average of around 140 hours a week and much of that with very little sleep so we were constantly tired. Despite my poor relationship with Mum and Dad in those days, I did what I could for them out of the money I earned on the tugs. I paid for and redecorated the entire house for them, installing new carpets or anything else that I thought was needed and would please them. I was blessed to be able to buy, what for them, were luxury items that they could never have afforded themselves. I surprised Mum one day by having a refrigerator, a washing machine and a Flatley dryer delivered. We'd never had any of these in our council house until then. Mum had done the washing in the kitchen sink using a corrugated washboard and a large bar of soap. Once a week the copper boiler would be heated up and the bed linen etc. boiled. To remove the excess water after being rinsed, the washing was taken into the back yard and passed through a mangle before being hung out to dry. She was so happy and seeing her happy made me happy. As a family, before I became a tugman, we were far from well off, as Father hadn't worked for most of my life and I only knew him as an aged, disabled, unemployed and rather unhappy person who'd experienced a life of terrible suffering. I hadn't realised just how tough he must have been in his prime until I decided to go down into the bowels of the tug and try my hand at stoking the furnaces myself.

One of our Firemen, Norman, went on holiday for two weeks, so I volunteered to take over his duties as the pay was higher than for deck crew and I fancied a trial run at something I'd never attempted before. A replacement Third Hand came aboard to fill in for me.

A Fireman's task didn't look too difficult when watching the experienced hands shovelling coal into the furnaces but I soon learned why they were allowed to rest for four hours after having sweated away for the preceding four. I'd ventured into the boiler room on many occasions but to find myself alone in front of the three roaring furnaces, all hungry for coal to keep the boiler producing steam, was an altogether different state of affairs. Air was needed to feed the fire and to allow ventilation for the heat to escape, so at deck level, a framework housed an iron grating that extended across the width between the side decks to a door on either side that was kept open, this area was known as the fiddley. The Firemen were tough men but the deck work had hardened me into a tough little teenager too, so when I first heard the orders issued over our radio for us to get under way for a towing operation, I felt confident. Alone in the stifling hot boiler room, I stood before the furnaces with the shovel at the ready. The telegraph rang, the engine thumped into life and I was then responsible for supplying the steam to power us along. I scooped the shovel into the pile of coal that had tumbled out of the coal bunker and swung around to throw it into the first furnace. The shovel clanged as it hit the framework and spilt the contents onto the floor, sending shock waves along the length of my arms. Turning back to the coal bunker, I quickly shovelled some more and clang went the shovel again and the coal spilt onto the floor adding to what was already there. I started to get concerned then; I hadn't been very successful at feeding one hungry furnace and there were two more waiting. The pile of coal on the floor grew larger as I continued shovelling frantically, striking the side of the furnace and spilling more coal. I was convinced that the shovel was too large to fit into the mouth of the furnace. It was a special skill to be able to twist the shovel whilst throwing the coal the length of the furnace but I mastered it as time went on. In addition to shovelling the coal into the furnaces non-stop, I had to gather up the spillage at the foot of the first furnace because it was hindering me. It was all very discouraging to begin with because it was looking increasingly unlikely that I would ever be able to get enough fuel into the furnaces to supply sufficient heat to produce the steam required. Even when I did master it and the coal landed at the back of the furnace, it disappeared in a puff and more was instantly needed - and that was just one furnace. Keeping all three going at once was hot, back-breaking work. When the tug was running at full speed, the furnaces were hungrier than ever and there hardly seemed time to stop for a second. I found myself shovelling away at breakneck speed, with perspiration oozing from every pore of my body just to keep them going. What a relief it was when we finally stopped and moored up.

The fires needed to be cleaned out regularly. For this a long handled metal rake was used to pile the fire to one side of the furnace and then with an equally long handled slice, the clinker was removed. When that was done, the fire was moved to the other side and the clinker removed. I kept this up for the two week period and became a proficient Fireman but at the end of it was glad to be back on deck. In reality, I was lucky to have lasted for so long because one night, moored alongside the pier at Woolwich, I was so tired that I went back to sleep after I had been woken to start my shift. The radio burst into life and we received orders to cast off and head to one of the docks. The crew were roused and started to prepare. I rushed down to the engine room to get the furnaces fired up and was horrified to see that the fires had gone out. We therefore had no steam and no power to move. My heart sank. I was so worried, I grabbed hold of some paraffin soaked cotton waste, threw it into the furnaces, set fire to it, piled some coal on top and blew and blew in desperation, frantically trying to get the fires going. It was never going to happen; it takes 24 hours to build up the steam. In truth, I don't understand why I wasn't sacked there and then. I felt for the Skipper who had to report to the office that we respectfully chose to decline the offer of towing the ship. I was embarrassed and ashamed to face the rest of the crew. I felt like squatting down in the corner of the stokehold where nobody could see me and hiding away forever. There was a consolation, however, in that we had an enforced day of rest.

It was not just the arduous work of a Fireman that caused me to oversleep; the situation was compounded by my nocturnal activities when I was ashore. I was hardly ever home, so partied and clubbed into the early hours. I played hard and it took its toll. "Do not feel embarrassed by your failures, learn from them and start again," said Richard Branson, but I'd decided that I would never again attempt to be a Fireman and I wonder now if this had ever happened to any other Firemen in the past.

....

The first known use of steam to provide motion goes back to the 1st century AD. However, the first commercially successful steam engine was used in 1712, to pump water from mines and it wasn't until 1802 that it was adapted for maritime use. The world's first viable steamboat was built in 1807. As technology developed, steamboats were used successfully on canals, rivers and for short coastal passages with the first Atlantic crossing taking place in 1819. Later that century, in 1850, the first iron hulled ships were seen, which over time replaced the wooden hulls and screw propellers began to replace the paddles. From 1870 onwards, the much stronger steel hulls replaced iron. As the ships became larger they required more efficient and complex engines, hence the development of the compound engine. The original steam engines used the steam once before recycling it back to the boiler; compound engines recycled the steam into larger, lower pressure cylinders before returning it to the boiler, thereby gaining more energy and enabling ships to be faster and more economical. The steam tugs were fitted with triple expansion engines, which were compound engines that expanded the steam in three stages through a Scotch boiler fitted with three furnaces. Scotch marine boilers were used in steam ships internationally. They were short, large diameter boilers with furnaces beneath and the larger and faster the ship, the more boilers were fitted. The Titanic had a total of 29 boilers, each with three furnaces.

CHAPTER 5
ON STANDBY

The first door

The knockaway was sometimes used maliciously by certain crew members for perverse entertainment. The toilet compartment on the Atlantic Cock was the first door on the port side deck immediately forward of the coal bunker and just a few feet from the towing hook. Once in there, you were confined in a steel enclosure with very little space and in a constant state of agitation. If you were seen sneaking in there for a "tomtit," you could expect at any moment to have every cell of your body reverberating from the holy terror of having the sledgehammer smashed down onto the steel roof. When this happened, the tremendous shock caused your whole body to shake, rattle and roll. The crash of the sledgehammer smashing down on the steel roof was magnified in the empty toilet compartment. Even the metal plates from which it was constructed vibrated. You would stumble out trying to maintain your balance, quivering all over as if your whole body had been turned to jelly. Your ears would be ringing, head spinning and teeth chattering. If anybody had difficulty passing a motion when they entered it was a sure way to loosen everything up. We had to devise ways to divert attention and one cunning ruse was to nonchalantly stroll along the opposite deck on the starboard side under the pretence of going to the galley for a mug of tea, avoiding eye contact with whoever was standing near the knockaway. A few clanging sounds were made in the galley in the hope of deceiving anybody who was eyeing up a victim then you would sneak out and head to the fiddly door leading into the stokehold. Nipping in quickly, you could then dash across to the port side and slide along to the toilet door, quietly open it and creep in. Feeling triumphant to have made it undetected thus far, trousers could be safely dropped and the required position assumed. Mostly this worked but if you gazed up at the porthole and saw a malevolent, grinning face eyeing up its prey, that's when you braced yourself, gritted your teeth and waited for the inevitable bone-rattling crash. Mercifully, this antic came to end after an overzealous crash with the hammer one day shattered the deckhead light in the toilet, showering the occupant in shreds of broken glass.

There was no such luxury as a flushing loo. Flushing was done by using a draw bucket. This was a galvanised bucket attached to a length of rope. The procedure was to hold the bucket in one hand and in the other, coil the rope so that there would be enough length to throw the bucket over the side into the river. The bucket would be thrown in upside down, whilst holding onto the rope with the other hand. As the bucket hit the water, an upward flick of the rope would tilt the bucket, filling it with water. It could then be quickly hauled back up and tipped into the toilet. That was easy enough even with a strong tide running but when the tug was steaming through the water at twelve knots, things got a bit more complicated. Then, you would have to calculate carefully, throw the bucket well forward of where you were standing to allow for the forward motion of the vessel, hoping that the bucket would be full and in the upright position, ready to be hauled up as rapidly as possible at the precise moment it was immediately below you. If you failed, your arms were suddenly jerked almost out of their sockets by the jolt as you took off and were dragged, skipping and hopping along the deck towards the stern, all the time trying to pull the bucket back up. All in all, going to the toilet could be both frightening and exhausting.

Peeing, (Jimmy Riddles) was always done over the side at the stern and downwind. One day, as we were steaming up river towards the London docks, I was in the galley making a mug of tea when nature called. I went out on deck and too idle to go aft, thought I'd pee over the side as there wasn't much wind and nobody around. The contents of my bladder was instantly whisked around behind me, missing me by millimetres.

"You fucking filthy, disgusting little bastard," screamed Tony the Fireman, who had decided to come up for a breath of fresh air and had popped his head out of the engine room entrance hatch. He had turned to look at me at the precise moment that the wind caught the steaming stream of urine, whipped it aft in a warm spray hitting him square in the face. I turned to see him frenziedly rubbing his hands over his face. His glared at me first in disgust then anger as he exploded into a torrent of unrepeatable profanities. Once he'd exhausted his vocabulary of expletives he screamed them at me for a second time before he disappeared back down the hatch. It took some time before he forgave me and I always pee'd over the stern after that.

Passing the time

The Skipper and Deckhand navigated the upriver runs as I've said before, whilst the Mate and I slept, despite the rumbling of the propeller shaft rotating directly beneath the cabin floor and the clanging of heavy chains that ran along the scuppers to the quadrant that turned the rudder. When Roy, the Mate and I did the downriver runs we had plenty of opportunities to chat, exchange ideas and get to know each other better and I like to think that we became friends despite the age difference. He taught me a lot. He was built like a bear but was a kind, considerate, gentle and a very forgiving man who was very aware of other people's feelings and would be deeply upset if ever he thought he'd embarrassed or hurt anybody in any way. He was also very much a team player as indeed we were all obliged to be. He'd not only join in with the rest of us in our onboard leisure activities but equally our socialising events ashore. He'd spent several years at sea in merchant vessels and had so many interesting tales to tell. Throughout my six plus years on the tugs, he is one of the people I most remember because of his gentleness, kindness and intelligence, yet he was as tough as they come. The down river runs were enjoyable but it was miserable cowering behind the dodger in bad weather. However, it was as it was and we just got on with it. Worse was the fog. The Thames in those days had a huge volume of shipping and with visibility down to virtually zero and ships blowing their horns alerting other vessels of their whereabouts, it was unnerving watching all the blips on the radar as we steered our way past them.

When the towing had finished, if we didn't have another assignment, we would either tie up at Woolwich pier or more frequently return to Gravesend where we had three mooring buoys. When we reached the buoy, if nobody was already moored to it, the Mate would steer alongside and I would jump on it, quickly thread the mooring rope or steel cable, depending on how long we would be staying, through the eye and get back aboard as quickly as possible to make the rope fast to the tug's mooring bits on the foredeck. If there were several other tugs already moored to the buoy, as the Mate steered towards the outer one, I'd throw a rope to lasso its mooring post then make it fast to our own mooring post. This helped the Mate manoeuvre to a position alongside it. The most difficult and scary part followed, for which I relied on the Deckhand for help. Once moored alongside the outermost tug, I'd clamber across them all until I was on the one that was the closest to the buoy. The next stage could be tricky, especially in adverse conditions, wearing thick winter clothes. I'd climb over the bow, and hold onto the stem whilst balancing myself on the large rope bow fender. The next undertaking required an athletic manoeuvre. I had to drop onto the mooring cable leading from the bow down to the buoy and balance in a horizontal position across the cable at a 90° angle, with it passing under my stomach. Face down, with my hands gripping the cable tightly on each side of me, I'd work my way down the taught wire, swaying one way then the other to reach the buoy, and holding on for dear life. The more I slid down the cable towards the buoy and the closer I got to the river, I'd straighten myself out as much as possible to keep my feet out of the water. Once on the bobbing, wet, slippery buoy, I'd sit down and make myself as safe as possible by planting my feet on the other mooring lines.

The Deckhand would throw me a heaving line attached to our steel mooring cable and shackle. I'd haul these to the buoy and with the shackle, fasten the cable to the buoy. To do this, I had to lean forward at a frightening angle because the mooring ring on the buoy would be almost at water level with the weight of several tugs pulling on it in the strong tide. Once the shackle was firmly fastened, I had to go through a reverse performance to get back aboard my own vessel. This mooring procedure was to be prohibited in later years due to Deckhands falling in and drowning, but I found the danger exhilarating.

If there was no more towing for a few hours and if it was cold, the coal burning stove in the cabin would be rattled into life and the cabin hatch closed. If there was to be a prolonged period of inactivity at night, the dynamo generator would be shut down to prevent it using steam. In the boiler room, the coals would be drawn to the front of the furnaces to stop heat getting to the boiler, furnace flaps were put on to stem the air flow and the funnel damper would be closed. The paraffin lamps were lit and the stove stoked up to the limit. Those of us who chose not to sleep would gather around the wooden table and enjoy hours of joking and laughing, smoking, playing cards, chess, doing crosswords, reading or whatever each person preferred in the warm ambience of the smoke-filled cabin. Some of us would spread a blanket on the table and set up a card school. I learned and enjoyed playing a variety of games, poker, brag, shoot, solo, rummy and a host of others. The stakes could be high and more often than not I managed to supplement my wages with the winnings. Whilst I was briefly acting as Third Hand before joining the Atlantic Cock, a mature Cook, Bill, joined temporarily. As a teenager, he'd served a short spell in prison as punishment for stealing cigarettes. His only request whilst serving time had been a pack of playing cards. I thoroughly enjoyed his company. He was a card fanatic and exceedingly competent when playing or performing card tricks. He had me hooked in no time. I enjoyed it so much that I would take books out of the library to learn as much as possible and spent a lot of time practising, learning how to cheat and deal from the bottom and the middle of the pack and do card tricks. This I would do only for my own amusement and to entertain others, it never occurred to me for a moment that I would ever actually cheat. In fact, I didn't need to because I usually did well enough, especially at poker.

As well as perfecting my card

10. Roy

playing, fancy dealing techniques and a host of card tricks, I became enamoured with chess. Roy was a keen and accomplished chess player so the two of us would spend many hours engrossed in games which would sometimes take place over a period of days. I found this to be a very enjoyable way to spend some of my free time. Another interest I had was in making bell ropes. It was Roy who taught me how to play chess and initially taught me how to make the bell ropes. As my interest and ability in the latter increased so did my desire to try more elaborate and complicated designs. I found an excellent book in the local library and became fairly accomplished at producing wonderfully decorative ones. It was a satisfying way to pass away free moments in the limited space of the cabin and is a pastime that had obviously originated from sailors spending lonely hours in tiny spaces during long sea voyages. Rope work is a natural and essential activity for sailors. Every Deckhand would be efficient at long splicing, back splicing, eye splicing, weaving Turk's heads and I took it a stage further. My skills in making bell ropes introduced me to some cleverly designed knots, such as pineapple knots, diamond knots, eight strand square sinnets and so on. Traditionally, bell ropes would always be painted to protect them from the ravages of the weather and mine were no different. All of the finished articles I ended up giving away as presents but I wonder if these gifts were ever appreciated or even wanted, apart from the one that hung on display in one of our local pubs, the Greyhound. Anyway, the objective was for me to have an interesting and constructive way of passing away my free moments. The Greyhound was one of the nearest pubs to the Royal Terrace Pier and consequently a regular for us as soon as we came ashore. The second pub, even closer, was The Crown and Thistle, commonly known as "The Crown and Crumpet". The landlord, Fred, behaved as if he was one of us and we had many a riotous time in both of the establishments.

One crew member who joined us temporarily had his own peculiar form of entertainment on board. He took a special delight in setting light to his farts. Suddenly, at any time of the day or night, whenever we were together in the cabin, he would shout out,

"Quick, somebody get a match, hurry up."

At the same time, he'd get into position, lying on his back, he put his hands behind his knees and pulled them up to his chest to stretch his orifice open to achieve maximum propulsion of gas. Usually, one person would oblige him by scurrying off in search of a box of matches, then position himself with arms outstretched waiting for the signal to place a lighted match against the expulsion point. When the moment was exactly right there'd be a shout.

"NOW!"

The match would be struck as the gas was released with an explosive sound and we would be exposed to a mini pyrotechnic display when it ignited. I hasten to say that not everybody was amused at his choice of entertainment and fortunately he didn't stay with us for very long. "Home is where the heart is, home is where the fart is. Come let us fart in the home. There is no art in a fart. Still, a fart may not be artless. Let us fart and artless fart in a home," - Ernest Hemingway.

The accommodation on the Atlantic Cock had the Skipper and Chief Engineer in their comfortable, wood-panelled cabins and dining room at the forepart of the vessel and the rest of us in the stern. Our bunks were set on either side of the cabin. We didn't have the luxury of wood panelling, just the riveted metal hull plates that were painted with a special paint containing cork to help prevent condensation and it was for the same reason that the steel decks above the fore and aft cabins were laid with teak planking. The hull plates were bitterly cold in winter and piping hot in summer but the section below the water line, always cold, was a useful place to keep perishable food. There was a long wooden table and wooden benches at the forward end of the cabin with the coal burner in the centre. The entrance ladder was at the stern end. It was referred to as a ladder but it was not how a ladder is usually visualised. It was actually a steep wooden stairway, rather like a cross between the two. Access was through a hatch from the aft deck. Because the ladders were steep, we were taught to always go down backwards, which was the sensible thing to do. That allowed you to place your foot on the full expanse of the step and hold on to the rail. Going down frontwards limits you to having just your heel on the step, with the step above that cutting into your calf and nothing to hold on to, unless you happen to be a contortionist, or, as a ballet dancing acquaintance of mine was capable of doing, turn both feet outwards at a 90° angle, a feat he was proud to demonstrate whenever the mood took him. I didn't know any burly tugman who'd ever had the inclination to ballet dance so the motto was, always go down backwards. When I was once in a hurry, I decided to neglect this sound advice and paid a painfully heavy price. I dropped down the hatch and started to descend frontwards and it didn't take very long before I found myself lurching forward into space. I flung my hands out in front of me and grabbed the first thing available to break my fall. I wished I hadn't done that. I yelped as my hands sizzled from being firmly clasped around the coal fire's blisteringly hot funnel that momentarily broke my fall until I released my hold in a flash and hurtled headlong downwards, landing with a painful crash on the wooden floor. I lay there for a while in shock. I was in pain from the fall and didn't quite know what to do with my smarting hands that had turned to an impressive colour red. Fortunately, nothing was broken except my spirit and I was so pleased that there had been no witnesses. I never told anybody what had happened; it would have produced howls of laughter. Aware that I would get no sympathy, I just got painfully on with my job, suffering in silence as if nothing had happened. My own stupidity had caused it and I had learned a useful and costly lesson. "A good scare is worth more to a man than good advice," – E. W. Howe

Another time when the crew's lack of sympathy was well demonstrated had to do with food – or lack of it. We were around the dinner table tucking into one of the renowned meat duffs. I salivated at the thought of sinking my teeth into the scrumptious plateful before me. The rowdy chatter and storytelling had gained momentum with much hand gesturing being used for emphasis. I got a little too excited, slammed my hands down onto my plate, which flipped over spilling the contents of the hot steak and kidney pudding, with its thick gravy and all the accompaniments, into my lap. This provided a wonderful source of amusement for the crew as I leapt up, tipping my longed for dinner all over the floor. Every one of them roared with laughter at my distress. The misery was amplified by the fact that before I'd sat down I was ravenous. I must have looked a pitiful sight standing there forlorn, a huge, hot stain spreading around my crotch area as I stared down in disbelief at all the lovely food splattered at my feet, knowing there were no seconds. I had to resort to heating up a packet of dehydrated Vesta curry that I had as a standby.

Don't panic!

Another lesson I learned from painful experience was that when disaster strikes, it's every man for himself. The old adage of women and children first in times of crisis is fine and may or may not be adhered to if women and children are present. However, when seven men are shut into a confined space and something happens that signals danger, anything goes and it's a case of survival of the most brutal and determined. It was a still, foggy night with visibility restricted so much that no shipping ventured on the river. We'd dropped anchor in a safe place to wait for the fog to clear and settled into our bunks to take advantage of the break in activity. It was deathly silent apart from the gentle lapping of the water against the steel hull, the hissing of the coal burner and the occasional fart or snore from the crew members. All was calm and peaceful and we appreciated being in our bunks, snuggled up under our rough blankets in the warmth of the cabin. All of a sudden there was a loud thump and the boat shuddered. Some of the crew instinctively leapt out of their bunks and onto the ladder as fear and panic spread. I decided I'd better do the same. I jumped down out of my bunk and rushed to the ladder where there was a writhing mass of fear filled humanity scrambling over each other intent on being the first one through the hatch to safety. Seven panic-stricken men could no way fit through one small hatchway at the same time. In desperation they were determined to prove otherwise. There were far too many at the top of the ladder so nobody could actually squeeze through. Each person seemed to be on the back of another. I got to the ladder but couldn't go any higher because I had somebody's arse in my face as another terrified individual with his head between my legs was doing all he could to shove me up further. Somebody else was climbing over my back. My fingers were gripping tightly onto something or someone and were being crushed so much I thought they'd break. Nobody wanted to be the last one out. In the ensuing havoc, hands were grabbing anything they could get hold of to gain enough purchase to smash their way past everybody else. We ultimately finished up on the aft deck dazed, scared and covered in scratches and bruises but somehow, we'd made it. We stood there shoeless, huddled in a group on the aft deck shivering in the cold, wondering why everything was exactly as it had been when we'd last stood there. We weren't sinking. Nothing but a ghostly silence and stillness in the dense, damp fog, and then somebody noticed in the murky darkness, a large piece of wood drifting away from our stern. The tide had carried it past the hull after it had bumped against it and created the panic in the cabin. We were so relieved to discover that the whole thing was just a false alarm and that we weren't going to be plunged into the icy cold, polluted water of the Thames. Had anybody landed in the water they would have had to be taken immediately to hospital. The pollution levels were so high that in 1957, the river was declared biologically dead. The only safe time to go in the water was during the brief period of slack water on the high tide.

I'd been through a similar event when I was ten years old. One of the older boys I knew promised to take us young ones to a popular cave that he knew somewhere near Northfleet. We'd heard other boys talk about crawling through it and so we were excited and raring to go. It was a nice sunny day when we set out on foot, filled with a sense of adventure. Northfleet was a five mile walk but then we walked everywhere in those days without giving it a thought. I would often walk to visit relatives in Northfleet and sometimes I'd walk the ten miles to Chatham to visit relatives. On arrival at the location in some barren land, we descended into a large, deep-set, sunken area similar to a quarry. We found the cave, which was set in the side of the steep bank, and we ventured inside. The older boy, Eric, carried a torch and led the way. The cave gradually got narrower until we were crawling along on our hands and knees in what was little more than a small tunnel. The rest of us followed the light up ahead and it was disappearing rapidly as the older boy, knowing the cave well, rushed off ahead of us four younger ones. Eddie, my best friend at the time, was in front of me and two more were behind me. Suddenly it was total darkness. We had no idea what lay ahead and no idea where Eric was. Eddie knew the leader well and called out but there was no reply. He started to panic and his cries were getting more desperate as he got closer and closer to tears. Still no reply came back so he started to cry and plead and this affected the rest of us. I'm not the bravest person but I wasn't overly concerned until my friend started crying and the two behind me began letting out little whimpers. Then Eric finally called out to us from somewhere way ahead.

"This cave is haunted and the ghost always grabs the boy at the back," he called.

Terror took hold. I wasn't sure about the existence of ghosts but being cramped on hands and knees in pitch darkness, with no room to move up, down or sideways and the possibility of being grabbed by some demonic apparition can be pretty upsetting. All of a sudden all hell broke loose. I'm proud to say that initially I wasn't too bothered until the other three went haywire. My friend at the front was now bawling and crying out for the light to be put on as he scampered ahead blindly on all fours. I didn't want to be left there and neither did the two behind me but the major factor that caused the ensuing mayhem was that none of us wanted to be at the back. The unfortunate boy who found himself there screamed out and tried to flatten the boy in front of him so that he could scramble over his back. The boy behind me was determined to do whatever was necessary to keep the boy at the back where he was and at the same time was doing all that he could to push me further into the ground so that he could scamper past me. I was whimpering then and kicking him back. Fear and panic had consumed us all - no, more accurately, it was blind terror. Our vision was absolutely nil. We swore, punched, kicked and scratched each other in the confined space of the black, narrow tunnel as we simultaneously scrambled onwards. None of us wanted to be the last one in reach of the ghost. Incredibly, the boy behind me, with staggeringly brute force and ingenuity, somehow made me disappear and got past me. That placed me one from the back! The fight that followed in the ridiculously confined space was savage as we scrambled onwards. Up ahead I heard a scream and we soon found out, painfully, what the scream was about as we tumbled headfirst on top of each other into a hole. It wasn't a very deep hole but at the time it felt like a bottomless pit. We were writhing around in an attempt to extricate ourselves from the mass of tangled limbs when the torch was switched on. Eric shone the light on us. We were dishevelled, tearful and bleeding. The torch beam was flickering to and fro as Eric tried to contain his laughter. I didn't go back into the cave after that. "I have, indeed, no abhorrence of danger, except in its absolute effect – in terror." - Edgar Allan Poe.

Bluetown

The towage company had stopped using the Ramsgate slipway so all refits were thereafter carried out at the Sheerness dry dock, or at least that was what we called it. In fact, the refits were carried out close by at a naval yard in Bluetown, which had developed around the time of the Napoleonic wars. The name derives from the wooden houses that the inhabitants had painted with blue paint. It was strange how as more and more houses were painted blue, less and less blue paint could be accounted for at the storage in the dockyard! Bluetown is a suburb of Sheerness on the Isle of Sheppey, at the mouth of the River Medway and around 20 nautical miles from Gravesend. The first building ever constructed at Sheerness was a fort that was built by order of King Henry VIII to protect the entrances to the River Medway and the Chatham Dockyards from coming under attack by enemy ships. A restricted depth at Chatham Dockyards, meant that vessels needing repairs or to replenish supplies could be delayed for considerable lengths of time awaiting favourable tides. So with this in mind, Samuel Pepys, the Secretary of the Admiralty, ordered the construction of the Sheerness Dockyards as an extension to the Chatham Dockyards. The town didn't achieve official status until near the end of the 19 century.

In 1944, the SS Montgomery, a United States merchant ship carrying a large cargo of explosives, ran aground on a sandbank 250 metres from the Medway Approach Channel. When the tide went out, she broke her back and now lies 15 metres below the surface with her masts still visible. The excessive cost and danger involved in attempting to salvage her and her cargo were considered too great so she still has 1400 tons of munitions in the hold. If they should ever detonate for whatever reason, apart from damaging buildings on the shore, the explosion would send an enormous column of water in the air and probably cause a mini tsunami. It was with that comforting thought in mind that we cast off from the Royal Terrace Pier and steamed down Gravesend Reach into Lower Hope on our way to Sheerness for our refit. The voyage was a gentle one all the way and as we steamed into the final stretch of the Thames Estuary known as Sea Reach I started to look forward to my stay there.

As soon as we were moored up in the dry dock and were able to get ashore, Roy went directly to the blacksmith's workshop and asked him to make up some harpoon tips, which he managed to do in double quick time. We attached these to broom handles and waited for the water level to go down enough for us to wade in in our sea boots and spear the fish that had been trapped in the dock. We were rewarded with a few fine specimens, one of which was a beautiful sea bass, which we enjoyed later that day along with the remainder of the catch. That night the crew went back to Gravesend and to their families. Some of them returned the following day to carry out maintenance work and that was the routine they followed until the refit had finished and it was time for the tug to be re-floated and sailed back to Gravesend. At lunch times we had fun filled moments in the local pubs. I stayed there for the duration and had a thoroughly enjoyable time.

It was on the last night before we left that some crew members, everybody in fact except the Leading Hand, the Skipper and the Engineer, joined the Cook, Alan and myself for a final celebration in one of the local pubs and it was there that Alan and I had a close encounter with two locals youths who would have dearly loved to make mincemeat of us. We were sitting around a table when I noticed two pretty girls standing at the bar eyeing me up and probably Alan as well since he, like myself, was as enthusiastic and successful with the opposite sex as I was. Alan and I were keen to make a move but hesitated because the girls were with two rather large men who were giving us menacing looks. Their intentions were unmistakable should we dare to return the girls' glances but the challenge was too great. The inviting looks were irresistible and so, emboldened by a few pints of beer, Alan and I decided to risk the wrath of the two bruisers at the bar. We strolled up to the flirting girls and engaged them in conversation. As expected, their male companions didn't take kindly to our intrusion. They pushed between us and the girls and stood directly in front of us. Their aggressive looks and threatening language left us in no doubt what their intentions were but we stood our ground, encouraged by the fact that the girls made it obvious that they would prefer to be with Alan and me. Peter, a Fireman in our crew, saw the altercation taking place and marched up to the bar and asked if everything was alright, at which point the two losers withered away. It was well worth the risk we took because when we left with the girls later that evening everything we'd hoped for came to fruition. They helped make the refit at Sheerness so memorable that I couldn't wait for a return visit.

.

CHAPTER 6
FAREWELL TO STEAM

The agony and the ecstasy

Since school days I'd dated a girl, Kate, on and off. As she matured, she developed into a beautiful, curvaceous young girl and I found myself becoming ever more attracted to her. She was a little smaller than me with shiny, wavy black hair, dark, laughing eyes, full, luscious lips and slightly coffee coloured skin, a throwback from her Maltese ancestry. We began dating more regularly until one day, I realised just how much she meant to me. It's strange that it seemed to happen quite suddenly. We were playing around and laughing and as I looked at her lovely, laughing face and bewitching dark eyes I became conscious of how much I enjoyed being with her and she felt the same way about me. We decided that neither of us wanted to be with anyone else and as time went on we both fell madly in love. The love I felt was so intense it was almost as much as I could bear, as happens to some teenagers when they fall in love for the first time. From that moment on I devoted myself entirely to her alone. "No there's nothing half so sweet in life as love's young dream." –Thomas Moore.

We became ever closer the more time we spent together until it became clear to us both that we never wanted to be apart so I proposed to her and she accepted without hesitation. I bought a ring for her and with friends gathered around to celebrate with us, I placed it on her finger. She cried tears of joy, and we hugged and kissed and were blissfully happy. Our engagement lasted for a year. I loved my fiancée very much but we had different ideas on which direction our lives should take. She wanted to settle down and have children, a natural thing for most women to want, I suppose, especially back then in those days. She would have been perfectly happy living in a council house with lots of children around and as long as I knew her, she was never enthusiastic about getting a job. I was more ambitious. I had been bitten by the travel bug and wanted to visit different countries and I could never envisage myself working on the tugs or remaining in Gravesend for the rest of my life. I'd decided a few years before whilst waiting at a bus stop in the cold rain that I wanted to go and live in an exciting, warm country. It didn't make sense to me that I should suffer bad weather when better climates were on offer. I equally could not imagine myself doing the same thing day in and day out for the rest of my working life. My friends seemed happy enough with their lot, going to the same pubs, meeting the same people, doing the same things that they did the day before and would do the same things the following day and so on. There were far too many other interesting adventures awaiting me and regrettably, my Kate was not prepared to move on. She was not interested in travel or leaving Gravesend or improving her education or seeking a better life in any way, all of which I was unaware of when I'd asked her to marry me. I agonised for a long time before telling her that I thought it better if we parted. I knew it would be painful for both of us but it was far worse than I'd expected. I could never have foreseen what the outcome would be.

I broke the news as gently and as rationally as I could. I felt wretched watching her hurting inside as she looked up at me pleadingly, her intoxicating, dark eyes filled with tears and her warm arms clutching me so tightly. My mind was in turmoil. I held her close and different emotions arose within me. As they melded together I became confused. I loved her so very much and yet I just knew deep inside that I could not spend the rest of my life in Gravesend. We stayed together for the remainder of that evening and made love with such an intense passion that I was tempted to reconsider. I was overwhelmed as I held her warm, young, naked body next to mine, that beautiful body that she surrendered to me so willingly. We lay silently, hugging each other. I was tormented inside. I imagined how the rest of my life would be with her and convinced myself that it would be better for us both if we each went our own way from that moment on. I walked her home. Outside her house, we stood clutching each other tightly and then, finally, with heavy hearts, we said our goodbyes. For a long, long time afterwards, I was haunted by the image of her walking away from me.

It was some time later that I had a message from her mother telling me that my dear, sweet ex-fiancée was so distraught and so ill that a doctor had been called in to see her. I was filled with remorse. What had I done? I went to see her and was pained when I saw her sitting curled up on the settee, her lovely face looking hurt and dispirited. I sat next to her for a while and when she seemed more relaxed I left her with the promise that we would stay in touch. A few days later things got worse. Her mother sent a message to me to say that after my darling had described her dreams and nightmares to the doctor, she had been placed in a psychiatric clinic. I was shocked. I felt responsible and didn't know how to respond. I sent a message back offering to visit her at the clinic and her mother agreed that it would be a good idea. We arranged a day and went there together. It was horrendous. The patients could be heard wailing and crying and the atmosphere was incredibly depressing. When Kate appeared, looking distraught, my heart ached for her as she sat before me with tears streaming down her cheeks, pleading to be taken back home. When her mother and I rode away together on the bus, she said that if I would take her daughter back the doctor thinks she would be better and could be sent home. Whether this was intentional emotional blackmail or a genuine plea for help I don't know but after a few days reflection, I felt I had no choice but to agree. She came home and we continued as we were before the split. I had mixed feelings, I wanted to end our relationship because long term I could foresee difficulties and yet I loved her so much.

As time went by, little by little, we both came to the understanding that we would eventually drift apart but it wasn't easy. Even after we'd officially split for the second time, I couldn't stay away from her completely and she felt the same. She lived in a street parallel to where I lived and although it was further for me, I'd go out of my way to walk past her house on my way home late at night. I never knew which nights I would be on leave but whenever I walked past her house, she was always there, waiting at the window. She'd open the door silently to avoid waking her parents, I'd go in and we'd spend heavenly moments in each other's arms and we'd make love. Sometimes her mother would call down to ask what she was doing or to tell her to come to bed.

"Kate, get up here at once," she called down.

"I'm just coming," Kate shouted between her heavy breaths and groans of ecstasy. It was a most appropriate thing to say, considering the activity we were engaged in at the time.

It was never easy saying goodnight, except on one occasion when her mother called to ask what she was doing downstairs so late at night and started clomping her way down the stairs to check on her. We were in the process of making love on the settee. Horrified at the thought of being caught, I jumped up and feverishly searched for my shoes in the dark, falling over in the process because my trousers were around my ankles. Whilst I was stumbling on the floor on hands and knees, I found my shoes. The clumping on the stairs left no doubt that Kate's mother was getting dangerously close. I had one hand clutching my shoes and the other trying to pull up my trousers as I attempted to run as fast as I could with ridiculous little movements because my feet were so restricted. I hopped my way through to the kitchen and fumbled in the dark for the door handle. I got the door open as I heard Kate's mother enter the sitting room. I dashed through the back door with just my socks on my feet. I hobbled into the alleyway between her house and the neighbour's and cried out in pain when I trod on something sharp in the process. Panting from the panic and the pain, I propped myself against the wall, pulled my trousers up put my shoes on my smarting feet and snuck out into the street and home. Our clandestine meetings went on for quite some time until I'd walked past several times and realised that she would no longer be there for me. I was devastated that it was finally over but at the same time pleased that we could get on with our lives and that the ultimate decision was hers. I have never forgotten her and she will forever have a place in my heart. "Ever has it been that love knows not its own depth until the hour of separation." – Kahlil Gibran." It could well be that when the life force has left our physical bodies and our spirits transcend to whatever realm exists after death, we may well meet again. Cosmology, physics, astronomy, philosophy, religion, many quantum physicists, forward thinking scientists and others such as renowned theoretical physicist and cosmologist Stephen Hawking, hypothesize that there is a Multiverse. If then, our universe multiplies into copies of itself at every quantum event, with copies of ourselves living out every possible outcome of every possible situation, then somewhere in that infinite number of universes, Kate and I are at this moment entwined in each other's arms, deeply in love and living in perfect harmony. And yet again in another of those universes we've never even met.

Precognition

During my engagement to Kate, I'd been promoted to Senior Deckhand aboard the Moorcock, the newest tug in the fleet. Built in 1959 (and scrapped in 1981), 272 tonnes, 113' long with a draught of 12' and with a 1280 hp. 8 cylinder diesel engine. She was so different to the old steam driven tugs. Instead of having a Third Hand (Junior Deckhand) and Deckhand (Senior Deckhand), she had two Deckhands, which for me meant another increase in salary. The Moorcock was absolute luxury compared to the coal burning steam tugs. The accommodation was forward and well thought out. The Skipper's night time cabin was on the starboard side of a through passageway at deck level, with his day cabin on the port side. Between these two cabins, a ladder went down to the Chief Engineer's cabin to starboard and the Mate and Leading Hand's cabin to port, with the rest of us forward from there. Leading aft from the passageway, the galley was to port with a diesel fuelled cooking stove. Opposite the galley, stairs led up to the wheelhouse and aft of that the showers and washbasins were to starboard and the toilet to port. After that there was a door leading into the engine room. It was such opulence compared to what I'd been used to. Everything was inside and to have a real flushing toilet and hot water showers was bliss.

11. The Moorcock

On the old coal burners, when we needed to wash, we each had a galvanised bucket that we filled with water then either plunged one of the hot plates from the stove into it to heat it or we carried it down to the engine room and heated the water from a steam jet then carried it along the deck and down into the cabin. We'd then place it on the wooden benches around the dining table, strip off, wash and prepare ourselves to go home. The Moorcock was fitted with a refrigerator, another luxury that hadn't existed on the coal burners where we'd had to make do with a safe on the boat deck, which was a simple wooden framework with wire gauze on the sides and doors to allow air to circulate. I'd always believed that I'd eventually be promoted to this tug. It was what I'd hoped for and would constantly say to my crew mates that I would be ordered one day to join the Moorcock. When it happened they wouldn't believe that I hadn't had prior knowledge. The vision I'd created in my mind had materialised into fact.

I was delighted to be on the Moorcock. No more misery enduring the effects of the cruel elements on the runs up and down river. Instead, the trips were made in a comfortable, heated wheelhouse without any need to go outside. The bunks were far more comfortable than they were on the old coal burners. Everything was new, clean and civilised. This fine tug was fitted with powerful water cannons and we were the duty tug for the Gravesend area, which meant that we were called upon to assist the fire service when required. The Kent and Essex councils subsidised this operation and firefighting officers would occasionally come on board to train us in the art of firefighting and instruct us on the correct procedure. Fortunately, the fires were few.

The crew on the Moorcock were a lively bunch and we got on well together. The Skipper, Arthur, was an interesting character. He had a French background and unusual for a tugman in those days, he liked to have the occasional bottle of Beaujolais when we were moored for the night. Apart from that, nobody drank much whilst on duty. One day, the Mate, Eddie and I were in the snug wheelhouse on the down river run, which meant that the Skipper was off duty. Approaching Gravesend Reach, he appeared on deck with a shotgun. He looked up at us like a naughty boy with a mischievous grin on his face, then he lay down on the foredeck with the barrel aimed through the eyes of the vessel and pointed towards a mallard floating up ahead. He fired and despite the spread of the shot, only injured the poor creature. By this time the blast of the gun and the slowing of the engines had brought some of the other crew members on deck. It was pitiful to see the wounded duck flapping around helplessly in the water. We stopped engines, drifted alongside it and hauled the poor creature aboard. We all wanted to end its suffering quickly - not so easy if you'd never done it before. Buck, the Engineer, tried breaking its neck by twisting it but only managed to strip the feathers and skin from the muscles and expose the red flesh beneath. Next, Chunky, the Leading Hand, had an equally unsuccessful attempt. One of the Firemen, Jack, took hold of its feet and with a couple of swings smashed the poor things head against the engine room casing. It was distressing to watch but nowhere near as distressing as it was for the now terribly injured bird. It was all done with the best of intentions but we were inexperienced animal killers. One final twist of the neck ended its life. Everybody was upset. Nobody wanted any more to do with it. I couldn't bear the thought of all that suffering for nothing so I took it, plucked it, cleaned it and roasted it for my dinner that evening with a few vegetables. When I sat down to eat it all by myself the rest of the crew, unable to comprehend how I could do such a thing, stared at me in disbelief as if I was some sort of heartless monster. At least the ill-fated bird didn't suffer in vain.

Fog was often a problem on the Thames and when we anchored and waited for it to clear, one of us Deckhands would keep watch and from time to time go outside and ring the ships bell to let other shipping know our whereabouts and listen for the sound of their horns. If we heard three short blasts from one ship followed by the same from another ship, it meant that each ship was going astern and a collision could be imminent and that meant salvage. We would also be permanently tuned into the open radio band 2182 kHz. This was the frequency used for "mayday" calls when ships were in distress. Mayday originates from the French "m'aidez" meaning "help me". The financial rewards for salvaging could be substantial for the company and the crew. The company share was 75% and the remaining 25% was shared out among the crew on a sliding scale, with the Skipper being given the highest share, five parts plus sixpence in every £1. The Engineer received four parts, the Mate and Leading Hand three, the Deckhands two and the Cook one. The total amount awarded increased for the first tug to get a tow rope aboard the stricken ship. As soon as we heard the mayday call and ascertained where the ship was, the Skipper would be alerted. The trouble was, so was each of the other Skippers. It would be a free for all among the tugs available, each one determined to be the first. There would be a wild scramble with no niceties as the rewards could be so high. Even being the outside tug on the buoy or the pontoon didn't necessarily provide an advantage because if you weren't quick enough off the mark you risked being cast adrift or dragged along with whoever managed to cast off first. All available tugs would charge towards the prize at double full speed. It was all very exhilarating. During my time on the Atlantic Cock, we once came across an abandoned, burning ship by chance. We went alongside and I jumped on board amidships and ran along the smoking deck with the tow rope, attached it to the foredeck bollards before running back and leaping back aboard the tug. Meanwhile, we'd informed the office at Gravesend and before we knew it other tugs, eager to be a part of the action, heard our call and started appearing from nowhere. It was a pleasant surprise when I received a cheque for a substantial sum of money eighteen months after I'd left the tugs.

The singer not the song

I went back to Sheerness dry dock on the Moorcock and had another memorable time with other crew members who'd stayed behind with me. Eddie, the Mate, had been posted to another tug and was replaced by Bert. Some evenings, he and I would fill in time waiting for the clubs to open by going to a local bingo hall and always won enough to partially or totally pay for the evening's entertainment. There was a holiday complex nearby so we never lacked a place to go for amusement. Ken, the second Deckhand and I went there one evening and drank more than we should have. We met a couple of girls who'd invited us back to their chalet for the night. One of them was more attractive and friendlier than the other and when the time came to go to bed she stood and said, "Right who's coming with me?" We both shot bolt upright at the same instant without the slightest hesitation and leapt towards her. Ken was a good deal larger and far stronger than me and pushed me back down onto the settee before disappearing into the bedroom with her. I sat there feeling dejected. By that time, the second girl was dispirited that neither Ken nor I were as eager to go with her so she refused to let me accompany her to her bedroom. I sat down alone on the settee wondering what to do next. After a while, Ken's girl came back out to see me and invited me to share the bed with her and him. I declined her offer but she didn't want to accept no for an answer. I assumed that Ken had passed out because she tried several times to persuade me but I refused and left, sulking my way back to the Moorcock. When Ken clambered aboard around breakfast time he had an anguished look on his face.

"What happened to you, you look dreadful?" I asked

"I feel sick," he answered.

"Why?" I said

"Ooh," he groaned "I was disgusted and felt sick when I woke up and saw her."

"Ha-ha, serves you right," I said showing no sympathy for his self-inflicted plight.

"Ooh, I feel sick. When I saw her in the daylight she looked fucking awful. She was covered in sores and, oh, it was just so fucking horrible," he said as he ran to vomit.

It's surprising how much perception changes the more you have to drink. It's like the best of the wine always being in the bottom of the bottle. Anyway, when he'd finished being sick he was so upset he decided to go straight home. The whole thing was compounded by the fact that he was married and felt so ashamed. Embarrassingly, on the way home, he had to ask the bus driver to stop twice so that he could step out and vomit. What I thought at the time as bad luck turned out to be good luck for me.

I was in the ballroom of the holiday complex on my own one night when I became entranced by the pretty redheaded singer. Not only was she pretty, she also had a good voice, getting plenty of applause for her interpretation of Barbra Streisand songs. As soon as she came off stage I rushed over to her side and engaged her in conversation before she became surrounded by other admirers. Naturally, I emphasised the brilliance of her remarkable vocal ability. She was a lovely girl and we both felt a connection. I discovered that she lived in London's East End and as that was one of my regular haunts we were able to continue dating for a while. We would meet up at the King's Head in the Old Kent Road where I'd been a regular visitor for some time. The entertainment there made it well worth the trip from Gravesend. There were musical nights, comedy acts and so forth. The pub would be packed solid, so much so that it paid to estimate how many pints of beer you wanted to consume and buy them all at once because it would be almost impossible to get back to the bar a second time. We were packed like sardines in the smoke filled bar and even the pavement outside was filled with people. Those were good days. I was also a regular visitor to the greyhound race tracks. Roy, the Mate on the Atlantic Cock had introduced me to the sport and we'd often go together wherever the races happened to be on our time off, be it Wembley, East Ham, Catford, Crayford or anywhere else. I found it more and more difficult to keep meeting up with the songstress in London and the affair gradually fizzled out when I met other girls closer to home.

CHAPTER 7
THE TRAVEL BUG BITES

The weaker sex they're not!

With plenty of money to spend, I made the most of my days off and the annual holidays. My first trip abroad was in 1960. I went with my friend Tommy to Lloret del Mar on Spain's Costa Brava when travel was more complicated than it is at the time of writing. The plane landed at Perpignan in Southern France and then a coach took us on a lengthy ride to the resort. I loved Spain. I loved the food, the sunshine, the people, the language, the Flamenco, the Spanish girls - even though I spent the majority of my time there romancing a lovely wanton German girl called Marina who was staying in a hotel not far from where we were staying.

Tommy and I had great fun playing practical jokes on the young chambermaid each time she came into our room. There was a time when Tommy hid under the bed and I let her in. Thinking it was safe to carry on, she started her chores and as she walked past the bed, Tommy flashed his hand out grabbing her ankle. She let out a piercing scream at the sudden fright. Later, at lunch, she and a group of her fellow chamber maids were peering through the window at us, giggling whilst we ate. When lunch was over, we left the dining room and headed to the exit to make our way to the beach.

"Pssst," I heard. A young boy grabbed my arm and indicated that something was amiss and that I should follow him. Concerned, I did as he bade, and he led me upstairs all the while beckoning me to follow him. He took me to my room and with a worried look and using sign language, implied that I should go in. I went in and immediately the door was slammed behind me. I was trapped in my room with a gang of young Spanish chamber maids intent on doing heaven knows what to me. A couple of them leapt at me. I dodged them and as more came at me from another angle, I briskly avoided them too, escaping to the other side of the bed. They ran around to try and seize me. I leapt across the bed and made it to the door and escaped. When I arrived at the hotel exit, Tommy was still waiting for me oblivious to what had been going on. Now, before any testosterone filled males start wondering why I didn't just take advantage of the situation, let me say that this wasn't the first time I'd been assaulted by a group of girls and in reality, whilst it wasn't entirely unpleasant, it wasn't good to feel powerless and at their mercy. In those days it was unthinkable for a man to strike or hurt a woman, which limited my self defence.

It happened to me once at a party. I'd become friends with a girl who lived on a different estate to myself and there would often be several of us teenagers at her home. Her father was mostly away working and her mother, being left on her own, would allow us kids to meet up and play rock and roll music and jive and generally enjoy ourselves, even joining in herself. As well as the usual teenage chatter, there would be plenty of sexual talk, confessions, boastings and fantasies spoken of and the mother encouraged some of it. As kids were coming and going in different rooms or the garden it wasn't easy to keep track of who was where. One girl invited me to go upstairs, so naturally, I obliged. When I went into the room, I was grabbed and pulled onto the bed by a group of squealing and playful young girls. Together they were surprisingly strong and some of them had definite intentions of a sexual nature. I do not intend to divulge in detail what happened next and leave my readers to draw their own conclusions; suffice to say that some of them were very inquisitive, experimental and resolute in satisfying their curiosity and desires. Why me, was I emitting some sort of aberrant pheromones that enticed the opposite sex to attack and take advantage of me? Anyway, I eventually staggered back downstairs dishevelled, exhausted and a little shocked. I can imagine what an outcry there could have been if an equally large gang of boys had assaulted a girl in the same manner! Even earlier I was the victim of a similar incident at the infants' school. It happened that once I was the last boy to leave the classroom and six girls were standing in a group nearby looking at me and giggling. They ran over and cornered me, got me on the ground and held me down whilst they took turns trying to kiss me to death. Of course, the Costa Brava incident had a perfectly logical explanation, revenge, albeit a playful one and it never happened to me again after that. As for the assault at the party, there were further developments. The mother once called by my home and asked for me. My parents had an inkling of what had been happening; it is difficult to keep such things quiet, especially if there's a likelihood of scandal. Anyway, she was standing outside and they forbade me to go with her. Later, for whatever reason, the police became involved and when the husband discovered what had been going on, they separated. Two years later, I met the daughter at the bus stop and we started chatting about the past. Her bus arrived before mine and just before she boarded she shoved a key in my hand.

"I'm at home alone tonight, come and see me about half past seven," she said and quickly got on the bus leaving me dumbstruck, holding the key.

That was the last thing I'd expected. However, the offer appealed to me so I pocketed the key and that evening duly went to her home. I hesitated at the door, instinctively. I had doubts about the wisdom of letting myself in, not knowing what the outcome might be, so instead of using the key, I knocked on the door. What a lucky escape I had because the door was opened by her father. We eyed each other up for a while. I don't know if he recognised me but I certainly recognised him and I felt very uneasy. I asked for his daughter and when she came to the door, she apologised, I handed her the key and we never saw each other again.

But back to Spain. I loved travelling abroad. I had well and truly been bitten by the travel bug. The following year, I went on my own to Torremolinos. The name means "Tower of the Mills". The Moors, who were of Arab and Berber descent, crossed the strait of Gibraltar in 711, and established the mills after they'd conquered Spain. The tower and the Alhambra Palace were both built during the Nasrid Dynasty, which lasted from 1230 until 1492, when they surrendered to a Christian Spain at the fall of Granada. Torremolinos was looted and destroyed by an Anglo-Dutch flotilla during the War of Spanish Succession and was rebuilt, together with the mills, in the early 19th century. The mill industry began to decline in the 1920's and Torremolinos became a poor, little known fishing village until it became the first tourist resort on the Costa del Sol in the 1950's. When I was there it was still a small resort and market day was a lively affair with the locals singing and dancing flamenco and the mules and donkeys attired in brightly coloured garments. Any small bar I visited would invariably have somebody singing and dancing flamenco and I've been passionate about the music ever since.

I took a bus to explore Malaga and having heard and read so much about bull fights decided to see what it was all about. The bus trip became interesting when locals boarded and took short journeys with their livestock. The prices of the tickets for the bull fight varied considerably and much to my regret, I chose to pay the cheapest price, which meant I spent the entire time in full sun envying the wealthier and more knowledgeable spectators who'd paid the higher price for the shade. The bull fight was horrendous. I am flabbergasted that such atrocities are still allowed to take place in the 21st century and I wonder how anybody could find it entertaining to watch a magnificent animal being tortured to death for twenty minutes.

I had a gratifying time with a mature woman for the first week and then I met a lovely, dark haired Irish girl. We spent wonderful romantic evenings alone on the beach and had such a good time together that our relationship continued in the UK for a while until she surprised me one day by talking about marriage as if it was a foregone conclusion. The thought had never crossed my mind, so I extricated myself as gently as I could.

My next trip was Paris. Paris in the sixties was an exhilarating place to be and I would go there as often as I could. Although my weekends and days off were infrequent and rarely consisted of a full two days, I would sometimes take the train from London to Paris so that I could spend a night and as much as possible of what remained of the my spare time there, rather than go on pub crawls with my friends in Gravesend. It was a 12 hour journey each way; leaving London Victoria at nine o'clock in the evening and arriving at Paris Gare du Nord at nine o'clock the following day. I visited as many of the famous sites as possible and I loved ordering interesting meals in restaurants. I wanted to taste everything new and felt as if I was floating through it all in a wonderful dream. It was the first time I'd had onion soup and I got into a right mess with it because I hadn't realised that there was a soggy mass of melted cheese at the bottom of the bowl. I plunged my spoon in and it came back up looking like a gooey yellow lollipop, making it impossible to scoop up any of the soup. When I tried to bite some of the cheese off and pulled the spoon back out of my mouth there was a lengthy stream of sticky cheese between my mouth and the spoon that I tried to separate with a fork. That just made matters much worse because I then had strands of molten cheese spreading out from both utensils as well as the bowl. It would have been funny if I'd been with friends but sitting on my own, I was mortally embarrassed and was sure that the eyes of the whole restaurant were riveted on me. Who was this idiot who didn't know how to eat soup?.

I particularly enjoyed the nightlife and the sounds of live jazz bands blaring out onto the street as I walked past the bars with their outside terraces thronging with life. I was supremely happy and somehow felt that I really belonged there. I have never lost my love of that wonderful city and of France itself. At that time I wouldn't have thought it possible that at a future date I'd be Captain of a beautiful eighty-foot motor yacht based on a mooring just outside the city centre.

Christmas Eve in custody

I had some terrific friends in Gravesend and would regale them with the delights waiting in Paris for a single young man. I convinced them that they or any single male should never consider marrying until they'd experienced at least one weekend in Paris. My enthusiasm influenced them so much that six of us decided to go there for Christmas one year. On 24 December, we took off from Lympne Airport in Kent for a flight to Beauvais. Lympne Airport had been chosen as the landing site for the arrival of a Focke-Wulf 200 on 25 March 1941. It was Hitler's personal plane and his pilot, Hans Baur, had indicated that he wanted to defect and fly the plane to England with Hitler on board. This audacious kidnap plot, however, did not happen because at the last minute he changed his mind.

Our flights had been booked with Skyways, which was the world's first low-cost air coach service. It was established in 1946 and the flight that we took from Lympne to Beauvais was a far cry from modern day transport. The aircraft was a Dakota, a smallish, twin propeller craft that carried only a limited number of passengers. Dakotas had been used as transport aircraft during World War II and were one of the first commercially viable planes to carry passengers. Thousands of them were converted for use as civilian passenger planes by virtually every airline company after the war because they were cheap and easy to maintain. We had an exceedingly bumpy flight in this aircraft and spent most of the time wishing that we hadn't drunk so much before we left. If the wartime pilots had suffered half as much as we did on that flight we may have lost the war. Each of us tried to act as if we didn't have a care in the world, snickering at the plight of the others until we started to turn a strange shade of green. The interior of the plane was small and very basic. We were a total of 12 passengers with my pals and I seated behind the pilot. Our fellow passengers looked uncomfortable from the buffeting we were being subjected to but they didn't seem as distressed as we were. We were pleased when we landed at Beauvais airport, 85 kilometres NNW of Paris. During the German occupation in World War II, this airport was captured and used by the Luftwaffe, principally as a bomber base. Later, the bombers were moved away and interceptor fighter units were stationed there to defend the airport against constant daylight bombing by the American air force. Consequently, the airport suffered sustained bombardment to keep the interceptors pinned down. It was liberated on

03 September 1944 by the allied forces and after the unexploded munitions and wartime wreckage had been removed, it was opened as a commercial civil airport in 1956.

It was late when we finally staggered off the plane and onto the coach which took us into the centre of Paris. We found our way to the hotel that we had pre-booked, wasted precious little time unpacking and headed off in search of the pleasures to be found in that amazing city. It was Christmas Eve and after our nerve wracking flight we were ready to celebrate. We didn't get very far. On the opposite side of the road to the hotel, we walked past a small family run bar/restaurant. It was a bitterly cold night and the warm glow of the interior lights attracted us. We peered inside. A middle-aged couple and some attractive young girls were singing, dancing, drinking and surprisingly, not a single male was in sight, with the exception of the proprietor. We stood gazing through the window and when the occupants saw us gawking they beckoned us in. To say there was no hesitation would be an understatement as we rushed to squeeze through the door as one. My companions must have thought that I'd brought them to wonderland. We did have a most entertaining evening joining our new found friends in their celebrations. We'd ordered a meal to begin with, accompanied by copious bottles of wine that we were more than eager to share with our hosts. After the meal, we went to our hotel and brought back the bottles of duty-free booze that we'd bought at the airport so that we could share them with our fellow revellers. Our new friends spoke no English and none of us spoke any French, although my pal Paul had given us the impression that he had some knowledge of the language; we soon found out that he was somewhat delusional. It didn't matter; we had a marvellous evening. We joined in singing with them, making up our own words as we didn't have a clue what they were singing about. We danced with the girls until sadly the time came when everything ground to a halt and we asked for the bill, which was placed before us. *It was one hundred times what it should have been!*

We were aghast and sat staring at it with horrified expressions. Naturally, we refused to pay and it is regrettable that the situation became increasingly unpleasant. We'd had an unforgettable time with wonderful, hospitable people and now it was utterly ruined. Heated words were exchanged with wild gesticulations. Nobody comprehended in the slightest what the other was saying or attempting to convey by frantic arm waving and an exhaustive panoply of facial expressions. The only word we understood was "Gendarmes" that cropped up every now and again and we repeated it back, it being one of the few French words we knew. Anyway, we knew we were being ripped off, so had nothing to fear. How wrong can one be?

One of our group, Derek, went outside, presumably back to the hotel. Shortly afterwards the door burst open and in rushed several gendarmes. Without further ado, they surrounded us, shoved our arms up behind our backs, bundled us into the waiting van and whisked us off to the police station. They made us stand up against the wall for over an hour. Standing upright for a lengthy period is not easy when you are inebriated and tired. I was standing to the left of my friend Sid.

"Pssst," he whispered.

I swivelled my eyes in his direction. He surreptitiously cast his eyes down to his jacket pocket on the side closest to me. I followed his gaze. He then looked straight ahead so as not to attract any attention and gently eased part of an apple up to the top of his pocket.

"I stole it," he mumbled.

"When?" I asked.

"When they overcharged us," he whispered. "I picked it up from a bowl of fruit, I hope they won't notice it," he whispered again, obviously worried, though why anybody would be so concerned about a single apple at a time like that was hard to imagine.

He let the apple drop back into his pocket. I snickered and that seemed to ease his fears because then a smile replaced his worried expression. The smile broadened. He looked at me and the sight of me stifling a giggle made him start to giggle.

Paul, feeling confident that with his spattering of French words he could ease, if not even resolve the situation, walked over to the group of gendarmes.

"Er, excusez moi," he slurred.

The next moment he was lying flat on his back on the floor. One of the gendarmes had socked him one and flattened him. The rest of us stared in disbelief. He was our only hope and he'd blown it. Sid and I looked at each other and I motioned with my eyes to the apple in his pocket with a worried look on my face. He almost wet himself.

Paul came to and stood up dazed, blinking his eyes. He was forced back to the wall with the rest of us and that's where they made us stand for the whole of the rest of the night. It wasn't how we'd imagined that we'd spend Christmas Eve. Before we left Gravesend, I'd convinced them that they'd have an unforgettable time in Paris, which was turning out to be true, but not in the way that any of us had expected!

Seven a.m., Christmas Day. We were sagging and still not allowed to move when in walked the proprietor of the bar from the previous evening. He went straight to the desk and slammed down his bill. The Gendarmes conversed with him for a while. There were a couple of nods and hostile glances in our direction. One of the Gendarmes went over to Paul. Paul quivered and went a strange colour as he was grabbed and pulled over to confront the bar owner. They chatted among themselves for a while then they broke into smiles and Paul was nodding and saying "Oui, oui." We understood that.

A few years previously, in 1960, the French franc had been revalued. The new French franc was valued at one hundred old French francs with the latter becoming centimes. In spite of that, the French population still quoted in old francs. In fact, this carried on until the introduction of the Euro in 2002, and even the younger generation who'd never known the old franc insisted on using them. It was very confusing to visiting foreigners. When dealing with matters with which one wasn't familiar and had no idea of the true cost, it could be startling to be told the figure in hundreds or even hundreds of thousands. That's what caused our misunderstanding in Paris. As soon as the misunderstanding became apparent, of course, we paid immediately and everybody was happy. Well, the bar owner was happy. We were thirsty, hungry, tired, fed up but most of all, relieved. After the bill was settled the Gendarmes metamorphosed into kindness itself. There was much laughing, no doubt a lot of it at our expense. We were escorted back to our hotel in the back of the police waggon and during the drive back they couldn't do enough for us. We arrived wearing their kepis and surprisingly they even gave us their guns to amuse ourselves with. We said our goodbyes with the customary French handshakes and went up to our rooms. Derek had spent the night alone having no idea what had happened. He'd looked through the bar door and not seeing us there, went to his room and slept. He was flabbergasted when we related our little saga to him.

From that moment on, things got better and better and everything I'd promised them came to fruition. We had a wild, hilarious, unforgettable time and the memories provided us with laughter whenever we met in the years that followed. Almost our entire time there was spent in the Pigalle area, famous for the Moulin Rouge and the Can Can, a dance that had originated there. It was the place to be to experience Paris by night with its night clubs, topless and nude shows, and live jazz and in one area, it was reminiscent of present day Amsterdam. We stood outside staring in amazement as four provocatively dressed prostitutes sat at a window looking out shamelessly at passers-by. We weren't saying much, just ogling and then we were surprised to see Derek stroll across the floor towards one of them. He had a habit of sidling off to do his own thing without discussing anything. It was the reason that he wasn't arrested with the rest of us on Christmas Eve, having decided to disappear to the hotel. He stood before the attractive girl that he'd slyly chosen whilst the rest of us were merely watching. There was a brief nod of their heads, then she slid from her stool and walked off bidding Derek to follow her. He glanced over his shoulder and looked at us with a lascivious grin. We gave him the thumbs up and a cheer then wandered over to the bar on the opposite side of the road to wait for him. It wasn't very long before he came over to us looking more than pleased with himself. We bombarded him with questions. We wanted to know everything that happened, all the minutest details. The more we quizzed him, the more excited he got as he relived the ecstatic time he'd had as he glanced continually across the street to the girls in the window. He got so excited in fact, that he couldn't contain himself any longer so he rushed back over there for a second go. So, we had to wait again. The second time he was even quicker and he came back subdued. He had been too hasty, allowing his enthusiasm to get the better of him and after having paid he was unable to perform. We then each went our own way. Paul and I stayed together and met two Parisian girls who took us back to their flat for the evening.

The next evening we went into a bar hidden in a dingy side street, and the only customers were attractive, scantily clad girls. We couldn't believe our luck. We discovered that they were performers in a strip joint close by and we had the most fabulous evening with them. At times, one or more of them went next door to the club to perform and when they came back another one or two would go. They were totally uninhibited and wild. One of them took a particular fancy to Sid, the apple thief and he couldn't take the smile from his face as she fondled him in front of the rest of us. We stayed there enjoying their raucous company for a long time that evening before we went around the city to see what else it had to offer us and we weren't disappointed. The trip turned out to be everything I'd promised my friends it would be. It was indeed unforgettable. After our time in Paris life seemed flat once we'd returned to Gravesend and I resumed my life on Old Father Thames.

A small role in history

Thirty million years ago, before Britain became an island; the Thames was a tributary of the River Rhine. Around 10,000 years ago, after the ice age, the melting ice swelled it to ten times its current size and about 3,000 years ago, it took the meandering course it has today. Men have traded on the Thames since the Bronze Age and when the Romans arrived in London and established a port, they discovered that the flood tide could carry them from the North Sea 50 miles up the Thames. At the spot where they came to a halt, they built the first bridge, which is the site of the current Tower Bridge. The only times we went upstream of the Tower Bridge was with one or other of the two ships operated by Naviera Aznar SA, the Monte Ulia and her sister ship Monte Urquiola. They were the largest ships to pass under Tower Bridge, carrying produce and passengers from the Canary Islands and would berth at New Fresh Wharf close to London Bridge.

The Thames is Britain's largest river and the most important gateway to the London docks. Gravesend, on its Southern shore, has been a town of considerable maritime activity for centuries. In 1401, a Royal Charter gave the men of Gravesend permission to carry passengers to and from London and it soon became a popular alternative to the dangerous route along the Dover to London road, which crossed Blackheath that had a reputation for its infamous highwaymen. Four hundred years after the Royal Charter was granted, the first steamboat began making the journey to and from London, which brought increasing numbers of visitors, making Gravesend one of the first English resorts for tourists.

On 21 March 1617, a ship left London carrying John Rolfe and Princess Pocahontas, bound for Virginia. Pocahontas was the daughter of Chief Powhatan, the predominant chief of around thirty minor tribes of the Tidewater region, Virginia. She had been taken captive and held for ransom during the Anglo-Indian war in 1613 and converted to Christianity whilst in captivity, taking the name of Rebecca. At the time of her release, she chose to remain with the English and in 1615 married a tobacco planter named John Rolfe, which helped bring about an end to the war. They went to London in 1616, where she was introduced to English society as a "civilised savage" and became a much-feted celebrity. Pocahontas, however, was unwell, and by the time the ship reached Gravesend she had fallen gravely ill. She was taken ashore and died of unknown causes very shortly afterwards at the age of 21. She was buried at St George's church at the bottom of Gravesend High Street where there is a life-size bronze statue in her honour. She is most famous for reputedly saving the life of Captain John Smith, a colonist who, with one hundred others, settled in Virginia in April 1607. In December of that year, he was captured by a Powhatan hunting party and when threatened with death, it is said that Pocahontas placed her own head in the way as the club was raised to shatter Smith's skull. Her story has been portrayed in numerous films and literature over the years.

Mary Shelley mentions the town in her novel 'Frankenstein', as does Charles Dickens in at least three of his novels. He lived at Gads Hill Place, two miles east of Gravesend and close to where I lived there was a pub was called the Dickens Inn. There is also a Dickens Road. General Gordon also lived in the town from 1865 – 1871 during the construction of the Thames forts that guarded the river downstream from Gravesend. One of them, Shornemead, was an artillery fort that was abandoned in the 1950's and we boys would go there regularly to use it as a playground. General Gordon decided to improve the lives of disadvantaged boys, supplying food and clothing from his army wages and installing a Sunday school. In his memory, Gravesend Promenade is known as the Gordon Promenade and the secondary school that I attended was also named after him.

In 1932 a civilian airport was established on the eastern outskirts of the town that became a Royal Air Force fighter base in 1939 and was heavily bombed by the Luftwaffe during WWII. In 1944, when the Nazi's began deploying the V1 flying bombs, the forerunner of today's cruise missiles, the danger was considered too great for flying operations so the airport was used as a base for barrage balloons instead. Although I could only have been 11 months old, I have a clear memory of being carried under the table in my mother's arms to shelter from a V1 that landed in Gravesend early in June. It must have been a truly terrifying ordeal to have had such a deep impact on my memory. I never discussed the circumstance with my mother but I know that there was another woman in the room who joined us under the table. Over the next three days, seventy-two V1's hit London and the South, killing and wounding hundreds of people. On 18 June, one landed just 100 yards from Buckingham Palace, killing 144 people and in total, almost 10,000 were launched from France. A fifth of them apparently either crashed on take-off or malfunctioned but nevertheless, approximately 100 a day hit Britain, killing a total of 22,000 and wounding 6000. The bombardment continued until the allied forces captured the launch pads in October. Hitler then began using the far more lethal V2 rockets. Over the next few months over 1400 were targeted on the U.K. with the last one striking on 24 March 1945. These deadly rockets had a range of 200 miles, flew at a speed of 3500 mph and were the prototypes for today's space program. Two of them hit Gravesend, one landing close to the Fort Gardens less than two miles from where we lived.

I'd been born just half a mile from the Royal Terrace Pier, in Gravesend Hospital, 500 feet from the edge of the polluted river Thames. In his novel "Little Dorrit," Dickens wrote that the Thames was a deadly sewer and in a letter to a friend wrote, "I can certify that the offensive deadly smells, even in that short whiff, have been of a most head-and-stomach-distending nature." And a journalist, George Godwin in a reference to the Thames foreshore, wrote, "in part, the deposit is more than six feet deep". Between 1831 and 1854 there were three cholera outbreaks and over 30,000 people had perished as a result of the horrific pollution. Raw sewage and discharges from factories and abattoirs had been pouring into the river since the 17th century. It reached a critical stage in 1858, the year of the "Great Stink", when an exceptionally hot summer sent the temperature to 35° and the level of the river, which was in effect nothing more than an open sewer, fell lower than normal, leaving piles of effluent on its banks. The smell was so overwhelming that in June, the curtains in the houses of parliament were soaked in lime chloride in an unsuccessful attempt to mask the stench and parliamentary members were unable to carry out their duties. Up to 250 tons of lime was spread onto the sewer outlets and onto the river banks at low tide to try to eliminate the overpowering smell. The civil engineer Joseph Bazalgette instigated a new system of interconnecting sewers to take the effluent clear of the city of London, which prevented further cholera outbreaks and saved thousands of lives. He also built the embankments over the foreshores, narrowing the river, which increased its flow, enabling it to more effectively remove the ever increasing amount of rubbish thrown into it. The embankments concealed the pipes for the new sewage system and allowed roads and raised walkways to be built. In 1878, the pleasure steamer SS Princess Alice collided with a Collier close to the sewer outlets and 650 people died mainly as a result of the toxins in the river. During the war, German bombs destroyed some of the Victorian sewage systems and post-war Britain lacked the funds or the inclination to restore them. When I joined Ship Towage, the Thames had been described as a "Badly managed open sewer" and "A vast, foul-smelling drain". The river didn't begin to breathe again until the late sixties then the sewage systems were improved as part of the post-war recovery.

I have played my small role in Gravesend's history and the history of the Thames, which provided us tugmen with our livelihood and sadly, all too often, an untimely death. I am privileged to have been a part of it and of the steam age. It's unbelievable the amount of power that was produced by boiling water. Those magnificent steam engines were built of high quality steel and polished brass, with wheels, valves, levers, dials and a maze of pipes carrying the steam to perform different functions to power the mills, agricultural machinery, trains and boats. I was also fortunate to have shared it with such wonderful, tough, hardworking, generous, and colourful characters. I'd learned a lot, and I'd had a good time but couldn't see a future for myself as a tugman and was ready for something new - so in the autumn of 1965, I left. Thus began a regular pattern throughout my working life. Every six or seven years or so, whether I was employed or had my own businesses, I would move on to seek a new experience.

Jill and me on the ketch in Cannes harbour

Part 2:
PLEASURE YACHTS

"Twenty years from now, you will be more disappointed by the things you didn't do than those you did. So throw off the bowlines. Sail away from the safe harbour. Catch the wind in your sails. Explore. Dream. Discover." – Mark Twain

CHAPTER 1
THE BLOODHOUND EFFECT

No, no Soho

I'd been spending many of my free evenings in London's West End and the Soho area and decided it would be fun to work and live there for a while, so I took a job in an office just a short walk from Soho. I never did live there and it wasn't long before I realised my mistake. I was so thoroughly bored living such a predictable, incredibly monotonous existence. Every day was the same. I caught the same train each morning and evening at the same time. I stood squashed between a heaving mass of commuters on London's underground. I walked along the noisy streets breathing in polluted air with thousands of others striding off to wherever they carried out their tedious duties. There were always the same people in the office. Each person performed the same routine day in, day out. The male staff wore the same dowdy grey suits whilst they sat answering telephones and shuffling papers. It's all right for some, somebody has to do it, but it wasn't for me. We took the same tea and lunch breaks at the same time each day and the mundane gossiping about other office staff on what I considered to be uninteresting topics was tiresome. What a contrast to the hectic, unpredictable, interesting, dangerous and enjoyable life on the tugs.

There was one positive aspect, the typing pool on the next floor down. I became accomplished at inventing excuses to go there as frequently as possible, with my visits culminating in a variety of dates. Complications cropped up at times as my philandering caused friction among the typists, but as the sparks flew at least something happened to contrast with the predictability of the boring routine. One morning a group of us were chatting in the reception area when the door flew open and an irate typist stormed in berating me for being unfaithful.

"I suppose you think you're clever," she shouted at me in front of the others.

"What, what have I done?" I asked, taken aback.

"You know perfectly well what you've done. If you prefer Brenda to me well you can go with her."

"I don't know what you're talking about," I said

"Oh yes you do. I saw the two of you walking here together." She was red faced and very angry.

"Yes, I walked to the office with her, so what, why are you angry with me for that?"

"Because you're a two timer and you've been leading me on. If you prefer to be with her, go ahead," and she stormed out, slamming the door in the process.

It was such a ridiculous situation. I had never actually dated her or asked her out, we had just shared our journey part of the way home and I periodically walked to the office with her. I was astonished at her anger and I had never at any time intimated that there would be anything else between us. She'd clearly interpreted something into our journeys together that simply was not there. The only thing I was guilty of was to walk to the office with another pretty typist, something that I'd often done before anyway. In fact, I think Brenda may have planned meeting me on the way to the office because she constantly sidled up to me making it clear that she fancied me. One day I was in the basement looking for a file and she appeared. There were two other staff members there. I went into the strong room where the most important files were kept under lock and key and she followed. The next moment the door was slammed shut and locked from the outside. Somebody had decided to play a little joke. When it became obvious that we were not going to be let out in a hurry I sat on the floor as there were no chairs inside. She came and sat down beside me and leant against me.

"What do we do now?" she said with a playful smile and a naughty twinkle in her eyes. I was trapped and her warm, sensuous body was being pressed against mine invitingly and it felt so good. I discovered later that she had cunningly planned for this to happen with one of her colleagues so that I wouldn't be able to escape her advances. Had the roles been reversed, I could well be facing charges of historic sexual harassment today

There were other enjoyable moments but I so missed the excitement, the unexpected and the danger. And how I missed being out in the open air. Having suffered the hardship of life on the tugs, I wasn't expecting to be craving a similar ordeal again so soon but anything was better than the banality of office work in a noisy, smelly, crowded city - so I left after a few months. After I'd given in my notice I was called into the main office where I was grilled by two senior members of the organisation, not because I was leaving but because one of the secretaries that I'd been dating had also given in her notice at the same time, unbeknown to me. They were convinced that I was involved, thinking, presumably, that we'd be running off together. They were devastated to be losing a valuable secretary. It was coincidental, nothing to do with me but it contributed to my last few days being rather unpleasant. I knew that I would miss the company of the typists but nothing else.

A eureka moment

Back in Gravesend with nothing to do and being a long time movie enthusiast, I went to the Majestic cinema in Gravesend's King Street. It was one of what used to be four cinemas in the town centre. In the 1960's, two films were shown at each sitting, with the Pathé News, a short clip on some interesting subject and advertisements by Pearl and Dean during the interval. I've no recollection of what the two films were but during the intermission, every cell of my body became electrified as I watched a brief clip of Prince Phillip sailing his ocean racing yacht, Bloodhound, a sixty three foot Bermudan rigged yawl, built in 1936 to conform to the twelve metre class. Twelve metre does not refer to the vessels length or any other specific measurement but refers to the formula governing design and construction. I don't think I've ever been so fired up about anything. I watched in awe as the yacht crashed through the waves and the crew were in constant action heaving on ropes. I knew immediately that that was for me. I could never have imagined then, that six years' later, I would be sitting with my wife in a restaurant in Cannes, enjoying a meal paid for by the gentleman opposite who was considering offering me the position as Captain of that very same Bloodhound.

I had never sailed before but I was determined that that was going to be my next venture. I left the cinema and went to the nearest newsagent where I scanned the shelves for yachting magazines. The thought of purchasing them was abhorrent to me; after all, I was unemployed. I picked up copies of Yachting World and Motor Boat and Yachting and flicked through the pages until I found the situations vacant columns. There was an advertisement for crew for an ocean racer which was under construction. Surely, it was meant to be. I bought a newspaper because it was cheaper than the magazines, returned to the advertisement, furtively took my fountain pen from my pocket and feigning interest in an article, noted down the details on the edge of the newspaper. I took the bus home and wrote a letter of application. I received a reply some days later inviting me to an interview in London. I went to the library and found a book on sailing, which I took home and read from cover to cover twice.

I was thrilled to be heading back to London with the vivid memory of the Bloodhound crashing through the waves under full sail and the prospect that I could be a part of that world. I arrived at my destination in good time. I tapped on the door and was bid enter by a gravelly voice. The room was smaller than the average office and immaculate. It was probably just hired for the purpose of the interviews. Seated behind a small desk was a smartly dressed, beefy man with a bristly ginger beard on a ruddy face. It was evident that he was an athletic, macho, outdoor type, the type I was used to working with. I didn't actually lie during the interview, if I had I would have soon been exposed as a fraud, but I did skip adroitly around the fact that I had never sailed. The job just sounded too good to be true. The yacht, designed by a well-known architect, was being built for my interviewer and his brother, who both had the ambition to enter races and needed someone aboard as permanent crew. The salary was way above the measly remuneration I received for my boring time in London and approximated what I was earning on the tugs. When I was told that I was also to be given a considerable "victualling allowance," I was champing at the bit and trying not to let it show. With every fibre of my being, I was willing him to offer me the job.

"Thank you for coming," he said, "I have other applicants to see. Let me know how much I owe you for your expenses."

I was disappointed. I wanted to start there and then, that very minute. Nobody had ever offered to pay my expenses before and if that was an indicator of things to come, I liked the sound of it already. I had to have that job. I waited impatiently for ten days and then the letter arrived. It outlined the terms and conditions of employment together with instructions to go to Warsash in eight weeks' time, where accommodation had been arranged for me. I was overjoyed. "All you need in this life is ignorance and confidence, and then success is sure." – Mark Twain.

....

The thought of sitting around for eight weeks was unappealing, so I applied for and got a job as a Deckhand on a small oil tanker on the Thames. It was our duty to refuel ships and it was a most disagreeable occupation. It was dirty, smelly, monotonous and cold and the crew, although not unpleasant, didn't seem to have much of a sense of humour, a far cry from the tug crews. I suppose I'd expected a similar atmosphere to that on the tugs but it was not so. At least I learned something new, the art of sculling, but I learned the hard way. At the end of my first day on the tanker, after we'd moored to the buoy for the night and the crew had jumped into the wooden tender to get ashore, the Skipper turned to me and in a brusque manner said,

"Can you scull?"

"No." I replied.

"Well, you'll fucking well learn now. Take us ashore," he bellowed as he handed me the single oar.

I took it and went to the stern. Never having sculled before I didn't quite know how to start. I slipped the oar into the single rowlock set into the transom and one of the crew set us adrift. I started waving the oar from side to side and it just jumped out of the rowlock each time I moved it. The art of sculling is to move the oar from one side to the other, twisting it each time with a figure of eight motion so that the boat is thrust forward on each movement. The problem for the novice is that the oar has a tendency to float up out of the rowlock with each thrust. The difficulty I had in mastering it was compounded by the group of experienced scullers watching my every move and particularly because I knew they were all anxious to get home. On top of that, the tide was whisking us away from where we needed to go. Frustrated and embarrassed, I tried without success. The oar took on a life of its own.

"Come on you dozy little Berkshire Hunt," the Skipper bawled, except he didn't really say Berkshire Hunt.

"The tide's carrying us away, if you don't get a fucking move on we'll be too far away," yelled another crew member.

"Pull yer fucking finger out," said another.

I struggled and struggled some more with instructions being yelled at me. I felt utterly useless. Eventually, I did manage to master it but we had by then been carried off by the tide and were a fair distance from where we should have been. I sculled until I was exhausted and finally the rest of the crew took over, taking turns to scull us to the jetty. When we eventually moored up and stepped ashore they all had a good laugh at my ineptitude and I had little choice but to see the funny side of it as well. I was pleased when the time came to leave the tanker and get on my way to what I really wanted to do more than anything else, ocean racing. The Skipper of the tanker was annoyed that I'd only stayed for the six week period but I'd learned another skill and had another experience.

Mum was worried and unhappy that I would be leaving home and she didn't make it easy for me. Having married a seaman, she knew what was involved and she was right because I didn't see very much of either of them in the years that followed. Dad was supportive; he could hardly be anything else considering his own life history. I, however, was thrilled and thus began an exhilarating life of immeasurable thrills, hilarity, fear, danger and boundless other emotions.

CHAPTER 2
GIVING A FINGER TO THE SEA

Thank you, Dakota Staton

Warsash lies at the mouth of the River Hamble, where it joins Southampton Water. It was a delightful place to be. Boating has been a major activity there in one form or another for hundreds of years. A shipyard was built there in 1807 where ships were built for the Royal Navy. It went into decline by the end of the 19th century when fishing and agriculture, in particular, the cultivation of strawberries, became an important part of the economy, together with yachting. The shipyard at Warsash was owned by the company Thomas Roberts, but since 1964 it was called the Morgan Giles shipyard following the purchase of the original Teignmouth-based Morgan Giles shipyard after the death of Francis Morgan Giles. My B&B was a house among numerous others of similar design in Shore Road, Warsash, very close to the shipyard. It was a warm, comfortable, homely house filled with many knick-knacks and a very obliging and motherly lady who served up superb food. With my victualling allowance I was also able to enjoy evening meals in pubs, restaurants and jazz clubs. The yacht was being built two miles upriver from Warsash at Moody's boat yard in Swanwick. Each of the brothers had a yacht already, both of which were chocked up ashore waiting to be placed back in the water and put up for sale.

When the two yachts were launched, they were brought to moorings in the River Hamble, offshore from Morgan Giles shipyard and I left my lodgings and moved on to one of them. The yacht was a medium sized fibreglass sloop. There was a cosy saloon and a snug fore cabin where I slept. It suited me to be afloat again, hearing the lapping of the water against the hull, the tapping of the halyards against the mast and the familiar smell of boats and the sea. It was a wonderful time for me, living aboard on my own with a motor launch supplied as tender so that I could go ashore for my shopping and for the evenings. I would occasionally dine at the Rising Sun Inn or the Silver Fern and on jazz nights at the Great Harry or the Jazz Club at the Dolphin Hotel at Botley - often with a local girl. I was particularly captivated by one of them; she was small and strikingly attractive, with curly black hair, dark eyes, impeccably dressed in expensive clothes and well-spoken. She was the daughter of a successful father and was used to luxurious things. I invited her to join me for dinner at the Rising Sun Inn one evening and as I was keen to impress her, we had a few gin and tonics before we ate. To accompany the meal, I ordered a ridiculously pricey bottle of wine, making sure to mention its vintage to the waiter when I ordered it so that my date would be suitably dazzled by my knowledge and sophistication. When it arrived and I'd ostentatiously sniffed and swirled it around in my mouth before nodding my approval to the waiter, I discovered that she didn't like wine. After the money I'd spent there was no way that any was going to be left. I drank the whole bottle myself, which evidently affected my comportment adversely because after we'd finished the meal and I'd escorted her home, she ignored me from that moment on. I was devastated but the wine was excellent.

I still had my passion for cooking and most evenings I would set a fishing line, pulling it up in the mornings so that I always had a supply of fresh fish whenever I wanted it. Cooking aboard was somewhat restricted on a two ring calor gas burner set down in a shallow well but with some creativity, I managed to produce delicious meals. I have never been a person to resort to processed or junk food; I enjoyed eating far too much and have never understood why some people just can't be bothered to cook fresh, wholesome produce. On waking up in the mornings after well spent late nights ashore, I'd stumble to the cooker to prepare my morning tea. One morning, I rolled out of my bunk on an especially lovely day and decided to have a lazy time sitting in the cockpit after breakfast. I sauntered dreamily over to the cooker, filled the kettle, leant over, turned on the gas and struck the match. The explosion was completely unexpected. It shook me to the core. I recoiled backwards in shock as flames shot up into my face and I heard and smelled the sizzling of my hair and eyebrows. Once I'd stopped quivering from the shock and composed myself after a fashion, I realised that there was a gas leak and as calor gas sinks, it had collected in the cooker well and ignited as soon as I'd struck the match. I never trusted that cooker again even after it had been repaired; all future uses from that moment on were with an outstretched arm as I stood as far away from it as possible and cautiously moved the lighted matched to the burner.

Moody's boat yard at Swanwick operated a refuelling barge that passed me from time to time as it motored up and down the river. The Deckhand was Janet, a friendly, buxom, red-haired girl and we began to shout out pleasantries to each other as she passed me. Over time, the barge passed ever closer to me and it didn't take long before I'd asked her for a date and she'd accepted. We had a good relationship, which continued for quite some time and I no longer sought out the company of other females, no matter how flirtatious they were. And then, one bright sunny day, the barge came into view heading downstream to my mooring with Janet standing on the deck, waving to me. I waved back totally transfixed, but not by Janet. I couldn't take my eyes off her stunning companion. As the barge came closer, my gaze was riveted on the long haired girl in shorts with incredibly long, shapely legs. I couldn't help myself. Janet had persuaded her Skipper to stop off at my boat for a while so that we could chat. Pleasantries were exchanged between the three of us, Janet, the bewitching brown eyed beauty with her, and me. I had difficulty focusing attention on Janet during the conversation because my eyes kept wandering to the other girl. They swivelled of their own accord. I couldn't seem to stop them. Every time I looked at Janet my eyes betrayed me by flicking towards her companion. The Skipper called out to Janet to attend to some task or other and I decided to take advantage of her absence. I just had to get to know the other girl, so started blubbering about anything at all to get her interest. It happened that the American female jazz vocalist, Dakota Staton, was performing at the Dolphin jazz club in Botley that night (I have always been an avid jazz fan and had regularly visited the Flamingo and the Marquee clubs in London). Whilst Janet was occupied with her chores, I mentioned the concert to her companion and was surprised that she knew who Dakota Staton was. So we had jazz in common. That sealed the deal. Her name was Jill and I invited her to have dinner with me that night followed by an evening of jazz, which she found too tempting to resist.

"Dakota Staton, wow, that's terrific," she said. From the tone of her voice I was under no illusions that the main attraction for her was an evening listening to Dakota Staton, but either way, it was to be the beginning of an enduring relationship.

They should have listened

The racing yacht, a sloop, was finally finished. She was a magnificent vessel built to Lloyds 100A1 specification with accommodation for seven. There were two bunks in the fore cabin, three in the saloon and two quarter berths. With the owners present, I stood on the deck in my smart uniform as she was launched and then we motored down to our mooring at Warsash. I so looked forward to sailing her and wasn't disappointed when the time came to do just that. After the launch party had finished and over the following few weeks, the owners came to Warsash whenever they could and we had trial sails in Southampton Water, putting the beautiful, sleek vessel through her paces until they felt they were satisfied with everything. I watched everything they did and joined in as if I knew what I was doing but all the time making mental notes on what was involved so that I could appear competent in the future. We were entered in the Cowes - Deauville race that year. It was my dream come true. The thought of going to Deauville was appealing because of my long standing love of France and all things French. Deauville, with its lavish hotels, had a reputation as the Parisian Riviera. It was popular with the rich and famous but by 1966 it was attracting more of the general population and I was looking forward to spending time there.

12. The Ocean Racer

Prior to the race, I checked through the extensive sail inventory and prepared as much as I could before the owners arrived with their friends who would be making up the full crew. We did some trial runs so that by the time it came to set off on the race we were familiar with each other and the plan of action. The race began well. There was a good stiff breeze and it was wonderful to finally realise my dream of racing. When the decision had been taken on which genoa would be the most appropriate for the wind conditions, it was hauled up from the sail locker and taken out of its bag. We headed into the wind with the engine ticking over whilst the mainsail was hoisted. The boom was left flapping around whilst we fastened the genoa to the forestay and hoisted it. The engine was switched off, the sheets were wound in on the cockpit winches, the wind filled the sails and we took off. We had to sail around trying not to stray too far from the starting line. The trouble was, so did everybody else. It was chaotic with all the participating yachts vying for position, each one sailing around, in and out and across all the others. It seemed that everywhere we wanted to go so did the others with the crews shouting out to each other and keeping an eye on their stopwatches, waiting for the starting gun. Too far forward and we'd be disqualified, too far back and we'd be starting at a disadvantage. The atmosphere was intoxicating. The gun went off. It was a relief that we hadn't miscalculated our arrival at the starting point. We rapidly winched in the sheets, the sails tightened, filled with wind, we heeled over and were off at the same time as the rest of the fleet, all aiming to reach Deauville harbour ahead of the others. Everything was going well as we set course for the French coast and ploughed through the waves with a comforting hissing sound as the hull sliced effortlessly through the water. Watches were set so that we could take turns at sleeping. There wasn't much time to relax as we kept a constant eye on the wind, tweaking the sails with each wind change to coax the maximum speed from the yacht and changing them for ones more appropriate for the wind strength whenever necessary. There was much heated discussion over the advantages of changing the headsails against the disadvantages of losing ground in the process.

The trouble started in the middle of the night. The wind strength increased and veered round slightly more to our starboard quarter. We were well up among the leading yachts. The waves were getting higher and we were pitching and getting wet from the salty spray from the wave crests blown onto us by the force of the wind. The turbulent water looked black and the lights of the other yachts around us were flickering as they were momentarily lost from sight due to the rolling and pitching movements. It started to rain and we donned oilskins. The English Channel is one of the busiest waterways in the world with 500 ships a day passing through on their way to Europe in one direction and the Atlantic Ocean in the other. They sometimes don't see smaller craft, so we also had to watch out for their steaming lights so that we could avoid them hitting and sinking us. It is not an uncommon occurrence for smaller craft to be sunk by large ships. Against the advice of everybody else on board, the owners of the yacht took the fateful decision to hoist the spinnaker. We hooked on our safety harnesses and made our way to the foredeck. The spinnaker was hauled out of the sail locker onto the pitching foredeck and the halyard, sheets and boom were connected. As soon as everything had been prepared, the genoa was dropped, the slack taken up on the spinnaker sheets and the spinnaker hoisted at the same time that the helmsman swung us back around on course. The spinnaker instantly filled with wind, ballooned out with a crack and swung out to the port side. We heeled over at a dramatic angle as the boom whipped around smashing onto the forestay with a savage twang. The boat shuddered and heeled ever more dramatically to port. There was an agonised yell. One of the crew buckled over onto the foredeck. He had been gripping the forestay to steady himself from the violent motion and when the spinnaker boom smashed onto the forestay it had sliced off one of his fingers. Some crew members were struggling to stay upright in order to take control of the spinnaker as the waves pounded us and we were lashed by the rain in the pitch dark of the night, with ropes and sails flailing around us in the strong wind.

"Get the fucking thing back down," came a frantic cry.

The injured man crawled along the leeward deck wailing as he searched in vain for his severed finger, hoping to see it miraculously floating before him. He left a trail of blood that spread in the water sloshing in the scuppers. Somebody else crawled along after him trying to coax him down below to safety. It was bedlam. The wind had been too much on our beam to set the spinnaker.

"What the fuck's going on up there?" the helmsman shouted out.

"David's been injured," somebody called back.

"Bring the bloody thing into the wind," another cried out to the helmsman.

"Let go the spinnaker sheet," came another cry.

We were crouched on the foredeck getting soaked from the spray and the rain as we tried to keep ourselves in one place and take control of the situation. The helmsman spun the wheel and when we headed into the wind, pitching violently, the spinnaker and its sheets were flapping madly over our heads.

Throughout it all the helmsman was screaming out, "What the fuck's going on?" as he tried to make himself heard amidst the noise of the wind, the sea, the rain, the flapping of the sails and ropes and the shouts from the rest of us.

The injured man was dragged clear of the mass of ropes and sails so that we could drop the spinnaker and re-hoist the genoa as quickly as possible. Some of us concentrated on sorting out the tangled sail and ropes whilst another crawled along the leeward deck that was awash with sea water, looking for anything that resembled a finger. It was hopeless, the finger had disappeared forever. The injured man was helped to his bunk and we radioed through to Deauville for medics to meet us when we arrived. We'd lost a lot of time and were well behind the leading yachts. The wet spinnaker was bagged and stowed; the genoa was set and the rest of the voyage went as well as could be expected. We eventually reached Deauville the following day having maintained radio contact so that the ambulance was waiting to take the patient to hospital as soon as we'd moored up. He returned several hours later, packed his bags and went home. The rest of the time in Deauville was spent relaxing and having a good time with all of the fleet celebrating either their success or at least their arrival! When the celebrations had finished, the rest of the crew went back to the UK and I stayed aboard waiting for the owners to return for the trip back to the Hamble. I had a great time in glorious sunshine and took the opportunity to practice the small amount of French I knew. I'd learned a bit of French from a language course I'd bought in my teens after I'd met a gorgeous, tanned French girl in Margate. I'd gone there for a day trip just to see what it was like and it wasn't long before I noticed her and asked her to join me for the day. She lived in Casablanca and I'd imagined that we might get serious and that I'd be invited to Casablanca sometime as a result of our journey together through Margate's tunnel of love. She obviously had other ideas and didn't get quite the same pleasure in the tunnel of love as I thought she did or the pleasure was so intense she couldn't bear to repeat it. Either way, the romance fizzled out. I didn't go to Casablanca and I got bored studying French with no further objective but had gained enough knowledge to make myself understood.

.

CHAPTER 3
GETTING SPLICED

Force 10 to Weymouth

I'd stopped seeing Janet, and Jill and I were seeing each other regularly, maintaining discretion so that Janet wouldn't find out. We both felt guilty, Jill more than me because she and Janet had been close friends for many years. Initially, Jill was only interested in the opportunity to see Dakota Staton live and hadn't expected to finish up in a relationship with me, at least that's what she says now and since I was having a good time on my own in Warsash, I had no intention of getting involved in a long-term relationship either, but neither of us had reckoned on fate. Inevitably, we were caught red-handed one day as we walked along Hamble Lane holding hands and Janet drove past us in the opposite direction with her parents. We stopped dead in our tracks as the car slowed down and we saw the three occupants glaring at us. Jill was devastated and the relationship between her and Janet soured from then on until one evening Janet got her revenge. She happened to be in the village pub, the Bugle, at the same time as me. Whether this was deliberately planned by her or whether we met by chance, I don't know but after several drinks, she invited me back to a boat moored just off shore that she happened to have the keys for. I accepted without thinking it through. As the evening wore on, she made advances towards me and the outcome was that I allowed myself to be seduced by her. Jill was a virgin and had every intention of remaining so until she was married, which was an admirable attribute and an uncommon one among the other girls I'd encountered in those swinging sixties. She was exceptionally attractive emotionally, intellectually and physically and whilst I longed to make love to her I respected her wishes so I was a frustrated young man. There was no excuse for my betrayal, however. The following morning I was so consumed with guilt I confessed immediately I met Jill. She was particularly hurt by Janet's act of retribution and no doubt by my own disloyalty. With hindsight, it does seem strange that Janet happened to have the keys to that boat on that particular night. The score having been evened between the two girls, the friendship between the three of us was ultimately rekindled and I was never again unfaithful to Jill.

....

The final sail of the season was a voyage along England's South coast to Plymouth. I loved the physical act of hoisting the sails and the moment when the wind filled them, the engine was switched off and the yacht sliced her way sweetly through the water with a satisfying hiss. Sailing was everything I'd hoped for and more and I was pleased to be entering another new harbour when we arrived at Plymouth. Plymouth was the departure point for the Pilgrim Fathers when they set sail for the New World in 1620 and founded Plymouth Colony, now called Plymouth, Massachusetts. It was also the home port of England's first slave trader, Sir John Hawkins. He was one of the 16th century's preeminent sailors, principle architect of the Elizabethan Navy and he helped design the ships that repelled the Spanish Armada. It was also the home port of one-time mayor of Plymouth, Sir Francis Drake, another slave trader who circumnavigated the world and introduced piracy on the West coast of the Americas. Drake was knighted in 1581 and was the second in command against the Spanish Armada in 1588. The English hailed him a hero but the Spanish considered him a pirate, and King Phillip II supposedly offered a reward for his life of £4,000,000 by today's standards. In time, Plymouth, meaning mouth of the River Plym, became an important commercial shipping port and naval base, taking city status in 1914. During the battle of the Atlantic in WWII, the German Luftwaffe carried out 59 heavy bombing raids, targeting the dockyards and laying waste to much of the city. 1172 civilians were killed and 4428 injured. After the war, the city was rebuilt and expanded to incorporate Plympton, which lay further up the River Plym and the commuter suburb of Plymstock.

Whilst in Plymouth we enjoyed a few nights on the town, as sailors do and as the time to start heading home to Warsash approached, the weather deteriorated. The yacht was powerful and could easily cope with any rough seas, so with gales of force 7 – 8 forecast, we set off under a reefed mainsail and a small jib, towing the inflatable dinghy. It was an exhilarating sail. The wind strength increased as we continued on our way and the forecast was for it to increase to force 10, so the decision was taken to make it as far as Weymouth and lay up there until the weather improved. The wind howled and one markedly strong gust picked up the dinghy from the water until it was flying from the stern like a kite. Two of us ran aft and pulled on the painter to haul it back but the wind was too strong and the dinghy was spinning around above us. We eased off the mainsail and jib sheets to reduce speed and managed to haul the wildly spinning dinghy aboard. We deflated it and stowed it safely away. With that little task accomplished, the sheets were winched in once more and we shot off at a pleasing rate of knots to Weymouth. We arrived there exhausted and coated in salt from the constant spray splattered on us by the strong wind. The harbour was crowded with boats sheltering from the storm in addition to the vessels permanently based there but we found a suitable place to moor on the outer side of two other boats. The middle boat that we were tied to was owned by a well-known and popular TV personality but we soon discovered that he was not the same wise-cracking and caring person that he portrayed on his game and talent shows. He was there with his pretty and vivacious accomplice from the TV shows and resented us crossing over his boat to get ashore. The owner of the boat that I was on was a tough, no-nonsense, ex-military type and it wasn't long before a raging row broke out between the two of them. After that, the TV personality never complained again.

The gales were set to last for some days so the owners decided to return home leaving me aboard until they could come back to make the return trip to the Hamble. I had a thoroughly enjoyable ten days on my own and have very pleasant memories of my time there and I especially remember having some excellent meals in the local restaurants. On our eventual return passage to the River Hamble, we stopped off for a night in Swanage bay. The gales had long since faded away so it was a gentle trip in hazy sunshine, so calm in fact, that we motored most of the way. That night was still and cold with a mist setting in when we went ashore in the rubber dinghy to celebrate our last night and what was to be our last sail of the season. As the evening progressed, we drank a little more than we should have. By the time we left to stagger to the dinghy, inebriated, laughing and singing, a thick fog had descended on the bay. With difficulty, we negotiated the delicate undertaking of installing ourselves into the bouncing, unstable dinghy, with every one of us falling over each time another member of the party leapt in and the dinghy wobbled and shot forward. Clinging to each other for support to keep upright, the starting rope of the outboard motor was pulled by one of us and we all fell into a giggling heap as the dinghy lurched forward heading for the yacht. The problem was that through the dense fog we couldn't see where it was anchored and each one of us had a different recollection as to its whereabouts. We kept motoring straight ahead to where the most likely spot would be. It seemed to take a very long time until finally, we all fell forward into each other as we ground to an abrupt, bumpy halt with an accompanying crunching sound from beneath. The helmsman, mistakenly believing he was holding a steady course straight ahead had steered, we knew not where, until we finished up shuddering onto the beach at Swanage, back where we'd started from. I have no idea how we eventually found our way back to the anchored yacht that night but we did subsequently get there. The following morning, hungover from the previous night's frivolities, we weighed anchor and set sail for the Hamble. We threw some lines over the stern hoping to catch some mackerel and were soon hauling them in non-stop. The fog had cleared and it was a pleasant day so we briefly anchored in Alum Bay on the Isle of Wight. The cool sea breeze had more or less helped us recover from our hangovers so we were able to appreciate the multi-coloured sand cliffs that have been formed over time by the oxidation of iron compounds. The sea was calm, the sky had cleared and whilst the rest of the crew relaxed in the sunshine, I prepared and cooked the fish in a white wine sauce. It was a nice way to finish the season and we even managed to stay sober for the final leg to Warsash.

Almost carried away

I was glad to be moored up and on my own again at Warsash, if for no other reason than to enjoy the company of my long haired, long legged, 17-year-old girlfriend, Jill with her alluring big brown eyes. She, her parents and two older brothers initially lived in a semi-detached house in Shirley, a large suburb on the western side of Southampton. The name Shirley is derived from the Old English "scir" (bright) and "leah" (cleared land in a wood). It was there that her Dad, a lovable, multi-talented musician and brilliant engineer/inventor, worked from his garage until he was able to afford his own workshop. It was there that he invented the Jupiter water pump, which was a popular installation in boats and caravans. Her parents divorced when she was two years old and three and a half years later her Mother remarried and continued to live in Southampton. The rest of the family, together with her aunt and grandmother, moved to the small, hidden, eighteenth-century village of Godshill with its pebbled roads and mixture of cob and thatched cottages and brick buildings with slate roofs. In antiquity, it was a tithing of Fordingbridge Parish, one and a half miles away. The area, situated in the New Forest National Park has been inhabited since prehistoric times and was a paradise for Jill and her brothers, Roger and Barry. They swam in the river Avon, played in the undergrowth and climbed the trees. Jill's Dad continued with his engineering business and her aunt and grandmother ran the village restaurant. Two years later they took possession of an ex-motor torpedo boat moored at Moody's boatyard and fitted it out to accommodate the extended family, comprising Jill, her father, two brothers, aunt, grandmother, a cousin, and an uncle. By the time I met Jill in 1966, ten years after they'd moved aboard the MTB, her Dad had remarried and moved to Shaftesbury where he'd bought and ran the Glyn Arms public house. Her brother Roger had moved to London and was the sub-principle viola player with Sadler's Wells Opera Company. Her much-loved uncle had sadly left the material world. Her aunt, a loving, caring nurse and her mother, Jill's grandmother, had moved to Southampton as live in carers for an elderly, disabled lady. Her cousin, Simon, a talented musician, was studying at Bristol University, was engaged to be married and went on to become a pharmacist, so Jill lived aboard the MTB with just her oldest brother Barry and his pregnant wife Sue. Barry was also a talented musician as well as being a precision engineer with IBM. Whenever I visited her and several of the family members were present, I was touched by the loving atmosphere that permeated every inch of the boat as a result of the affection they all had for each other. Something I had sadly never felt in my own home. I found myself being drawn deeply into the harmonious ambience. Her father, both brothers and cousin were all jazz musicians so we had a common interest – jazz, as well as boats. It was through Jill's deceased uncle's legacy that I discovered Buddhism, which set me on a lifelong spiritual quest for the meaning of life, death and the thereafter.

················

For the remainder of that year, I pottered around maintaining the three vessels until the two that were for sale, sold and only the ocean racer remained. I still had the motor launch and would make frequent visits to Swanwick to meet up with Jill to whom I was becoming increasingly attached. For the second time in my life, I was perfectly happy to remain completely faithful to one girl. Moody's management team wanted to build a marina and Jill's boat had to leave the mooring. It had no engine so had to be towed to the Bruce Campbell Marina at Badnam Creek, further downstream to where the river bends and heads towards Warsash. This suited me because it was closer to where I was moored. I would take the motor launch to visit her and stay until late, leaving when it was dark, to head downstream to my bunk aboard the yacht.

I left her in the early hours of one still, moonless night. I jumped aboard the launch and spun the starting handle of the diesel engine that was set amidships. It was a reliable engine and it burst into life readily. I slipped the painter, pushed the gear lever forward with one hand, grabbed the tiller with the other and motored out of the creek and into the darkness. The engine was chugging away nicely as I headed out from the marina. There was no other activity anywhere on the river. It was flat calm and absolutely silent with the exception of the chugging of my engine, and it was cold. The tide was ebbing so it would carry me down the river in double quick time. As I was exiting the creek into the open river, the tiller suddenly shot downwards out of my hand and the boat shuddered and momentarily stopped before it sped forwards again. I'd run over an underwater mooring cable and the lower pintle had been ripped off the transom, leaving the rudder flapping around at a crazy angle behind the stern. I tried wiggling the tiller in different directions but the launch just kept speeding ahead on a course of its own.

When I cleared the inlet and entered the tidal stream, the bow spun around and I was getting washed down river. I was no long running the show. There was nothing I could do. The rudder was half out of the water, hanging just on its upper pintle. I throttled back to tick over speed, hung over the stern and pushed the rudder back down, holding it in position as best I could. This was no mean feat as the wooden rudder had the natural tendency to float back up again, which pulled the tiller down onto my legs so I had to remove it completely. I was determined that the rudder should stay underwater and it was determined to float back up again and leave me to be taken wherever it and the tide decided to take me, which, if I didn't get control, would be out into Southampton Water and beyond, maybe never to be seen again. I gritted my teeth, tenaciously plunged the rudder back down each time it sprang up again. I pointed the launch towards a moored yacht. Hanging over the stern, glaring at the wayward rudder and thrusting it down with a grunt and a curse, I couldn't see where I was going and I was unable to reach the gear lever and throttle. My clothing up to my armpits was drenched in icy cold water. I had my left hand on top of the rudder; my right hand was thrusting it downwards, trying to keep it underwater. My trunk was twisted, with my head swivelled over my left shoulder to peer into the darkness at the distant yacht on its mooring. I bumped into it as gently as I could and made fast. I cut the engine and sat down dejected to review my predicament. I was wet, tired, and cold and there was nobody to call for help. I couldn't spend the night sitting there. There was no chance of repairing the rudder. I was not in a happy situation. I reasoned that if I could keep the rudder held in position long enough and manage to see where I was going and keep the engine running to give me the steerage I needed, I could get to my boat. The dilemma then would be what to do next. The tide would be pushing me way past it at a rate of about 5 knots. In the ideal situation, on arrival, I would have been able to spin the launch around and head into the tide whilst I calmly motored alongside and made fast. Turning the launch against the tide with no rudder was not an option. I prepared myself for the unknown, started the engine, cast off and shoved my hands under water, once more gripping the rudder. The engine and tide immediately whisked me away downstream. I was off like a rocket with a combination of the tide and the propeller pushing me along, but despite that, the journey seemed to last a lifetime. I finally saw my boat ahead. I prayed that I would be able to get alongside her in time to grab hold of something before I was carried off to who knew where. I drew closer at a daunting speed, fighting to keep the rudder underwater and at the same time turning it as best I could to steer the launch in the right direction. I pointed the bow directly at the yacht and when I got as close as I possibly could, I let go the rudder, cut the engine, rushed to the bow and grabbed hold of a stanchion of the moored yacht, holding on as tightly as I could as the tide spun the launch around and alongside. I breathed an enormous sigh of relief. I'd made it. I secured the painter and stern line, pulled in and stowed the dangling rudder, jumped on the deck of the ocean racer and went down to my bunk with a big thank you to my guardian angel.

The next day, I unpacked and inflated the rubber dinghy using a foot pump, then attached its painter, threw it over the side, mounted the seagull outboard motor on the stern and towed the launch to the shipyard to be repaired. The dinghy was to be my means of transport for the next few days. The following morning, I decided to go ashore to do some shopping and treat myself to lunch in one of the pubs. I jumped down into the dinghy and twirled the starting cord around the flywheel of the outboard motor. Seagull outboard engines were always in gear so as soon as they roared into life, the propeller spun wildly and the boat would take off. To go into astern, the whole engine was spun around at a 180° angle and the boat would go in the opposite direction. I yanked on the starting rope, the engine roared into life and the dinghy shot forward. Unfortunately, I'd forgotten to let go the bow line. With a twang, it went bar tight but the dinghy didn't stop moving and with the bow firmly attached it had nowhere to go but upwards. As the bow rose into the air like a whale bursting out of the water, the stern and the outboard motor disappeared under water and I found myself scrambling up an almost vertical dinghy to get to safety aboard the yacht. The outboard motor, submerged, stopped working. I reached the bow of the vertical dinghy and clung on tightly. With no more momentum from the outboard motor and me hanging on to the bow, the distribution of weight had changed and the dinghy plunged back down again with a mighty slap as it hit the water, soaking me in the process. I sat bewildered for a while, looking around hoping nobody had witnessed what had happened. I had to rely on the local ferry picking me up after that. After a couple of days, I tried again and remarkably, the amazing seagull started for me. Shortly after those two demoralising circumstances Jill started work as a coder in the hospital inpatients department at the General Registry Office in Titchfield. To make the commute to Titchfield easier, she moved off the MTB and went to live with our mutual friend, none other than the Janet whom we had both deceived. That meant that it was easier for us to meet – no more boat trips to Badnam Creek for me.

A commitment

In September of 1966, I enrolled at the Warsash School of Navigation to study for the Board of Trade Yacht Master Certificate. The school was established in 1902 and is part of Southampton University and it claims to be the world leader in maritime education. The course was intensive, covering the international regulations for preventing collisions at sea, general seamanship, navigation, chart work, meteorology, magnetism, and semaphore and Morse code signalling, followed by celestial navigation. The owners of the yacht had no further plans to use the boat during the winter so I rented a flat in the Broadway in Hamble and throughout that winter concentrated on studying. I enjoyed the subjects and was determined to pass the exams. My fellow students were mature males and all were taking it very seriously; consequently, there was no socialising between us. One loner, a small, rather scruffy, scraggly bearded, dark-eyed individual always seated himself in the corner of the classroom as far back and away from everybody else as he could get. I never spoke to him or him to me throughout the course and exams but he was to have a significant effect on my life.

I was surprised and flattered when one day I received a letter from the secretary that I'd dated and who had resigned from the London office at the same time as me, offering to come and stay for a weekend. She'd made me an offer I had to refuse! She was such a lovely girl and we'd shared some wonderful moments together so I hoped I hadn't hurt her feelings. I'd been privileged to have been a young man in the affluent swinging sixties, arguably the most exciting decade to date. Parents of teenagers of that period had survived the war and wanted their children to enjoy life. Conscription had been abolished just one year before I would have been eligible for service and there was a cultural revolution by the young that influenced a break from tradition in fashion. It was the age of miniskirts and hotpants, Mods and Rockers and Dolly girls with false eyelashes. Women started to wear trousers and denim jeans arrived. The first arrival of original Levi Strauss stovepipe jeans from America was advertised on our black and white TV's and within a few days, two friends and I took the train to Tooting Broadway and bought a pair each. It was the decade of the emergence of the Beatles, the Rolling Stones and Woodstock, youngsters looking for fun, peace and love and the mantra "Make love not war". Until the sexual revolution of the sixties, sex was a taboo subject with the ever present fear of unwanted pregnancies - and then in 1961, the contraceptive pill was introduced in the U.K. and with it, feminism and sexual freedom. There was also the emergence of amphetamines, LSD and marijuana. With the exception of drugs, which I'd never been tempted to try, I'd had my share of all that that decade had to offer in abundance.

Jill had something special that set her apart from all the other girls I'd dated. As time went by I got ever closer to her and I came to realise that I would be happy to spend the rest of my life with her, so I asked her to marry me and she accepted. The next obstacle was to ask for her father's consent, the thought of which filled me with trepidation, but I knew it had to be done. A date was set for us to meet in his pub in Shaftsbury. When we arrived in the afternoon, I was surprised to see that Jill's brother Barry and his wife Sue were there. I'd expected a private chat with her Dad. Greetings were said and with a pint of beer in my hand, I silently rehearsed what I would say to him. Next, Jill's stepmother Claire came into the bar accompanied by her daughter and her husband. It wasn't looking very private. I slunk away from the bar feeling embarrassed and pressurised but it wasn't over. It wasn't very long before Jill's second brother, Roger arrived with his fiancée Liz and shortly after that, in came her cousin Simon with his fiancée Linda. I knew that Jill's family were very close and loving but I hadn't envisaged that I would need the consent of the entire family before she and I could marry. Feeling overwhelmed, I hovered in the background in an attempt to make myself inconspicuous. A party like atmosphere soon developed and whenever I peered over the top of my glass of beer I could see them staring expectantly at me with amused grins on their faces. I was embarrassed and after a long, uneventful wait, Roger decided to take out his viola, Liz sat at the piano and they entertained us with some classical music. Every now and again I plucked up some courage and rehearsed my speech, but when I looked at the anxiously awaiting entourage smirking, their eyes riveted on me, I decided to have a few more sips of beer instead. Her amiable, patient father was eyeing me in earnest, clearly amused by it all and I could see an understanding twinkle in his eyes. And so it went on. The outcome was that what was to have been a momentous family occasion became a momentous family non-event; I'd blown it. By the evening, I suggested to Jill that we leave it for another day so we bid our farewells and left. The next opportunity arose when Jill's Dad visited us in the flat I'd rented. He was sitting in one of the armchairs looking at me. Jill was standing next to me smiling and jogging me with her arm. I did it. I finally found the nerve to ask him. He didn't want to disappoint us but his face registered concern because Jill was so young, only 17, but in a roundabout way, he inferred that we had his blessing. It was a beautiful moment. I was happy. My gorgeous Jill would be mine forever and I would be her's forever. We got engaged that Christmas and flew to Palma to spend two weeks alone together. I should have realised that it wasn't the most auspicious date when Jill chose 1st April for the wedding. It was to take place at the small, picturesque Church of St Leonard's in Bursledon, a village on the Hamble that also has a maritime history. It was there, at the Elephant Boatyard, where Henry VIII's fleet of ships was built. When the shipbuilding came to an end in 1870, the cultivation of strawberries became a major industry.

The wedding almost never happened. My best man Paul and other friends, including Sid the apple thief, came from Gravesend and they thought it would be amusing to spike my drinks on my stag night. Totally unaware of what was going on, I was happily drinking with them and with each drink I had they poured in a generous shot of vodka. The following

13. *Managing to stand upright!*

morning I could hardly get out of bed I was so ill. Wobbling around in a daze, I somehow managed to get myself together and with Paul driving us all in his tiny Fiat 500, we arrived at the church at 15.30 hrs with no time to spare. I spent that entire day in a daze, shaking and feeling dizzy and sick and sadly the wedding is still a hazy memory for me. I was swaying at the altar and had to confess to my beautiful bride that I felt sick. At the end of the service I was shaking so much I was unable to write out the cheque for the vicar. I had to apologise and arranged to pay another day. By the time we were at the reception in the Oak Hill Hotel I was feeling dreadful and don't know how I managed to last the day. When an appropriate moment arose, we made our getaway and travelled to the Bridge Hotel in Fordingbridge in the New Forest for our honeymoon. I find it difficult to forgive my mates for their stupidity.

Jill and I didn't want to bring attention to ourselves, so after we'd checked in, we quietly went to our room without saying anything to anybody. The last thing we wanted was for it to be known that we were on honeymoon. The next morning at breakfast, we sat glancing at each other across the table, smiling and feeling smug about our little secret as we looked around at all the other unsuspecting guests.

"Jill, you should have told me," the landlady bellowed across the room as she sauntered towards us. "Your Dad called to say you were married yesterday, congratulations."
We both blushed and sank down lower in our chairs in a desperate attempt to conceal ourselves from the knowing grins of the fellow hotel guests whose eyes swivelled towards us. We hadn't known that Jill's dad knew the hotel owner.

A little knowledge

My studies went well, although practising the signalling wasn't easy as it couldn't be done alone, so teamwork was arranged with two others from the boatyard who had also enrolled on the course. During the lunch break, for privacy, we climbed the ladders and boarded the boats that were chocked up in the hangar. We had rigged up a system so that one person seated on the deck of a boat, could tap out the shorts and longs of the Morse code on one apparatus, which caused a light to flash on another apparatus further away on the next nearest boat where two of us sat in the cabins. One of us watched for the short and long flashes and called out the letters of the alphabet that were transmitted and the other wrote down what was being sent. My friend Dave had volunteered to send the messages on one particular day and with the contraption on his lap, in the silence of the hangar, he began tapping his message but the tapping was audible which distracted me as I watched for the flashing lights. I complained to him so he threw his leather jacket over his lap to muffle the sound. Concentrating on tapping out the messages, he didn't notice until it was too late, the two men walking out of the hangar, whispering to each other, glancing back at him occasionally with a mixture of disbelief and utter disgust on their faces. They had been watching him sitting alone, engrossed in jiggling his hand up and down beneath the leather jacket over his lap and had put their own interpretations of what they'd seen.

Way into the night in our rented flat, Jill patiently tested me over and over again as we worked our way through all the navigation lights and rules and regulations that I had to learn parrot fashion. It was a long, hard slog. The exam was scheduled for May and I had already quit my job aboard the ocean racer to focus full time on studying and getting my Yacht Master Certificate. Jill meanwhile, continued working for the General Registry Office to support us both. She cycled through the woods each day from Hamble to Bursledon where she met a fellow worker who drove them both to Titchfield. At weekends, she would sometimes go with fellow workers to netball matches that she had organised, whilst I stayed at home studying. It was Jill who had taken it upon herself to put together the team in the first place. I particularly enjoyed learning meteorology and was so good at it that when Jill had planned an away match for her team one Saturday I was able to confidently predict the weather for that day.

"I'm off then," she called to me.

"You'll be OK today, darling, it's going to be a lovely day, no need to take extra clothing," I told her.

"Are you sure? We're going to be gone all day."

"Trust me; there is a temperature inversion today so it can't rain".

"How can you be so sure?", she asked. That gave me the opportunity to impress her with my expert knowledge.

"The earth is warmed by the sun, which in turn warms the lower level air. This has to rise and cool for the water vapour to condense before it can fall as rain. The temperature inversion today means that the upper atmosphere air is warmer than the lower atmosphere air, so as the lower atmosphere air cannot rise, it cannot cool, that's how I know you'll be OK. The ground level air can't cool at altitude today. When the sky is like it is today it is known as an anticyclonic gloom," I explained sanctimoniously. The logic of it was indisputable and it felt good to be able to predict with such confidence what was going to happen. I wouldn't always be able to receive a weather forecast at sea so my expert knowledge of the subject was essential. It was satisfying for Jill too to be able to assure the coachload of players that they could now comfortably go in light summer wear, secure in the knowledge that all would be well as they had their own expert weatherman to advise them. "It is certain because it is impossible (Credo quia impossibile)." – Tertullian AD 160 -225.

I continued all that day engrossed in my studies until the doorbell rang in the evening. I hurried downstairs and threw the door open anxious to welcome Jill home. I knew I was in trouble when I saw her standing dripping wet in the pouring rain, in her light summer clothes. Her scowl said it all as her eyes bore into me. I could at least take comfort in the fact that the whole netball team wasn't with her.

"Thank you for the expert advice," she said ominously.

"I don't understand," I stammered, "It can't rain if there's a temperature inversion."

"Can't rain, what are you talking about, can't rain, CAN'T RAIN, LOOK AT ME. I'm soaked to the skin and so is the rest of the team."

"I don't know what to say, I just can't understand how it happened," I pleaded, red-faced with embarrassment.

If the build-up of energy below a temperature inversion does break through for whatever reason, it can result in severe thunderstorms. Nobody had taught me that part. The torrential rain that fell on Jill and her team that day was proof and I realised that I had a lot more to learn about meteorology! Instead of trusting in me implicitly, Jill would have been wiser to have recalled the words of Oliver Cromwell when he said "I beseech you, in the bowels of Christ, think it possible you may be mistaken."

．．．．．．．．．．．．．．．

The exams duly took place over a few days in May. We were sat in pairs for the signalling section and were required to be able to read the Morse code at a set number of words a minute. My partner, who was a stranger to me, had already failed his signals test the two previous years and he was a bag of nerves. He badly needed to pass because his job was dependant on it. As the lamp started flashing it wasn't long before he went to pieces and gave up. He put his head in his hands and was on the verge of weeping, having failed once more. At the end of the test, he turned to me with a pained expression, totally distraught.

"Oh bugger! I'm sorry, I totally lost it. My mind went blank as soon as the signalling started. Oh bugger and shit, I don't know what'll happen now. I've really ballsed it up again," he moaned.

"Maybe not," I told him, "When you stopped calling out the letters, I just wrote down whatever I heard everybody else whispering to their partners, so you could well get full marks."

He beamed at me and I swear there were little tears of joy and relief in his eyes. He passed his exams and was over the moon. He couldn't thank me enough and immediately offered me a job as his second in command on his oil tanker. It was a good offer financially but it wasn't what I wanted. It didn't appeal to me at all, so. I thanked him and declined.

CHAPTER 4
TIME TO REFLECT

All the fun of the fair?

Congratulations Captain," my instructor said as he shook my hand and presented me with the letter of confirmation. I had successfully passed all the exams. I was elated. I'd moved on from my childhood days of living on a rundown council estate where a lot of my friends and their brothers and fathers had ended up in prison. When I began attending the infants' school, I became friendly with a boy, Eddie, who lived in the same street as me, just a few houses away and I was captivated by the tales he used to tell me. He would go eeling with his father and uncle on the disused Thames and Medway canal, which was originally built to link the River Thames to the River Medway at Strood, to avoid the sailing barges having to navigate around the Hoo peninsular and the Thames estuary. It was conceived in 1799 and was finally completed in 1824 but was a commercial failure so was sold to the South Eastern Railway Company in 1846 when it was filled in and a railway line built over it. The only section that remained navigable was between Higham and Gravesend and that was closed in 1934. Eddie's Dad would stretch nets across the canal, and then with his brother went a good distance away before wading in and walking back towards the net thrashing the water with eel beaters, which were basically long poles, driving the eels into the net. When they were gathered up they were piled into a barrow, which was wheeled around the neighborhood where the contents were sold to eager purchasers and I would sometimes accompany Eddie.

He also told me tales of rabbiting. His father kept ferrets and they would go to the marshes a few hundred yards from where we lived and send the ferrets into the entrances to the rabbit burrows after placing nets over the exits. The panic stricken rabbits scarpered to what they thought was safety only to be gathered up in the nets, killed and sold on to the local population. The same marshes provided an endless supply of turf, which Eddie and his brothers and other locals would dig up and sell on. They were a close family and his father and elder brothers taught him so much. Not only was I enamoured with the stories he told me, I also envied his close knit family so spent a lot of time in his company and was always thrilled when I was allowed to join them in their escapades.

I was initially a clever lad in school, always among the top few boys but as time went on and I hung around with Eddie and his cerebrally challenged, tearaway friends, I wanted to be accepted as part of the clique and allowed myself to be influenced too much by them. It was evident where their futures lay judging by the behaviour of the older youths. I used to wonder frequently why I allied myself with them as I stood back and watched another nose being broken in a drunken brawl or another burglary being planned or another innocent person being tormented and beaten up for the sheer, misguided pleasure of the unenlightened perpetrators. I felt such deep sorrow for the victims and I never participated in their brutal forms of amusement but did suffer the consequences when I was badly beaten up at a fairground one night.

The secondary modern boys' school I attended was next to the girls' school. They were in the same building and during the lunch break both sexes would meet up in the recreation ground behind the public swimming pool on the opposite side of the road. One particular girl was by far and away the most stunning in the school and all the boys would talk about her and hope to date her. I was the lucky one for a while.

When we stopped seeing each other she found another boyfriend from a different school. He was a nice boy and I had no hard feelings. One evening when I was out and about with two of the gang of lawbreakers, we saw the boy get onto a stationary bus.

"That's the boy who's dating my ex-girlfriend," I said as a simple matter of fact.

"Right, we'll sort him out for you," they said.

"No, I'm not with her anymore, it doesn't matter, he's OK. I quite like him," I tried to reason with them.

They ignored my protestations and just laughed when I tried to stop them. They rushed upstairs on the bus and proceeded to pummel the poor unsuspecting boy. I stayed on the pavement, ashamed to be involved. He looked out of the window when they came back down to join me and because we were all together, he naturally assumed that I had put them up to it. I deeply regretted what had happened but knew I would never have been able to stop my friends from passing up the chance of a punch up - especially if it was in their favour, two against one. It so happened that the boy's brother was an amateur boxer. He came across me one night at the fairground, accidentally I thought, but in reality, he'd been seeking me out as I learned later. He challenged me to a fight and I didn't stand a chance. I was with my friends who'd created the problem. They'd attacked the boy on the bus but it was me who was to pay the price. My opponent, surrounded by his band of eager supporters, stood facing me with a hostile stare, swinging his muscular arms in anticipation and almost drooling at the prospect of smashing me into a pulp. It was dark and a crowd had started to gather. There was a smell of hot dogs and onions, the fairground music blared, generators whirred, lights were flashing and I heard the screams and laughter of the crowds having fun as I was pushed forward by my friends. I don't really recall much of what happened after that except the cheers of encouragement from the baying crowd. At one stage there was an extra loud cheer and I have no idea if I'd managed to clobber him or if he'd landed yet another expertly timed and placed punch into my face – almost certainly the latter. I have never been a violent person and hadn't been involved in a fight before then or since, so I didn't stand a chance. Thankfully, my next door neighbour, a huge, tough character, happened to hear the commotion and rushed over and flattened my punisher and then turned on the rest of the onlookers.

"Ain't you bleedin' big enough to stop this?" he said as he floored the biggest of them.

They all disappeared rather rapidly after that, even my so-called friends. Bill, the neighbour, tended my wounds. When he had stopped my nose from bleeding and finished wiping away the blood from my face, I made my way home. By the time I arrived the blood had covered my face once more. Fortunately, Mum and Dad had already gone to bed.

I didn't commit any criminal offences myself but often stayed out late with some of the boys, occasionally all night. There was a riding stable close by and from time to time we'd sleep in the hay loft waiting for the horses to be put out in the fields very early in the morning. As soon as the stable hands had departed, we'd pick up the rough bridles we'd made up from bits of rope, go to the field, catch a horse, slip the bridle on and have terrific fun riding around on their backs before going home to get ready for school. However, these escapades were short lived because a group of boys from a nearby estate set light to the hayloft and the whole barn burnt down. Mum and Dad were not happy with me for staying out all night and also because of the type of delinquents I was associating with, but I was terribly unhappy at home and welcomed any excuse not to be there.

A traumatic time

Mum and Dad were stuck in an ill-fated marriage but in those days divorce was rarely an option and it would never have occurred to either of them to do anything other than make the best of a worsening situation. After Dad received his compensation for the loss of his eye, "mince" Dad would call it, and other injuries, he took to drinking heavily. He was awarded £2500, which was a considerable sum at the time when a house could be purchased for a couple of hundred pounds. He gave half to Mum and the rest he squandered on booze and what he thought at the time were his mates, "china's" he called them (china plate = mate). It will come as no surprise to learn that they faded away at the same time as the money. I don't know what happened to Mum's share but that too disappeared quickly. I lived in fear during those years, dreading Dad coming home drunk and creating hostile scenes, especially when he was accompanied by his objectionable, scrounging, so called friends who were equally smashed out of their heads at Dad's expense. I used to plead with Mum to leave home with me before he returned and she always refused, which only made matters worse for everybody. Mum was a fiercely stubborn, independent woman who had no qualms about telling people what she thought of them, which resulted in her having very few friends. She neither smoked nor drank and was determined to stand her ground against Dad. She would berate him for his drunken behaviour and he, in turn, would retaliate and I hated every minute of it. Dad had married late in life so my cousins from his seven sisters were all adults; consequently, I had nobody to turn to for guidance or comfort. I once went to a pub where I knew he would be and begged him to come home. His response was to offer me a glass of beer and encourage me to drink it. It was repulsive to my young palate and I showed my disgust at the vile tasting liquid by spitting it out and grimacing, much to the amusement of Dad and the drunken spongers surrounding him. The emotional wounds from those years pierced deeply into my heart and took a long time to heal and the scars remain. On reflection, Dad did what worked best for him at that time. He'd suffered much in his life and he was stuck in an unhappy marriage. My sister is five years younger than me so she was spared the pain of those tumultuous years. However, whatever perceived faults my parents had, I never heard either of them swear and the only time Dad ever hit me was when I swore at home when he and Mum had guests. After that I never swore at home again throughout my childhood and adulthood. They drummed into me over and over again not to lie or steal and begged me to sever my ties with the delinquents, and I appreciate the fact that they tried so hard to protect me. Under the influence of my friends, I once stole some paints from school because I so wanted to paint pictures at home and we couldn't afford to buy them. Mum and Dad were horrified and insisted that I return them the next day.

They had each suffered harrowing lives. Mum's Mum, Nin as we called her, the only Grandparent I knew, was a positively evil woman. She lied and concocted all manner of schemes to cause maximum hurt and embarrassment to people, so heaven knows what she had been through herself to make her behave in that way. She lived in Liverpool and when she became homeless, Mum and Dad paid for her to come to Gravesend. They welcomed her into our home and cared for her selflessly. I was in the sitting room with her one day whilst Mum and Dad were in the kitchen, preparing our meal. The meal was brought in and placed on the table and my parents returned to the kitchen. The next instant, Nin called out to them and when they both came back she told them that I had stolen food from her plate, which was a malicious fabrication. Mum and Dad insisted that I apologise, except that I hadn't done anything wrong, so I refused. I pleaded my innocence and the vicious old woman beside me contradicted everything I said. It was a stalemate. Neither of us budged in our story and that placed Mum and Dad in a tricky situation. When neither of us gave in, Mum and Dad went back to the kitchen and left me with the hateful old hag.

Sometime after accepting Mum and Dad's hospitality, she moved in with a family a few doors away and we heard that she was telling lies, wicked lies, about Mum and Dad. What makes some people so hateful, I wonder? Without knowing their full history it is unwise to attempt to pass any form of judgement on them but being on the receiving end of their behaviour is difficult. All of my childhood experiences though have helped form my present personality. It was as it was and it is no more. I have no cause to complain now; had it been otherwise, I probably wouldn't have had the wonderful experiences of my later life. The crime writer Sue Grafton put it well when she said, "People who've had happy childhoods are wonderful, but they're bland. An unhappy childhood compels you to use your imagination to create a world in which you can be happy. Use your old grief. That's the gift you're given."

Beefy Banks's barrow

I had no trouble with the 11 plus exams and should have gone to grammar school but chose to go to the same secondary modern as my wayward friends. The headmaster of my infant's school was not happy and summoned me to his office to explain myself. I got no encouragement from my parents.

"If you don't go to grammar school, you'll be able to leave school and can start earning money a year sooner," was Dad's only comment.

Consequently, my education didn't advance as well as it could have. At the Secondary Modern, I was one of six boys chosen to attend free lessons at the art school on Saturday mornings but once again my parents showed very little interest in my work. I quit and instead delivered newspapers for a local newsagent each morning before school. On Saturday mornings, I also collected the money for the week's delivery, which took a lot longer. I had one of the two largest rounds, which meant that I earned a little more than the other paper boys but it also meant that the bag filled with papers was that much heavier and it took much longer to deliver them on the circuitous two-mile hike. On Sundays, with the papers being much thicker, the bag was even heavier but mostly I had the use of my bike. I had to get up and be at the newsagent by five o'clock each morning to sort out which papers I needed and mark them with the addresses before piling them into the bag in the order that I would need them. I have vivid memories of arriving home cold, wet and tired and Mum having to dry out my clothes and shoes in front of the fire so that I could wear them to school. The newsagent eventually found himself in trouble for allowing me and the other schoolchildren to start so early in the morning before school and was told to cease doing so, but my paper round was so huge I had to continue beginning at an unearthly hour.

Although I hung around with the wrong crowd because we were in the same class at school, my main friend was Tommy who was a year older than me and lived just a few houses away. For many years we were inseparable and he was so different to the others, who to my knowledge never read books or took much interest in anything other than fighting and other mindless activities. Tommy, by contrast, was intelligent and like me, artistic, so we passed many hours drawing, painting, reading, modelling, cycling and any number of imaginative and resourceful pursuits. For my thirteenth birthday, Dad had bought me an old second hand bike from one of his nieces, for a token price of half a crown. Tommy was one of eight children and his parents couldn't afford to buy him one, so we went off together on mine. We took turns, with one of us standing peddling and the other sitting on the saddle.

We both had a love of the cinema and because neither of our parents were wealthy, Tommy and I would find ways to make enough money to indulge in our passion for films. Friendly neighbours would sometimes buy my paintings and in those days, empty beer bottles were returned to the pubs and for each one returned there would be a payment of one penny; we would collect them whenever and wherever we could until we each had enough to earn sixpence (a tanner), which was enough for us to go to the children's Saturday morning matinee. Sometimes we would pilfer empty beer bottles stored in crates in the back yard of one pub and then take them to another pub and collect the money, which was the closest I ever got to criminality. We would also knock on doors in the neighbourhood, asking if anybody had any old rags that they didn't want. When we'd collected enough, we'd borrow a barrow from a friendly neighbour, a man called Beefy Banks, and pushing Beefy Banks's heavy barrow, we'd set off on the two mile hike into town to exchange the contents for money with the rag and bone man. I was impressionable and immersed myself into the films, partly to escape the unpleasantness of being at home. I loved the glamour and the lure of the exotic locations. I have colourful memories of Gregory Peck and Susan Hayward in The Snows of Kilimanjaro, Burl Ives and Christopher Plummer in Wind Across the Everglades, Burl Ives, Alec Guinness and Maureen O Hara in Our Man in Havana, Stewart Granger and Deborah Kerr, trekking across Africa in search of King Solomon's Mines, Humphrey Bogart in Casablanca and Jack Hawkins and Joan Collins in Land of the Pharaohs and a multitude of other films. I longed to visit those places. I wanted to cross the desert, to see the pyramids, to trek through the jungle, to go on safari, to browse in the souks. Coming from a poor family living on a rundown council estate I could never imagine it happening. Now, however, I've not only visited them all but many, many more fabulous and compelling countries.

Under arrest

When we moved to a new area, although it was still a rundown place to live, it was infinitely better than where we'd been previously and I was away from the bad influence of my former friends. My life changed for the better once I'd started working on the tugs and spending more of my free time with Tommy and more balanced people but I would still spend as little time at home as possible. On the few days or nights that I wasn't working, I'd rather be with other people, either drinking with friends, nightclubbing, going to the greyhound races or the cinema or indeed anywhere but home and in any case the vast majority of my week was spent with my fellow tugmen.

I'd stayed clear of the criminal activities of my school friends but that didn't prevent me from being thrown into a cell one night. It was around one thirty in the morning and I was on my way home with an acquaintance that I'd met during a fun evening at the South Bank Club. We'd stopped to peer innocently through the window of a car showroom.

"Copper," my friend hollered and scarpered off before I could react.

Why he did that has always remained a mystery because he never gave a satisfactory explanation. I presume he thought we'd be in trouble for wandering the streets at one thirty in the morning. I wasn't even aware of a policeman until the constable grabbed me by the scruff of the neck and marched me off to the nearest police phone box. These were painted blue, placed in strategic positions around the town and were linked directly to the police station by a telephone accessible from the outside via a hinged door. The interiors had enough space to enable the police to make out reports or even hold prisoners temporarily. They were phased out in the 1970's when two-way radios were being issued. I struggled and complained to no avail whilst he called the station. After a brief discussion with whoever was at the other end of the line, he bundled me off to the police station. I was forcibly pushed into a tatty room with painted walls and shoved down onto a wooden chair next to a desk. There were two policemen. One was the arresting officer and the other, who wasn't wearing a uniform, was large, loathsome and clearly ruthless. He had a round, pimply face and grotesque blubbery lips that had spittle around them when he spoke. They thought my friend and I had intended to break into the showroom, though what we would have done in there I can't imagine. I was ordered to empty my pockets, which I obediently did. They both fired questions at me over and over again, trying to get me to admit that I had been up to no good but I couldn't give them the information they'd hoped for because I was innocent. I started to get annoyed and back answered the loathsome one. He responded with a violent smash of his hand on my jaw.

"You call me Sir when you speak to me you miserable little sod," he yelled. I guess that maybe he didn't overly like himself and took out his self-loathing on others and that night it sadly turned out to be me. I refused to call him Sir, which didn't help my predicament. He fumbled through the contents of my pockets hoping to find some incriminating evidence and found pictures of some of my past and present girlfriends.

"How many of these have you poked?" he said.

"None," I protested.

"Don't give me that load of bollocks, how many?"

"None," I insisted.

"Why have you got all these pictures if you haven't poked any of them?"

"I just have."

"And I suppose you're going to tell me you've never stolen anything either."

"No, never."

"You're not telling me that you haven't taken the odd thing from Woolworths at times," he said

"No, never," I said. Try as he did, he had nothing on me and never would have because I wasn't guilty of anything.

"Lock the lying little bugger up," he told his associate.

I was led to a cell, shoved in and the door was locked but not before the thin, brown blanket was taken away from me. I spent a cold, lonely night on a horrible thin, green plastic mattress, locked in the stark, bare cell. Shortly after daybreak, they let me out, returned my possessions and sent me on my way. When I got home nothing was discussed because Mum and Dad had got used to me staying out and I probably wouldn't have told them anything anyway.

Ali the Imam

Some of my happiest childhood years were spent in Liverpool. I don't know why I was sent there. I have a memory of travelling on the train with my Aunt Ethel, Mum's sister, with whom I stayed. She was married to a Muslim, Ali, and I adored him. She had converted to Islam when she married her first husband, also called Ali, with whom she had three children, Ali, Amina and Norma, who were all cared for by the second husband along with two adopted children, Maria and Mohammed. I shared a room with Mohammed. My Uncle Ali was an Imam and in addition to the five children, the large house where I stayed with him was always filled with other Muslims coming and going about their business and prayers. These were very happy years for me, living in a calm, loving, happy environment. I never witnessed any anger or heard a raised voice. Because of my Uncle Ali's status, he regularly received important members of the Muslim community and once I was asked to wait in a separate room because he was to receive King Hussein of Jordan.

As well as other properties, he also had a few halal butchers' shops and personally killed all that was on sale. I was taken by him to the abattoir on more than one occasion and accompanied him whilst he slaughtered the sheep that had been set aside for him. The noise was disturbing and the smell was nauseating as he took me on a tour of the various sections. The pigs that we wouldn't go near, squealed, the cattle bellowed and the sheep bleated in panic as they stood crammed in their pens awaiting their brutal slaughter. He took me up alongside the executioner and I watched as the terrified cattle were prodded into the tight enclosure. Unable to move, the executioner placed the gun on their foreheads and fired the bolt into their brains. As the animal collapsed in a lifeless heap, a trapdoor was opened sending it crashing to the floor below where somebody would shove a rod into the hole left by the bolt and turn its brain over, which cause the beast's legs to lash out. A team of men would then start ripping out the innards. We sloshed our way through blood and guts to Uncle Ali's area. His sheep were brought to him and placed on their backs in a rack one at a time with their heads pointing towards "Qibla," the direction that Muslims face in prayer. With the knife held behind his back, he would invoke the name of Allah, "Bismillah," then with one swift, expertly executed motion, slice through the carotid artery, oesophagus, trachea and jugular veins, leaving the nervous system intact so that the unfortunate beast would bleed to death. The consumption of blood is forbidden In Islam. The sheep were then not allowed to be touched until all life had drained away. To westerners, this seems a barbaric method of slaughter but they have no moral high ground to stand on. Despite this horrific experience, I never wanted to leave his side and I loved everything about his lifestyle. I loved the communal meals with so many people laughing and chattering away around the huge table as the bowls of food were passed around and we scooped the portions up with our fingers. I loved the frequent trips to Wales and other places in his Ford Consul, and to hear Uncle Ali singing in Arabic as he drove. We never had any family outings at home. (I can only remember one occasion when I was taken out with Mum and Dad as a family.) I loved it when visitors would arrive and Aunt Ethel would go to the back yard, pick out a chicken, kill it, pluck it and prepare a meal. The hospitality that they offered to everybody was overwhelming and the house was always full of love and laughter.

The gene drd4-7r

The time came, sadly, for me to return home to Gravesend. After Mum and Dad had squandered every penny of his compensation, Dad stopped getting drunk and his true character of a quiet, gentle man was revealed. This meant that Mum wasn't nagging him so much. Being at home became more bearable and the mental pain and turmoil I'd suffered lessened. We were still not a close family though and never had been. A couple of years after I returned, my sister went to Liverpool to stay with Uncle Ali and Aunt Ethel. She stayed for a few years and went to school there. By the time she came home, I'd begun working on the tugs so we never really had a childhood together; we had such totally different characters anyway. I'd inherited Dad's wayfaring genes. I looked the spitting image of him and just like him, I respond to confrontations or stressful situations calmly or not at all. I am a risk taker and crave constant changes in my life. My sister has equally fallen heir to Mum's behaviour patterns, neither of them ever had any inclination to travel or even obtain a passport or driving license. The desire to travel and take risks mainly originates in childhood imagination and that was certainly the case with me, and scientific research has concluded that approximately 20% of the population have a gene DRD4-7r. This gene is linked to curiosity and restlessness and by association travel. It would seem that Dad and I have that gene activated and Mum and my sister do not. It is intriguing that my half-sister has also never travelled.

For many years I resented the fact that my parents didn't do more to guide and inspire me but now I have no regrets. I would have been thoroughly unhappy had I qualified at something boring and spent my life in a conventional job year after year with not very much to look forward to other than a nice pension (although a nice pension would be much appreciated now!) I enjoyed my freedom as a youngster and on reflection wouldn't have wanted it any other way. It's made me what I am today. Mum and Dad may not have lived up to my expectations and I probably didn't live up to theirs, but they did what they felt they had to do in the circumstances and despite Dad's drunkenness in the early days, he was never violent and I love and miss them both.

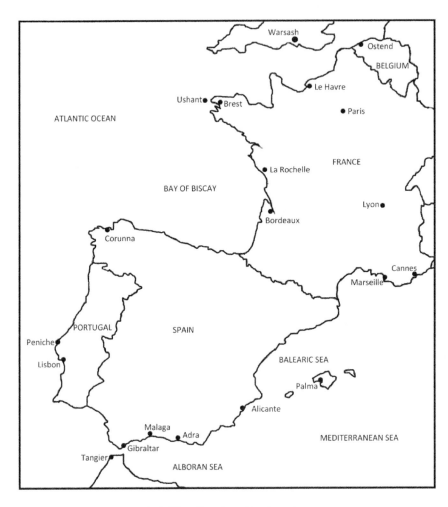

14. The Iberian Peninsular

CHAPTER 5
FOR BETTER AND FOR WORSE

To love, honour but not obey

I'd studied for and received my license in radiotelephony whilst waiting for delivery of my Yacht Master Certificate and in June 1967, with both certificates in my possession, I was raring to go and embark on what was to be a charmed life of adventure and deep satisfaction. There is no better way to describe what I felt than to use the words of Henry Wadsworth Longfellow - "My heart is full of longing for the secret of the sea, and the heart of the great ocean sends a thrilling pulse through me."

I didn't have long to wait. Within two weeks I was offered the chance to sail to Majorca for the season aboard a 62-foot yacht moored offshore at Warsash. Charlie, the Captain, was the son of the landlady who had been so kind to me when I first arrived in Warsash. We knew each other well so he knew I'd successfully passed my exams and I was competent enough to take command of a yacht. We were standing in the Morgan Giles shipyard when he said to me;

"How would you like to join me on a run to Majorca?"

"I don't know, tell me more," I replied.

"We'll have to leave shortly to take a motorsailer there so that the owner can have a month's holiday on her with his family and then we'll bring her back here."

"Sounds interesting, what sort of yacht is it?"

"There she is," he said, pointing to a beautiful looking vessel moored midstream. "She was built four years ago a short distance from here at Moody's boatyard."

As soon as I saw her, I decided to accept. The shiny white hull was glistening in the sun. She was cutter rigged and looked like a good seaworthy vessel.

"Why not, sounds like a good idea but I'll have to square it with Jill first," I said, "I'll let you know as soon as I can."

I had to explain to Jill, my wife of just 9 weeks, that I would be leaving her for a couple of months. I rehearsed all day the most appropriate way of breaking the news but couldn't find the courage to do it. At the very last moment, when we were in bed about to wish each other goodnight, I dropped the bombshell.

"I've got some good news, darling; I've got a job already. I have to leave in a week or so for Majorca," I said hesitantly.

"What?" She demanded, shocked.

"I've got a job on a motorsailer moored nearby. I know the Skipper and he wants me to help him take her to Palma and stay there until September and then we'll sail her back to the Hamble."

"Well, you're not going without me. If you're going, I'm going with you. You're not leaving me here on my own," she said.

"But I'm a sailor, you knew that when you married me," I pleaded. "Sailors go to sea. That's why I went to Nav. School. I've got my qualifications now and I've got a job offer. I have to go."

"You are not going without me," she stressed.

"How can you come, the job is for me, not the two of us?" I explained.

"I don't care; I'm not staying here on my own. If you go, I'm going with you," she insisted, even more forcefully.

"But you have a job here, we have the flat and I have to work, you knew I'd have to go to sea sometime," I said.

"If you go, I'm going with you and that's that." She was laying down the rules, starting out as she meant to go on. Jill had refused to include the word obey in her marriage vows, so I had no legal justification to punish her most severely!

"What would you do aboard?" I asked.

"I don't know but I'm going with you."

"Well, it' just not possible," I said with conviction and we went to sleep. One of us had to surrender to the other and I'd made up my mind. I was going to accept the offer and go to Majorca. Period. I wasn't prepared to give up everything I'd been looking forward to.

"I was wondering if there was any chance that my wife could come with us," I asked Charlie the following day.

"Oh, I don't know about that, I'll make the suggestion to the owner and let you know what the answer is," he said.

The next day when I went to see him he told me that Jill could be employed as cook. Week nine of our marriage and the result of our first difference of opinion was a resounding one nil to Jill. And so began our adventure together. In hindsight, losing the argument with Jill was the best thing that could have happened. Without Jill by my side supporting me in every way, the years that followed would never have been anywhere near as enjoyable. We shared so many periods of side-splitting laughter and also shared fears and danger. We became inseparable from that moment on.

The Spanish intimidation

We set sail from Hamble for Majorca at the end of June. Charlie's brother John and an older, grumpy but experienced old seadog, Ted, joined us as extra delivery crew. Charlie had arranged for our stores to be delivered, which consisted of cases of butter, tins of milk, fruit and vegetables, boxes of Carr's Table water biscuits and other brands, meats, whole blocks of cheeses, drinks, alcoholic and otherwise and anything else so that we took aboard enough food to feed the five of us for three weeks. Some of these, such as the tins of milk were stowed in the bilges under the galley and forecabin soles. The duty free goods that we were entitled to were sealed by customs officers and we were not allowed break the seal until we'd cleared U.K. waters. The cutter was a magnificent vessel, classified 100 A1 by Lloyds, with a mahogany hull on oak frames, teak decks and 1100 sq. ft. of sail area. She was powered by twin six cylinder Gardner engines of 150 hp. each and had a cruising range of 1500 miles. There were three double cabins and one single, plus accommodation for Jill and me in the forecastle. We were thrilled to be at sea together and looking forward to the summer in Majorca. When we'd cleared the English Channel and headed south for Gibraltar I had a number of opportunities to practise my Morse code signalling when passing ships flashed messages to us to pass the time of day practising their signalling and to satisfy their curiosity. Fresh from spending hours learning to identify and send the flashing or tapping messages, it felt good that the time wasn't completely wasted. However, it didn't work out so well when Ted decided to join in and make his contribution. John and Jill were at the wheel, Charlie stood by with pencil and paper and Ted and I were relaying what the flashes were telling us. The trouble was that Ted and I had different interpretations. On each flash, I would call out "A," for instance, and Ted would call out "M," and so it went on as we both concentrated on the flashes. Charlie was trying to write down what each of us was saying.

"What does it say?" I asked when the flashes stopped.

"I'm fucked if I know," Charlie said throwing the paper and pencil away in despair. It was utter gobbledegook. Since Ted and I were never going to agree, we didn't bother anymore after that, instead, we chatted to the

passing ships on the radio telephone.

The voyage went well. We didn't hoist the sails much as the engines were thrusting us along at a steady eight to ten knots and we didn't want to waste time. There were some rough spells, especially crossing the infamous Bay of Biscay and as Jill had the

15. Charlie and me

responsibility of feeding us, she had the unenviable task of crawling around in the bilges to retrieve some of the stored goods whilst the boat was being thrown around. There she was on all fours as the bow of the vessel rose violently upwards and then as it crashed back down again with a loud bang, the cans of goods took on a life of their own and leapt up at her knocking her off balance. As I listened to her astonished yelps, I wondered if she regretted insisting that she come with me. Mostly though, the sea was tolerable and there were reasonably clear skies. On the calm, clear nights when there was not another ship in sight and nothing to see in either direction but the sea in the moonlight it was breathtakingly beautiful. Moonbeams glistened on the water and the sky was littered with millions of shining stars. The only sound was the gratifying throb of the engines.

We didn't stop until we reached Gibraltar, where we moored up for a few days to stock up on stores and more duty frees. The rock of Gibraltar is such a prominent landmark that it can't be missed. It was captured from Spain in 1704, by an Anglo-Dutch fleet during the War of the Spanish Succession. It was subsequently ceded to the British in perpetuity in 1713, to secure Britain's withdrawal from the war and ever since, successive Spanish governments have attempted to regain sovereignty. The Straits of Gibraltar is only seven nautical miles across, so the rock has great strategic value because the entrance and exit to the Mediterranean Sea can be controlled from it. It has served as a base for The Royal Navy and played an important role in 1805 during the battle of Trafalgar, and in 1854 – 1856 during the Crimean war. It was strengthened as a fortress in World War II, and the inhabitants were evacuated to England, Morocco, Madeira and Jamaica. In the 1950's, the Spanish dictator, General Franco, claimed sovereignty and restricted travel between the rock and the Spanish mainland but his claim was rejected by the U.N in 1963 and 1964. Franco was so outraged that he sealed the border completely in an attempt to bring about economic ruin to the rock. Moroccans replaced the Spanish workers and the border remained closed until 1982. The year we arrived, the Gibraltarians were holding a referendum on whether to remain part of the United Kingdom or pass under Spanish sovereignty and the Spanish government was sending its fighter jets out daily to harass incoming and outgoing shipping and aircraft. In a threatening display of provocation, they constantly flew low over approaching ships, including us as we drew nearer. We were tired after having been at sea for several days and were very much looking forward to a respite in Gibraltar and if the pilots of the jets that screamed threateningly low over us as we punched our way through the waves to enter the harbour thought that they would scare us away, they were so wrong. What they expected to achieve by threatening a 62-foot motorsailer, I can't begin to imagine. The harassment of aircraft arriving at Gibraltar as they came into land was altogether another matter. Each time a plane arrived, we watched spellbound as the pilots negotiated their landings, avoiding the fighter jets screeching around them.

The door of Africa

It was a good feeling when the engine stopped and we stepped ashore again after our days at sea. We took advantage of the stopover and booked a day trip on the first ferry to Tangier the following day. It was an early start and we'd timed it perfectly. However, with the heightened security in Gibraltar, the heavy metal dockyard gate was locked so we couldn't get out. It was still dark and nobody was around, so we had no alternative but to climb over the gate if we wanted to catch the ferry that we'd already paid for. I almost made it over and was balanced precariously on top of the gate when I heard a bellow from the guard. He came running over in a threatening manner. I froze in position for a moment wondering about the consequences of my breaking out without permission. Would I be arrested or worse still, shot? The guard was not happy with me, but after giving us a severe dressing down he relented and opened the gate to let us through in time to catch the ferry.

Being in Tangier for a day was a fascinating experience. Morocco was partitioned in 1912, with Spain occupying the north and south of the country and France occupying the remainder. In 1923, it was declared an International zone, administered jointly by both the occupying countries. Tangier had long had a reputation as a spying and smuggling centre due to the safe haven offered through its political neutrality. Consequently, all manner of crooks, gamblers, spies, and other unsavoury characters were attracted to it and had I not had the wisdom to escape from my childhood friends, I may have had to eventually seek refuge there myself! There was plenty to see and not enough time to do it all. We wandered further away from the town centre to the edge of a desert area where we were accosted by a tall, lean, wrinkled Arab who had a shaven head and was dressed in tatty trousers and a black leather jacket. He was leading a mangy, disagreeable camel that looked as if it had died and been recently brought back to life. He pointed to the unfortunate beast and rubbed his thumb over the two fingers of one hand and held out the other indicating that for a small fortune we could mount the beast, whilst it walked a few steps, so that we could take a photograph. How could anyone resist such an offer? Not us, so Jill bravely decided to play the tourist game and attempted to climb up onto its back. The man couldn't contain himself. He visibly drooled as he spied Jill's lithe, bronzed, bare limbs. On the pretext of giving her a helping hand, it looked to me as if he took advantage and helped himself to a quick grope of her thighs, at the same time as he spread his lips in a toothless grin. I was furious, especially when he didn't take his hands off Jill's thigh until she dismounted.

The market was lively and intriguing and as the day went by hunger started to creep in, accentuated by the pungent smells from the amazing array of spices and street food that stimulated our digestive juices. We discovered an irresistible looking restaurant in a small side street, the smells of the spices and the sound of the Arabic music was far too enticing to bypass. We entered and were shown to places at a long table already occupied by numerous people of various nationalities. The delights that were served to us were exquisite and all the while we were entertained by a group of musicians in traditional dress. Afterwards we visited the Kasbah and all the usual tourist attractions. On either side of the shaded narrow streets, merchants were selling all manner of interesting and colourful objects. Jill was rather taken with a black silk Moroccan dress. We rather foolishly showed an interest and were instantly joined by the young Arab store holder and the bargaining began. It continued until we came to the conclusion that an agreement wasn't going to be reached, so we left and continued exploring the town. We were so intoxicated by the exotic atmosphere that we were startled to discover that there was hardly any time left to catch the last ferry back to Gibraltar. Panic set in and we sped through the streets, running as fast as we could. Wherever we went, men would always admire Jill's exceptionally attractive long legs and on that day in Tangier, I discovered that not only were they attractive but also that they had uncanny propulsive power. She sped away into the dark, narrow and sometimes foreboding streets, disappearing into the distance towards the ferry terminal at something approaching the speed of light.

Meanwhile, following the dust of Jill's trail, I was surprised when the street vendor suddenly materialised alongside me carrying the dress. We carried out a transaction whilst sprinting at full speed. I managed to bargain whilst gasping for breath and swivelling my head from side to side in rapid succession to look both at the insistent vendor and to ascertain where Jill had disappeared to. We exchanged money and goods on the run and as soon as the transaction was concluded, the little Arab vendor dematerialised as quickly as he had magically appeared. Einstein said that the closer you get to the speed of light, the more time dilates. Jill proved his theory correct that day because when she reached the terminal, remarkably, the ferry was still there. We'd made it, albeit in a distressed state. We panted and wheezed as we tried to get more oxygen into our lungs. We were soaked in perspiration and exhausted but Jill had gained her dress. Even though I'd paid a fraction of the asking price with what little cash I had left, I was in no doubt that I'd still been conned but I wouldn't have missed that day for anything.

During our stay in Gibralter, we took the opportunity to visit the tourist attractions, taking the cable car to the top of the rock to see the apes and visiting the caves. After a few days rest we took on stores, water and fuel and set sail into the deep blue Mediterranean. The name of the sea is derived from the Latin Mediterraneus, meaning the middle of the land, medius (middle) and terra (land). It covers an approximate area of 970,000 square miles and is subdivided into a number of smaller seas, one of which is the Alboran Sea, lying between Spain and North Africa, and that is where we began our journey to Majorca, Spain's largest island. The Alboran Sea is the habitat of the largest population of bottle nosed dolphins in the Western Mediterranean and is Europe's most important feeding ground for loggerhead sea turtles, the world's largest hard shelled turtle, which is now an endangered species. We were often accompanied by pods of dolphins leaping out of the water alongside and in front of us and playing in the wash we created. We also saw turtles as well as many flying fish, with some of them landing on deck. The typical flight of these fish is 50 metres but by using updrafts, they can travel up to 400 metres at 40 miles per hour.

We had plenty of opportunities to hoist the sails but mostly the wind was of insufficient strength to thrust the 55-ton cutter through the water fast enough to make it worthwhile. After two and a half days we arrived at Palma and dropped anchor in the bay, a short distance from the harbour entrance. We stayed there for a further two days until a berth became available on the main quay. At that point, John and Ted left us and returned to the U.K. It felt good for Jill and me to be in Palma once more. We'd got to know it fairly well during our two weeks stay over the Christmas period. Palma was founded and governed by the Romans until the collapse of their western empire, after which there was a Byzantine period prior to the arrival of the Moors in the early 8th century. The Moors remained in control of the city from 902 – 1225 and their occupation becomes evident when walking through the narrow streets of the old town. During their rule, they relied mainly on piracy as the major contributing factor to their economy. The town fell under the control of James I of Aragon on 31 December 1229, after a three month siege. The economy today relies principally on tourism, which in some incidences is a different form of piracy. We still had two weeks to spare before the owner and his family were due to fly out to join us, so enjoyed making the most of that time visiting various places of interest. I've never forgotten a most delicious lunch of red mullet that we were served at the yacht club where we used to go to collect our mail from a Spanish señorita called Carmen.

Circumnavigating Majorca

When the owner arrived we spent a month cruising around the island, anchoring in some beautiful bays and creeks. Making phone calls home wasn't easy in the small towns around the coast before the construction of yacht marinas. To reach the post office, we had to walk along sandy tracks, passing people selling live chickens for the meal table and queue up to book a call to the UK at a fixed time. We then had to return later to make the call. If we were lucky it worked out as planned, but not always.

Cruising around the island and staying in places where most people

can't get to easily was an unforgettable experience. The weather was settled, sunny and hot for most of the time. However, we did get caught in a violent squall when we were anchored in the bay of Andratx. All seemed to be fairly peaceful for the first day but on the second day, the clouds started to build up in

16. The cutter anchored in Majorca

the afternoon. As the sky darkened more and more, we started to prepare for rain when we heard a cry. Charlie saw it first. Thick, dark clouds were rolling in fast and there was a clear demarcation line in the sea beneath them where the water had become agitated in the wind.

"Quick, collect up everything that's lying loose," he shouted.

We rushed around the deck to bring in anything that wasn't lashed down but we weren't quick enough. The wind struck us with a sudden, unexpected force and towels and cushions were becoming airborne. We grabbed at them wherever we could just as the rain pelted down. Charlie, Jill, the guests and I rushed around grabbing at anything that looked as if it might disappear in the wind. Glasses and other items either crashed to the deck or disappeared over the side. By the time the squall had passed, everybody was soaked and the wheelhouse was crammed with soggy cushions and towels but no serious damage had been caused so we were able to laugh about it afterwards. Later on in the day, the thunderstorms started and lasted well into the night. The rain was torrential and the wind howled. Lightning flashes were frequent, lighting up the sky throughout the night. The storm was far more violent than anything we had ever seen in the U.K. and we stayed up late into the night watching it. After that, the weather improved. The trip along the west and north coasts of the island was idyllic and the anchorages in the beautiful bays were such lovely places to spend the nights. We had the chance to do some sailing but recognised that the cutter wasn't ideally suited for sailing in the Mediterranean where the wind seemed to be either too strong or too light.

Jill spent a lot of time down below in the galley producing delicious meals for everybody. That is until I decided to help out on a day that the owner and his guests were exceptionally hungry and requested a huge bowl of spaghetti for the six of them, as it could be prepared quickly. The work surfaces were cluttered so when the pasta was cooked I held out a large receptacle with a colander placed on top so that Jill could pour out the pasta to drain it.

"Jill, how much longer will it be, we're starving up here?" somebody called from the aft deck.

Maybe it was that that distracted us. Jill poured and I winced as the hot water and some strands of spaghetti escaped and fell on my hands. Jill apologised and giggled.

"Stop giggling and concentrate," I said.

That was a silly thing to have done. Telling Jill to stop giggling would produce only one certain result - more giggles. She was holding the pan of hot spaghetti precariously.

"Don't," I pleaded as I started giggling myself.

This caused her to giggle even more as she tipped the pan up and sent the entire contents into the colander, which I dropped. The pots clanged when they hit the deck sending the hot water and a kilo of hot pasta slithering all over the floor. Jill doubled over with laughter. I'd seen her take up this position before and it signalled that she was no longer able to control herself. It was so infectious that I knew we were doomed

"What's going on down there, how much longer will it be?" The cry came again.

Well, hearing that didn't help in any way, in fact, it just made us laugh even more. We cracked up as we looked at the swirling mess of hot, slippery spaghetti strands slithering across the floor in all directions. What to do? They were calling out impatiently for food from above. We looked at each other and there was no choice. We began to scoop up the mess from the floor, shovelling it into one of the large pots. We managed to salvage the pasta by rinsing it in hot water and mixing it with the sauce. Jill took the finished mixture and walking with a peculiar gait, struggled to stop laughing as she took it to the aft deck and placed it on the table.

When we arrived in the attractive horseshoe shaped bay of Puerto Pollensa with the Tramuntana mountain range as a backdrop, it was so lovely that we stayed for several days. It was there that Jill learned to water ski and in the process, performed some truly remarkable acrobatic manoeuvres, entirely unintentional but very impressive, which had me in fits of laughter, but she succeeded in the end. One of the male guests was persuaded to try and found it difficult to stand upright so was pulled through the water at a rate of knots in a squatting position. He was so low down that the water filled his shorts and when he did finally manage to get himself upright, the weight of the water pulled his shorts down so he immediately let go the rope and tried to resurrect his dignity but it was too late, we were all in fits of laughter.

On the journey down the east coast, we experienced one more ferocious storm, far worse than the one in Andratx. It was late afternoon, the wind was freshening all the time and the forecast was frightening. We were already rolling badly in the easterly swell and the guests were beginning to feel decidedly queasy so we were forced to seek shelter in Porto Colom, a natural harbour on the south-east coast. We motored in as close as we could to the small fishing port to look for maximum protection from the approaching storm. It was already crowded with a variety of other yachts taking shelter and there were no moorings available. A number of yachts had dropped anchor in the bay, close to the port and we did the same. As the day and evening wore on, more and more yachts came in looking for shelter and with very little room left, they had no alternative but to anchor close to each other. After sunset, the wind howled as it increased in strength and a swell rolled in causing anchors to drag, consequently, some of the boats risked bumping into each other. Since the late comers had anchored too close to the others already there, there was not enough room to heave in the anchors and motor forward to re-lay them without causing chaos, which was exactly what happened. It was indeed chaos. Yachts started their engines and motored around with the occupants shouting and heaving in and re-laying anchors wherever possible and some simply let out more chain in the hope that the anchor flukes would dig in and hold. Some of them collided. Our anchor dragged also but by paying out extra chain it did hold and it helped us avoid somebody else hitting our bow by a matter of a few feet. Charlie and I set watches throughout the night just in case the situation worsened. We were storm bound there for two days before it was calm enough for us to continue cruising.

We returned to Palma after a month away. The owner, his family and guests left and we enjoyed a welcome rest for a few days whilst waiting for Ted and Charlie's brother John to re-join us. They were to help us sail back to the U.K. so that we could always have two men on watches of four hours at a time throughout the day and night. Jill had the worst job in my opinion because she was responsible for feeding us during the voyage home. That meant that she had to stay below decks cooking in the galley, the worst place to be when the sea was throwing us all over the place. Our crew duly arrived and after a few more days we prepared for sea and cast off to sail back to the River Hamble.

On the return voyage we were unsure whether we had sufficient fuel to reach Gibraltar, so pulled into Adra on Spain's south coast. Adra was the last stronghold of the Moors and it is where they were finally defeated and their occupation of Spain brought to an end. It was a small, dusty harbour with no fuelling facilities. Our arrival turned out to be a welcome diversion for some of the locals who were standing around watching us. After we'd told them the reason for our visit, one of them disappeared and later returned, rumbling along in a dilapidated truck with another rough looking Spaniard at the wheel. John and I were whisked off with them to a local garage where we filled large containers with diesel, then rattled back along the track to the yacht, tipped the fuel into the tanks and repeated the procedure until we had sufficient to get us to Gibraltar with no further fear of running low.

It was September and the Gibraltarians were due to vote in the referendum. We docked in the harbour on the 8th, two days prior to the big day. As an enticement for the Gibraltarians to vote to become a part of Spain, General Franco offered them an irresistible proposition. If they would ignore the democracy, freedom of speech, economic stability, wealth and security that they had in Gibraltar, and vote to become part of Spain, they would be allowed to live under his dictatorship. In return, they would be stripped of all of their civil liberties and allowed to live in abject poverty in an uncertain economic environment like the rest of his working class citizens. It was a no-brainer. Practically every single building was decorated with union jacks and those that weren't were raided during the night so that the proprietors awoke to find Union Jacks painted on their facades. It was perfectly obvious that virtually nobody had any intention of forsaking their wealthy existence for the one that Franco was offering them. Of the 12,672 inhabitants who voted, 12,237 chose to remain as British citizens and just forty-four chose Spain. Fifty-five votes were invalid. The atmosphere was electrifying, with wild celebrations taking place throughout the town. Jill and I enjoyed a riotous time in the Bull and Bush until it started to get too rowdy for comfort so we returned to our bunks aboard the yacht. When things quietened down, we stocked up with stores, water and fuel and set off once more, bound for home.

Death Wish

The return voyage to the UK was horrendous from the moment we left Gibraltar and it got even worse once we'd rounded Cape St Vincent and sailed into the Atlantic. We crashed and shuddered our way north through the howling gales and huge seas. The wind was relentless. We rose up to the crests of the waves and crashed down again with a shudder as the sea cascaded over the bow and sloshed along the decks. We spent a lot of the time on our knees in the toilet compartment vomiting. When we weren't doing that we were praying for death. We climbed into our heaving bunks whenever possible, not always an easy task when the bunk is rapidly rising and falling. We gripped it tightly and heaved ourselves up, flopping down flat on our backs as quickly as was possible in the vain hope that it would make us feel better. As the yacht crashed down into the troughs taking us with it, it seemed as if our stomachs took several seconds to catch up with the rest of our body and just as it did we were rising back up again with a vengeance. And so it went on and on and on until we had to fly out of the bunk and rush staggering to the toilet again with arms outstretched to grab hold of anything that would prevent us from falling as we were thrown violently from side to side. We kneeled over the toilet bowl, grabbed the sides tightly so that we wouldn't find ourselves flying through the air and then vomit and vomit, even though there was nothing left in our stomachs to eject. We made our way back to the bunks only to rush off and vomit again shortly afterwards. We felt utterly wretched. Most of the time we could only stomach dry Carr's Table Water biscuits and sips of water and that was vomited either back into the sea or into the toilet, and I recalled Dad's words of wisdom passed on to me before I left home to join the Cervia. They were of no comfort and served no purpose other than to keep me conscious of the appearance of the little red lump.

When it was time for me to go on watch, I made my way to the wheelhouse erratically as I tried to maintain my balance, slewing from one side of the boat to the other. John and Ted were about to leave as Charlie and I took over from them when we saw through the Kent Clear View that the continuous, savage crashing down into the troughs had caused the wooden tender that was lashed in its chocks on the foredeck to break loose. It was rising and falling independently of the yacht. Charlie was steering, he eased up on the throttles and headed into the approaching waves. John, Ted and I donned oilskins and crawled our way forward to the tender. It was like trying to hold onto a wild beast as we struggled to get the tender back into the chocks and securely lash it down, all the while being thrown upwards and downwards and from side to side ourselves and getting a good soaking from the rain and the waves crashing over us. When the task had been accomplished, we saw that the tender's repeated rising and crashing back down had punched a small hole in the foredeck. Because of the slight damage and the terrible sea conditions, we were forced to seek shelter for a few days in Peniche on the Portuguese coast. Peniche had been constructed on a rocky peninsula and is well known for its sandy beaches and excellent surfing conditions -

one of the best in Europe because of the constant wind. How pleased we were to see it! It was a great relief to be secured in the safety of this picturesque harbour. Jill and I felt dreadful after the appalling conditions we had sailed through and we couldn't wait to set foot on terra firma. As soon as was practical after we'd moored up, we wasted not a single second before we jumped ashore, still reeling from the battering we'd taken. When our heads stopped spinning and we'd regained our equilibrium and taken on a feeling of normality, we ventured into the town. That was not a wise decision. We hadn't cleared customs control. We were pounced upon by uniformed officers and taken to an office where we were grilled vigorously, then marched off to another room where the authorities insisted on injecting us with an unknown substance. It was just what we needed after all that we'd been through. We didn't see much of Peniche. As soon as we were released we slouched dejectedly back to the cutter feeling thoroughly miserable.

After the deck was repaired we waited a further two days hoping for a more favourable weather forecast. When it became apparent that it wasn't going to improve, Charlie took the decision that we couldn't wait any longer. Although it was a relief to leave Peniche with its unpleasant memories, we weren't looking forward to what lay ahead. We still had to navigate the notorious Bay of Biscay. Dad had told me horror stories of this stretch of water, one of the fiercest in the Atlantic Ocean due to the many shallow areas where the continental shelf extends well into the bay. Atlantic depressions roll in from the west causing very rough seas, and rapidly deepening depressions can create hurricane force winds that come screaming violently into the bay. Winter storms can be disastrous and in the past, many ships have foundered, making the most hardened sailors fear this treacherous stretch of water. Years later, I would regularly sail in this bay delivering sailboats from La Rochelle to the U.K. and one year, one of my friends, doing the same thing, disappeared forever.

Once we'd left the harbour entrance it started and the further we went the worse it got - if anything it was even worse than before. We were thrown around like a cork and the wind howled and the rain pelted down. The halyards clanged against the mast and the engine rumbled away as it struggled to push us through the huge waves; the smell of diesel and exhaust fumes were constant companions and made us feel even more nauseous.

Charlie, John and Ted slept in the fore cabins and Jill and I occupied the owner's aft stateroom for the trip. Under normal circumstances that would have been a privilege but under those conditions we weren't able to benefit from it. There was a single bunk on one side of the cabin and a double on the other with a table in between them. The table was mounted on a solid stainless steel pillar and could be removed but we left it in position for safety reasons. Jill and I decided that getting in and out of the bunks and struggling to stay in them once there was too much effort and that it would be better to just crash out on the cabin sole under the table. It was uncomfortable but at least we couldn't be thrown out of our bunks. We lay on the floor doing our best to wedge ourselves in position to stop sliding from one side to the other. The propeller shafts rumbled beneath us as the engines struggled to push us up to the crests of the exceptionally large waves and when we heard a rapid increase in the engine revolutions as the yacht plunged violently back down into the deep troughs, we were certain that the propellers had come out of the water. We hardly slept at all. "A sure cure for seasickness is to sit under a tree," said Spike Milligan. I would have traded anything to be able to do that. At times, I peered to the east to see if I could make out the coastline, but it was nowhere to be seen. All I saw was a wall of water as we rolled over onto our side and then I saw only the threatening dark sky as we rolled back the other way with a brutal shudder. The torrential rain lashed down and reduced our visibility, adding to our misery.

After two days of praying to die, it became obvious that our prayers were going to be left unanswered so we changed them and prayed to be saved instead. I promised God that if I survived I'd never go to sea again. I didn't know for certain if there really was a God and if there was, whether He or She really cared very much about my promises but in that time of danger it seemed like a good option. I didn't know what else to do, I felt so utterly wretched. For years afterwards, I would offer up the same prayer on many a similar occasion and each time I got safely back to harbour I went back to sea again. It sounds like a ridiculous thing to do and probably only a fellow seafarer would understand why we do it. In the dead of night, it was far worse because we couldn't see the waves approaching. One enormous rogue wave hit us with such force, it threw the vessel sideways. John and Ted, on watch together, were thrown off their feet and smashed into the side of the wheelhouse landing in a crumpled heap. The steering wheel spun wildly in both directions as the boat was thrown from one side to the other out of control. I was off watch in the owner's stateroom with Jill and Charlie was in his forecabin. The dramatic lunge sideways alarmed us and we rushed to the wheelhouse realising something was wrong. Charlie had already arrived, taken hold of the wheel and was struggling to get us back on course. John and Ted, dazed, fought to stand upright, as another wall of water hit us. After we had gained control of the situation and John and Ted had recovered enough to resume their watch. Charlie, Jill and I went back to our cabins until it was time for us to relieve them.

The Pointe de Raz is on the coast of Brittany and eight miles offshore lies the Ile de Sein from which there is a perilous reef stretching east to west for thirty miles. There is a precarious passage between the Ile and the point known as the Raz de Sein, which is the usual shortcut to Ushant and there are many buoys, beacons and lighthouses marking the dangers that have to be negotiated. The sea there can rise quickly and be very rough, making the area a place to be avoided in any but the most settled conditions. It goes without saying that many ships have been wrecked there, and even in a moderate wind it can be a very dangerous place with the seven-knot current and violent sea conditions. The alternative is to head out to sea for a further thirty miles to clear the reef extending from the Ile de Sein and that's exactly what we had to do. It was the last thing any of us wanted, but it would have been extremely unwise to attempt the Raz de Sein passage in the weather that we were experiencing. With heavy hearts, the course was set to take us those thirty extra miles further out to clear the reef and then set course towards the Isle of Ushant.

The Isle of Ushant is a mere 15 square kilometres, surrounded by several smaller islands. It lies 15 nautical miles from the French mainland and marks the entrance to the southwestern approaches to the English Channel. It too has a fearsome reputation and is considered to be one of the most difficult navigational passages in the world because of its many outlying rocks and dangers and a tidal stream of more than ten knots. Because of the dangers, there are six lighthouses, one of which has a beam that can be seen for an astonishing distance of eighty miles. Many ships have foundered in these treacherous waters, probably the most well-known being the Amoco Cadiz, which ran aground nineteen miles from the island in March 1978. It resulted in what was at that time the world's worst oil pollution drama, which devastated the Brittany coast.

The main village on the island has about 900 inhabitants and in the cemetery, the names of the ships lost and of the sailors who perished are listed. There is an inner passage that at the best of times, poses a considerable challenge even to the most experienced navigator and it would have been impossible for us to attempt it under such conditions. We, therefore, had no alternative but to extend our passage by going around the outside of the island. Ushant was yet another area that Dad often spoke about with trepidation.

After we'd made the alarming rounding of Ushant, we rejoiced when we altered course to take us into the English Channel and homeward bound. The English Channel presented no problems to us after all that we'd been through. We still had to cope with a rough sea but it was a fantastic feeling when we set a course for the Isle of Wight. We were shocked; however, to discover that the relentless pounding we'd taken from the savage sea and wind over the previous days had resulted in us taking on water at a frightening rate. Charlie and John searched for the leak without success and eventually concluded that the hull planking must have spread somewhere. The bilge pump was working almost constantly on the final leg home in an effort to keep the water in the bilges at a safe level.

After many more hours, the Needles finally came into view in the distance; it was such a wonderful sight and such a relief. As we got closer, we took turns to shower to save time when we eventually moored up at Warsash. Ted went first before we reached the Needles. Unfortunately for him, there was still a fair sea running as we approached and we could hear him cursing and swearing as he was being thrown around in the cubicle. Feeling jubilant to be so near to home, we were in high spirits and

Ted's venomous cursing sent us all into hysterics as we imagined him trying to wash his overweight, naked body whilst trying to stay upright. We rounded the Needles and the rest of us had our showers as we cruised along Southampton Water and into the River Hamble, battered, exhausted and at the same time elated to have safely made it home. The horrendous conditions had slowed us down from our normal cruising speed so that the voyage home took far longer than the voyage out. At times it seemed that we almost stood still as the walls of water crashed into us. What with that and the detour to Peniche, the time we spent there, the mishaps along the way and the extended sea passage to clear the reef and Ushant, it had taken us eleven days to do the 1200 miles from Gibraltar. It was a taster of what to expect In my successive 25 years at sea. Thomas Aquinas once said "If the highest aim of a Captain were to preserve his ship, he would keep it in port forever."

We hoisted the yellow flag to request customs clearance, and once moored, tidied up and packed our bags whilst we waited for the customs officers. When we'd been cleared, we said our goodbyes and disembarked. Charlie, John and Ted went their ways and Jill and I, feeling wobbly, made our way to the home of our friends, Adrian and Mary, where we had stored our personal belongings after leaving our accommodation at the Hamble Broadway. We found the hiding place for the key and let ourselves in. Adrian and Mary were on holiday and our hearts sank when we discovered that there was no food in the house. Weary, hungry and disheartened, we left and travelled to the Oak Hill Hotel where we'd had our wedding reception. We booked a room for the night and ordered a well-earned three-course meal and an excellent bottle of wine. Staying awake long enough to finish the meal took a great deal of effort but we did manage it, only just. After all that we'd been through, any sane person would have vowed never to set foot aboard a boat again. However, Jill and I at the time must have lost our senses, because the following morning we discussed the prospects of doing it all again and where and how we could find somebody who needed a Captain and Cook/Deckhand. We knew from that moment on we were going to continue as a husband and wife team. Although Jill's upbringing had been unorthodox, the expectation was that she would marry, settle down and have children, so less consideration was given to her career possibilities than that given to her brothers and cousin. Her Aunt had hoped however, that Jill would travel, expand her view of the world and fulfil her dreams and we weren't about to disappoint her. I knew that Jill was an unconventional girl when she insisted on omitting the word 'obey' from her marriage vows and she clearly had a sense of humour to have chosen 1 April for the wedding. I was therefore not too surprised that she was as eager as I was to set off once more on a new adventure. The monumental character building exercise that she had endured for the past three months had given her a new vision of what could be and it was to have a lasting impact on the rest of her life. "The best of life is to embark on an adventure with a woman who is interested in having an adventure with you." – Oleg Cassini, a Russian fashion designer who worked for Paramount Pictures

.

CHAPTER 6
THE PASSING FANCY

A surprise encounter

We'd vacated our rented accommodation in Hamble Broadway when we left for Majorca and needed a base, so we rented the bottom floor of a house next to the Bugle, a pub/restaurant in the lovely village of Hamble. They were happy days. We'd spent very little throughout the trip to Majorca as everything we'd needed had been provided by the owner of the yacht, so it was a special day when we received the wages that had accrued whilst we'd been away. How we enjoyed spending it!

We couldn't wait to find another yacht on which to satisfy our desire to travel. However, the proprietor of the house, who lived on the top floor, was a mature spinster who had planned a nine month world tour and we had agreed to remain as caretakers until she returned. After a lengthy spell of relaxation, we looked for employment in the Southampton area. I found work in the office of a company in Southampton city centre that sold clutch and brake linings to local garages and delivered them in their fleet of vans. Jill found a job as a wages clerk at Hawker Siddeley in

Hamble, very convenient as it was within walking distance of our new lodgings. After a short while, I was virtually running the small office on my own. It was an enjoyable time, the storeroom staff and the drivers were terrific fun to be with. One of the drivers left, so we needed a replacement and a young girl applied. After I'd interviewed her, she sat in my office waiting for her boyfriend to come and collect her in his car. An old green Triumph Roadster came rattling along the road and who should be driving it but the scruffy, unsociable individual from my Navigation School days. He was still as scruffy as ever with a scraggly dark beard and dark piercing eyes. If he'd been of larger stature he would have looked quite sinister. We were surprised to see each other and chatted about our mutual interests. It was the beginning of a friendship that has endured for more than fifty years. He had passed his exams and he and his partner, like Jill and me, were hoping to find a yacht that they could work on together. They were living aboard a boat moored at Kemp's Shipyard on the River Itchen at Southampton. We saw each other regularly after that and made a decision to pass on to the other any offers that we didn't want to accept ourselves, or any offers that came in after we'd accepted what we wanted.

Jill and I had come to the conclusion that we needed more skills in preparation for the jobs to come. If anything went wrong whilst we were at sea, there would be nobody to call on for help and I had to be able to deal with any emergency myself. I took out books from the library and studied as many subjects as possible that I thought would be relevant, electricity and electrical installations, plumbing, engine maintenance and anything else that I felt would be appropriate. I also enrolled on an engineering course at the Gardner establishment in Manchester. Gardner's reputation was unrivalled. Their engines were renowned worldwide for their reliability, economy and longevity and the 6LX diesel engines installed on the cutter were considered the finest heavy duty diesel engines ever made. Since Gardner engines would often be the first choice for yachts it was important that I had knowledge of their manufacture and maintenance. Jill took driving lessons and passed her test so we bought a second hand Austin A30 for £60. These small family cars were manufactured from 1952 – 1956 and had a top speed of around

60mph. When the time came for us to go to Manchester, Jill drove us there on the M1, Britain's first motorway, which had no speed limit in those days - although this was of no advantage to us in our little A30. We stayed in a rented house with the sister of Jill's brother's fiancée and Jill drove me in each morning to the instruction centre and picked me up at the end of each day. When we returned to Hamble, Jill started taking cookery lessons in the evenings, which she excelled at. I salivated on those nights in anticipation of the culinary masterpieces she'd be bringing home. Our new bearded friend Bob and I encouraged Jill and his partner, Tina, to practice as much as possible, taking turns to dine at each other's homes - and boy did we eat well! Jill and Tina became very competitive; each determined to better the other, which was just wonderful for Bob and me. He heaped praise on Tina for her efforts and I couldn't help but lavish well deserved praise on Jill. She had a natural talent. The meals were exceptional and the more Jill and Tina tried to outdo each other the more Bob and I emboldened them. Jill was a no expense spared cook but Tina was inclined the other way, because Bob counted the pennies on his hosting nights. The meat was mostly offal, which Jill was not at all fond of; in fact, it would be fair to say that at times she found it distressing looking at heart, liver or kidneys on her plate but with an English stiff upper lip she politely ate it. I, as usual, just devoured everything in sight. I'd eaten plenty of offal at home and on the tugs and some of the healthiest and longest living individuals in other countries eat everything from head to tail because they know that the organs are the most nutritious part of the animal. The concentration on eating only muscle meat, which has the least nutritive content, is a relatively new, western concept.

Working at Hawker Siddeley had advantages; it was near to where we lived, they had sports facilities, a club house, the pay was more than I was getting in Southampton and Jill was there, so I left my job and went to join her. The car spares company made me a better offer to try to keep me; more money and more amenable hours, but I declined. My job at Hawker Siddeley was to tour each department, collect the clocking in cards and calculate the wages. Jill was in a different office and her job was to make up the wage packets. I wasn't there long before I upset my co-workers. It was routine for them to work late on Friday nights and again on Saturday morning. They had always done this and then I came along. I had no trouble finishing everything I had to do by four o'clock on Friday and I'm quite sure that everybody else could have done the same, except they wanted the overtime. I, however, wanted to go home and be with Jill. By Friday I'd had all I could take of being shut up in a stuffy office under unhealthy fluorescent lights. They decided to gang up on me one morning and tell me what they thought of me disrupting their "nice little earner". I stood my ground.

"You're making things difficult for us, we've always worked on Saturday mornings," the senior staff member said.

"But there's nothing to do, you just sit around pretending," I replied.

"No we don't, there are always things to sort out."

"There's nothing that can't be finished easily by Friday afternoon."

"Well, it doesn't look good for us if you never come in on Saturdays and you never stay late on Fridays either."

"I'm not going to spend precious time sitting here twiddling my thumbs when I could be at home with my wife. I've got a life and I am not going to hang around here bored out of my mind, pretending to work just to please you and to earn a few more measly pounds when I could be enjoying myself doing what I want to do. No amount of extra money is worth me losing valuable me time."

We agreed to disagree and after that, there was no further animosity. They carried on working unnecessarily to increase the amount in their wage packets and I had my weekends free with Jill. We made the most of our time there, regularly taking advantage of the facilities provided.

I was offered an unexpected bonus one day. One of Jill's co-workers, a very attractive, dark haired, married girl would regularly call into my office to bring or collect paperwork as our two departments worked closely together. She would stand next to my desk chatting. My co-workers said that this had never happened before I came along and they hadn't known who she was until she began those weekly visits. She must have somehow gathered information about my routine because one day as I was cycling along one of my regular routes I saw her standing on the roadside. I stopped to say hello and she revealed her cunning plan. She invited me to visit her in her home the following day whilst her husband was away at work. I was surprised because I thought she was happily married and just liked to flirt. I was happily married however, so I declined in as gentle a way as I could but obviously not gentle enough because her visits to my office ended after that.

An exciting offer

We'd replied to an advertisement for a Captain and Cook and had been invited to dinner at the Montague Arms Hotel in Beaulieu, a small, unspoilt village at the edge of the New Forest, to discuss taking command of a yacht based in the South of France, owned by a gentleman living in Jersey. Unfortunately, he was looking for an experienced Captain and I was only 24 years old with limited experience. I needed a permanent Skipper's job to gain the experience that the yacht owners wanted. It was a typical chicken and egg situation. The meal was outstanding though as was the excellent Pouilly Fuissé. Bring on some more interviews, I thought, who cares if I miss out on a few jobs, I could force myself to suffer a few more meals like that.

Bob and Tina had two possibilities of employment. They accepted command of a motor yacht that had been built in Sweden three months previously and had been brought to the Hamble and moored at Moody's boatyard at Swanwick. They gave Jill and me the contact details of another yacht being built in Belgium, so we applied for the post and very shortly afterwards were invited for an interview. We received a letter asking us to meet the owner in the lounge area of an elegant hotel in London. Seated on one of the comfortable red armchairs in the warm atmosphere, was Hervé, a small, slightly overweight, balding Belgian wearing glasses. We joined him and took to him immediately; he was amiable and smiling constantly, obviously very proud and pleased with his project. He spread out the plans of his yacht on the shiny wooden table between us and handed us a couple of glossy, colour brochures. On the front cover was an artist's impression of a beautiful motor yacht under way on a calm blue sea.

"I've bought a 62 ft. steel hull that has been built by a renowned shipyard in Holland and it's lying at Kortrijk where we're fitting out the interior to a very high standard," he enthused, proudly passing his hands over the papers that he'd spread out on the table. "It has twin 250 hp. Vosper Thorneycroft engines and the propellers have been specially designed and built by Lips to give us a cruising speed of 16 knots. I've planned a 10-day cruise catering to the American market. You'll pick them up in Sorrento and take them to Capri, then on to Rome, then La Spezia, Portofino, the South of France, and Corsica." On and on he rambled as he laid out his captivating plan.

He explained that he owned a coach company operating tours and had come up with the idea of doing a similar thing with yachts. The itinerary he had drawn up was based on his experience of operating coach tours where strict timetables can be adhered to and distances and speeds can be calculated with a fair amount of confidence and certainty. At sea, unknown and unexpected factors have to be considered, such as the wind strength and direction which affect the vessel's progress and have a subsequent effect on the waves. When the violent Mistral wind blows, which could last for as much as ten days, it may be necessary to remain in harbour for safety reasons. Then there are thunderstorms and some anchorages could be untenable in adverse conditions. His schedule was based on the vessel achieving the 16 knots he hoped for but the chances of always being able to achieve that speed were remote.

"Have you taken into account the bad weather factor?" I asked. "It may be that there will be difficulty sticking to such a tight schedule."

"Oh, it will all be OK, it's going to be a good strong seaworthy boat and I've already ordered a second hull which I hope to have ready to sail next year so there will be two cruises operating."

The cutter was a strong seaworthy boat too and it didn't help us much when we were thrown around like a little toy boat in the stormy conditions of the Bay of Biscay and I doubted that people who'd paid a high price for a relaxing cruise would want to go through a similar experience. I was sure that they would prefer to remain safe in a harbour somewhere but Hervé couldn't envisage anything upsetting his wonderful plan so we went along with him. The plan of the finished yacht looked impressive as did the classy brochure outlining the cruise. Jill and I exchanged glances, wondering if this guy was for real and if he had any idea of just what was involved. Even if we could cruise at 16 knots every day we would be hard pressed to keep to his itinerary.

"We will take eight paying guests and they will be expected to eat ashore so the galley area is small but adequate for most purposes."

He was exceedingly enthusiastic and we listened and listened and bit by bit we got pulled into his dream. In addition to Jill and me, he would be employing an engineer and another female crew member. On completion of the construction, we would sail the magnificent vessel from Ostend to the Mediterranean Sea via the French canals. It sounded appealing and we accepted his offer. He paid us our expenses for the day and we left him still beaming with pleasure and pride with a jubilant twinkle in his eyes.

On the train journey home, Jill and I discussed the whole proposition, wondering if it would work as he'd hoped but as we'd discovered from the interview at Beaulieu, we needed the experience and at that time would have accepted almost anything to get our feet on the rung of the ladder. Once back in Hamble, we reluctantly went back to our mundane jobs at Hawker Siddeley. It wasn't easy to get enthused about wage packets at the best of times and knowing that soon we would be setting sail on a journey through the French canals to a heady life in the Mediterranean just made us even keener to finish there as quickly as possible and say our goodbyes to everybody and everything.

The Calamities begin

At last the letter arrived with our tickets enclosed and the date that we were to be in Kortrijk. Over a year had gone by since we'd arrived back in the U.K. from our Majorca trip and we were more than ready to be moving on. Accommodation had been arranged for us at the Ibis Kortrijk Centrum Hotel, close to where the yacht was being fitted out by the shipyard, in conjunction with the workforce from the coach company. We took the Townsend Thoresen ferry from Dover to Zeebrugge, Belgium's most important fishing port, where we were met by a chauffeur who drove us inland to our hotel. Kortrijk lies on the banks of the River Leie and is the largest city in South West Flanders. It has some interesting medieval architecture, although much was destroyed in 1944 when 300 Lancasters dropped 5000 bombs on the city centre, which had been a significant railway link for the German army. The city's economy had been largely dependent on the wool and flax industry since the Middle Ages, and it still has an important role in Belgian textile commerce.

We were left to amuse ourselves for two days before the jovial Belgian came to take us to the yard to see the boat. After having seen the lovely glossy brochure depicting a fine, luxurious motor yacht, we were disappointed to see a dirty, unfinished vessel with no wheelhouse. It was a miserable day, overcast with light rain. Workmen were milling around inside and outside of the vessel, shouting out instructions, some of them running, some of them deep in thought as they conversed with each other. There was plenty of banging and noise from machinery and there was a strong smell of oil, and wood and metal being cut and welded. The Belgian's optimism, however, was contagious and we were buoyed up after spending the morning listening to him enthral us with his wonderful ideas. The inside at least was impressive. Descending into the saloon, immediately on the starboard side was a large bar taking up a lot of space. From the thick slate surface to the saloon floor, it was covered in a brown and white cowhide. Behind that was the small galley. The plush carpet was dark blue and there were light blue velvet L-shaped settees with matching light blue velvet bucket seats at the bar. The curtains were in a heavy blue and green patterned fabric, hanging from the deck head to the cabin sole and running the full length of both sides of the saloon. It certainly had the air of luxury. In the centre of the saloon were steps leading down to two twin berth cabins, one on each side of the companionway. From the wheelhouse or rather where the wheelhouse would eventually be, other steps led down to the aft section where there were two additional twin berth cabins, one on each side. Jill and I had a cabin in the forepeak, accessible from a hatch on deck and the engineer and fourth crew member would be sleeping wherever happened to be practical. In the centre of the wheelhouse floor was a hatch, that when lifted, revealed a ladder that descended to the engine room. There was little we could do whilst the work continued for a further nine days, so we took advantage of the Belgian's hospitality, during which time he introduced us to an 18-year-old, curvy, pretty blonde called Sophie. He told us that she would be our third crew member and the fourth, the engineer, would be joining us in Paris.

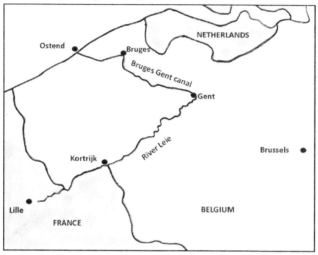

17. Belgium

When everything was almost finished we left Kortrijk, still with no wheelhouse, which we were informed would be fitted, along with the mast, when we reached Chalon-sur-Saône; it was to be a long journey with no protection whatsoever from the weather. The vessel was already higher than the average motor yacht and with the wheelhouse in place it would not have fitted under all the bridges on our journey through the canals. After Chalon-sur-Saône height would no longer be a problem.

We were accompanied by Hervé and the attractive blonde, who it transpired, was Hervé's girlfriend. A couple of workmen came along as well to continue working on the unfinished jobs. It took us six days to motor the 88 kilometres along the canal route to the coastal town of Ostend, passing through the beautiful city of Bruges and making occasional stops along the way for the workmen to get parts they needed. At Ostend, we moored alongside a quay to await the arrival of the field surveyor from the American Bureau of Shipping. Lloyds of London (Lloyds Register of Shipping), we were told, had passed on the opportunity to classify and register the yacht. They obviously knew something that we didn't but were about to find out. The design and construction of the yacht had supposedly already been witnessed, including the materials, machinery and electrical systems and the next stage was for the surveyor to accompany us on sea trials, prior to having the certificate of classification issued. Most of the interior work had by this time been finished.

It was another grey, miserable day when he arrived and there was a fairly brisk wind that created a moderate swell. Under his instruction, I started the powerful engines and eased the vessel out into the North Sea swell with Hervé on one side of me, the surveyor on the other and Jill watching from behind as I steered straight ahead. The tests went well as we motored further out leaving the harbour entrance receding behind us. To shelter from the cold wind, Hervé left my side and crouched down in the entrance to the saloon with just the top of his head exposed as he tried to peer over the coach roof into the distance, leaving the rest of us to endure as best we could. The wave seemed to come from nowhere as it abruptly lifted the bow high to the crest, sending Hervé rolling backwards, slithering along the deck on his back with his legs in the air until he reached the casing of the stern section with a thump just as the bow dipped down into the trough sending him spinning back the other way, heading straight for the saloon entrance and the three foot drop to the floor below. As he spun and slithered, he grabbed at anything he could reach to stop his momentum, which happened to be our legs. The wave passed, the boat steadied and he pulled himself up with a nervous, embarrassed giggle. The surveyor and I tried to stifle our laughter but for Jill, it was impossible, she erupted into a fit of unashamed laughter, which she was prone to do at such times. After composing ourselves the surveyor spoke.

"Put the wheel hard over and go full astern, Captain," he instructed.
The dishevelled little Belgian pulled himself together as best he could, shuffled alongside me and whispered in my right ear,

"Don't do it."
I couldn't defy the surveyor; it was the final test, so I stopped the engine, spun the steering wheel hard to starboard and pulled the single lever

controls to the full astern position.

"OK, Captain, stop the engines." the surveyor said after a while, which I did, and we wallowed in the swell.

"Right, that's it, all done, turn around and let's go back," he said.

With the wheel still hard a starboard, I pushed the throttles forward and we were homeward bound, except that we weren't turning. We were going in the wrong direction and heading straight ahead, for Holland. Jill, Hervé and the surveyor stared at me. I tried turning the wheel more but it was already at maximum lock. I pushed the throttles further to gain more steerage but we just kept heading further out into the North Sea with Ostend harbour behind us. I spun the wheel the other way, hard to port and increased the revs even more but we just went ever faster towards Holland. It was then that we realised that the last manoeuvre had snapped both rudder shafts and the rudders had plunged to the bottom of the North Sea, leaving me with a steering wheel as useless as a gigolo without his manhood. The surveyor and I looked at each other in disbelief. By using the twin engines, one ahead and the other astern to spin the boat around, I steered back to Ostend harbour by tweaking one, then the other of the twin engines to hold the course.

The wind strength or direction hadn't changed so we made our way back through the grey, murky water without any further difficulty and found a place to moor up alongside the quay. The surveyor had a discussion with Hervé, explaining what was required for the yacht to be granted the certificate of seaworthiness and went on his way. Hervé was not pleased and after sitting down alone in the saloon for a while looking dejected and deep in thought, he left us and went off to make the arrangements for the supply of two new rudders and the replacement of what was left of the shafts for sturdier ones that met the recommendations of the surveyor. The boat was hauled out of the water and we had to wait another week for the work to be done. I benefitted from the week long wait to stock up with the charts and navigation equipment I'd need when the time came to cast off for the long haul to the Mediterranean. When the work was finished, the boat was launched and we went out again for the final sea trial, which went well. We moored up once more and prepared to get under way immediately the following day for the journey to Le Havre. The rudder incident had caused an unexpected delay and Hervé was anxious that we get to Cannes in time for the season. We should have realised then that the yacht was prone to mishaps but that was only the beginning.

I needed to top up the water tanks so took off the filler cap, shoved the end of the hose in the hole, turned on the tap and then, with Jill, concentrated on checking that we were ready for sea. We made sure that everything was securely stowed away and lashed down, the portholes closed and the engine oil and water levels OK. When I was satisfied that we were ready to depart, I was surprised that nothing had come out of the water tank overflow to indicate that the tanks were full. It had seemed a long time ago that we'd started filling the tanks and I wondered how it could possibly be taking so long. I noticed that the quay was a fair bit higher than when we arrived. Hang on, I thought to myself, the quay can't get higher. No, but the boat can get lower. We were sinking! I rushed down below to see what had been going on and saw that the bilges were filled with water.

"Somebody turn the hose off!" I yelled from the bowels of the boat.

The panic in my voice startled Jill who sprang into action and rushed to turn off the water. Jill and I were fast coming to the conclusion that the portly little Belgian and his band of merry men had not the faintest idea about boat building and were fitting it out as if it were a coach, making things up as they went along. We had a permanent and very pronounced list to starboard because they hadn't calculated for weight distribution, doubtless thinking that it wasn't important and that a boat would be as stable as a coach and therefore one could do whatever one liked. This was going to be an interesting journey, I thought. So how did we finish up with the fresh water flooding the boat instead of going into the water tanks? The plastic hose from the filler cap to the water tank had been laid directly over the exhaust pipes, so it must have burned through within minutes after the engines were first started way back in Kortrijk. Even worse, unbelievably, the exhaust pipes were unlagged, leaving us with two exceedingly hot metal tubes under the cabin soles running half the length of the boat, so that anything nearby could melt, or worse, burn. A new plastic pipe was fitted well away from the dangerously hot exhausts but nothing was done about the exhaust pipes themselves; we topped up the tanks and were finally ready to cast off, wondering what the next disaster would be.

Hervé stepped ashore leaving Sophie on board with Jill and me, though what her role was meant to be we weren't sure. Probably she just fancied a trip to the Med. and as she was Hervé's girlfriend, attractive, and about thirty years younger than him, he obviously didn't want to upset her.

"Good luck with everything. Have a safe journey and I'll see you in Chalon-sur-Saône," he said.

The vessel had been registered in Panama for tax purposes, so the Panamanian ensign was hoisted on the flagstaff at the stern. I started the engines. We slipped the mooring and I motored out of Ostend whilst Jill brought in and stowed the fenders and mooring ropes, explaining the routine to Sophie.

Ostend to Paris

 It felt so good to finally be at sea again with the gentle breeze, the steady rolling motion of the vessel in the swell, the smell of the salty water, the thumping of the powerful engines, the steering wheel between my hands and seeing the coastline of Belgium slip away in the greyness of the North Sea as we headed towards Le Havre. Laying off courses on the charts wasn't easy since no space had been allocated for such a vital activity. Hervé, it seemed, had given little thought as to how I would get the boat from A to B. I suppose he thought I'd just jump aboard and drive it to wherever he wanted us to be, following signs as in one of his fleet of coaches. What a pity there weren't signs in the English Channel with arrows pointing me to Le Havre. There was no stowage area allocated for the charts and no chart table to lay off my courses and plot the tides, I had to kneel on the saloon floor, try to cope on the minute table, or use the irregular and

even smaller slate surface of the bar. We had no navigation lights. Everything, Hervé told me, would be connected in Chalon-sur-Saône when the wheelhouse and mast were installed, so we couldn't travel by night and I only had a temporarily installed compass.

We didn't have long to wait to discover the next serious problem; the sixteen knots cruising speed we'd hoped for turned out to be just eight knots at full speed, so we didn't get further than the 90 nautical miles to Boulogne-sur-Mer on the first day, arriving late just before it got dark. It is approximately half way between Ostend and Le Havre and is France's largest fishing port, specialising in herring. It lies at the mouth of the River Liane on the section of France's North coast known as the Cote d'Opale and it was there that Sophie intimated to me how she thought she may be useful on board. After a tedious passage, we'd made fast in the harbour and Jill cooked up one of her delicious meals. Sophie sat on the inside next to me, leaving the other side of the table free for Jill to serve up the food and seat herself. As soon as we started eating, the promiscuous eighteen year old started rubbing her leg against mine, making it perfectly obvious what she wanted it to lead to. She certainly hadn't wasted any time. In my bachelor days I would have been eager to respond but now as a married man with my wife sitting opposite I briskly moved my leg away. I'd had the most wonderful bachelorhood but I was then and am now, a faithful person, so I made it obvious from my body language that I was not going to respond to her wanton gestures.

The following morning, we left at first light to travel the 98 nautical miles to Le Havre. The name simply means "The port". It is the second largest in France after Marseille. The town and harbour were founded in 1517 by King Francis I and during WWII it suffered more damage than any other port. We made fast alongside the quay, assessed how things had gone and stocked up with provisions ready to begin the journey along the River Seine to Paris the following day. It was an enjoyable and fairly relaxing cruise along the 124-kilometre leg to Rouen with no further mishaps.

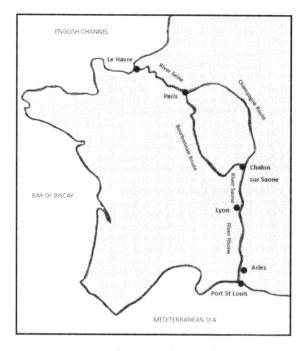

18. The French canals

This section of the river is a major French commercial shipping route so the wash from the many passing ships occasionally caused us some discomfort. The tides are very strong with a substantial rise and fall between high and low water and there used to be a powerful tidal bore at flood tides known as the Mascaret, which had caused numerous deaths; one of the most prominent was the daughter of Victor Hugo, the French poet and novelist who wrote Les Miserables and The Hunchback of Notre Dame. The violent bore is now mainly controlled by dredging. I timed it to run with the flood tide behind us so that we would reach Rouen before nightfall. Rouen is renowned for its cathedral that had been painted many times by Claude Monet. The town was the command base of the English when they occupied France for thirty years and in 1430, Joan of Arc was sent there to be tried by the church court. She was sentenced to be burned at the stake, which took place in May 1431. Rouen was eventually recaptured in 1449 by Charles V1, the King of France. During the Nazi occupation in world war two, approximately 45% of this lovely city was destroyed. It was eventually liberated on 30th August 1944 by the

Canadians, following the D-day invasion of the Normandy beaches by the Allied forces.

We stayed in this city, the capital of the Normandy region, overnight and for a few hours the following day to top up with more stores.

Our next leg of the journey was the 191 kilometre stretch from Rouen to the city of Paris, with an overnight stop en route. It was good to be back in Paris again and it was an extraordinary experience to arrive in this most beautiful of cities by boat and to be moored up on the banks of the Seine. We stayed there for two days but our pleasure was marred when we sent Sophie ashore early in the morning to buy extra food and the shop keeper short changed her by a large amount. Sophie knew she was correct in the denomination of the note she handed over. She couldn't have been mistaken because we only had ones of large denomination. Arguing with the shopkeeper got her nowhere and as we had to account for our expenses, Jill went with Sophie, who spoke some French, to the Gendarmerie. After my previous experience with the Parisian Gendarmes, I wasn't very optimistic about the outcome and was proven right. A fat lot of good it did us. The gendarmes accompanied Jill and Sophie to the shop and after listening to the unpleasant swindler espousing her side of the story they chose to believe her. Whilst Jill and Sophie were away, she must have taken the large denomination note out of the till and with feigned irritancy showed them the contents of the much smaller denomination notes. Jill and Sophie were told by the gendarmes that there had clearly been a misunderstanding or worse still that they were lying and were told to be on their way without further ado. They returned to the boat furious and with a bitter feeling about Parisians.

Whether or not it was relevant to the above circumstance I don't know, but we were there the year after a period of civil unrest that virtually brought about the collapse of the French economy. The state of affairs was so bad that the politicians feared a civil war would break out. Fuel was unavailable and it was difficult to withdraw any money from the banks. It all began with a student revolt against capitalism, consumerism and the institutions. The unrest then spread to 11 million factory workers, which was 22% of the French population. The aggressive response by the police and university administrators inflamed the situation, resulting in violent street clashes and wildcat strikes across the country. It was so serious that President De Gaulle fled the country on May 29 for the French Military headquarters at Baden-Baden in Germany. He took all of his personal papers with him and told nobody where he was going, leaving the Prime Minister, Georges Pompidou to deal with the turmoil as best he could. So serious was the situation that the Prime Minister was offered a weapon to defend himself with, which he refused. Other officials planned escape routes and burned all documents that could exacerbate the situation. General Jacques Massu, in Baden-Baden, persuaded De Gaulle to return to France, which he did the following day, 30 May. That same day, up to half a million protesters marched through Paris protesting against him. There were genuine fears that a full-scale revolution would take place and preparations were made to respond to it with tanks which had been placed on standby. By the afternoon, De Gaulle had called for an election on 23 June and told the workers to return to work, otherwise, a state of emergency would be declared. As news spread that the army was stationed outside Paris with tanks, the communist party, who had fuelled the trouble in an attempt to overthrow the government, acquiesced and the revolutionary-minded students and workers stopped demonstrating and went back to their daily routines. De Gaulle won the election by a wide margin despite the fact that the French population considered him too old and too authoritarian. On Bastille Day, there was a further uprising by communists, socialists and anarchists, which resulted in bloodshed when the police responded to the rebellion with brute force. The whole episode subsequently brought about a social revolution in France, rather than a political one, with the after effects lasting many years. On 27 April, shortly before we went to Belgium, De Gaulle was defeated in a referendum on constitutional reform and resigned the next day. The temporary presidency was held by Alain Poher until 15 June when an election was held during the time that we were navigating the canals. George Pompidou became the new president. It was against this backdrop that we cruised the length of France. Jill and I had no way of knowing then that in 1971 when everything had settled down, we would once again be in Paris, based there as Captain and Cook on a 25 metre motor yacht.

With the unpleasant monetary experience behind us, we stayed moored in Paris to await the arrival of our engineer who flew out from the U.K. to join us the following day. He was a huge fellow; over six feet tall, with a thick mop of dark brown, curly hair and a round smiling face. Fully crewed, we set off on the 14 day run to Chalon-sur-Saône. Despite our introduction to the hostile attitude of some Parisians we couldn't help but enjoy cruising along the River Seine through Paris. Thousands of tourists pay small fortunes to see the sights from the crowded Bateaux Mouches and we were being paid to do it on our own private boat. It was a privilege to have seen the famous attractions from the comfort of the yacht, most of which are almost on the river's edge. Gently cruising past the majestic Eifel Tower, Les Invalides, the Louvre, the awesome Notre Dame and passing under the famous bridges, of which there are 37 in the city and many more on the outskirts, was an unforgettable experience. When the sightseeing had finished we knew that we had to face the arduous task of negotiating 155 locks and another 495 kilometres on the western Bourbonnais route, which I'd chosen as the best route for us to reach Chalon-sur-Saône as quickly as possible. The other option, which I'd estimated would add at least one extra day to our journey, was the eastern Champagne route, which had a few less locks but an extra 50 kilometres of waterway and a five kilometre long tunnel.

CHAPTER 7
A BRIDGE TOO LOW

Fighting gravity

We headed South East on the Upper Seine, a wide, busy river with numerous craft navigating in both directions. After a few kilometres, at Charenton, the Seine met the River Marne that ran to the East. We continued on the Seine to Melun, running around the south side of the island and passed through Dreveil, Chartrettes and Avon to complete a 48 kilometres run. The bridges, with headroom of 5.2 metres posed no difficulties for us but I was concerned about the low bridges to come, some of which were as low as 3.5 metres, with the passageway through them no more than 5.0 metres wide. We passed through 7 locks to reach St Mammès, which is located on the banks of two rivers and is an axis point for river transport between the Seine and Burgundy. From there we joined the Canal du Loing, which joins the upper Seine to the Briare canal. The building of this canal began in 1720 by Phillippe II, the Duke of Orléans and it was finished five years later. It is 49 kilometres long and has 19 locks with a total drop in height of 35 metres. The longest distance between locks was a mere 4.7 kilometres. We followed this pretty, wooded route, passing through the picturesque, fortified town of Moret, which has royal connections going back to Louis VII. The lock there dropped us down 2.4 metres. After a further 800 metres, the Bourgogne lock dropped us another 2.37 metres. Another kilometre on, at Ecuelles, there was a few shops and as it was just 800 metres from the next lock, I decided to tie up to the canal bank for the night. We had travelled just 4.3 kilometres on this canal and having passed under five bridges I realised that we were going to have difficulties and needed to get the yacht lower in the water. We hunted around on the canal bank collecting as many large boulders as we could find and placed them all around the deck to take us lower into the water before relaxing over an evening meal.

The next morning, shortly after 06.00 hrs, we were woken by a loud splashing of water against the hull and a strong rocking of the boat as the canal barges navigated past us vying to be first through the lock as they began their daily voyages delivering their cargoes. This became a regular routine for us, to wake up and start moving by 06.00 hrs. We would have been woken by the swell and noise of the numerous passing barges anyway whether we liked it or not. It wasn't a bad thing as we needed to reach our destination in Cannes in time for the season's cruising. I also decided that I would always try to moor each night as close as possible to the next lock to avoid having to wait too long for our turn to pass through.

We set off once more, passing under the bridges and going through the locks, stopping to collect any large rocks that we happened to see as we were still too high in the water. It became difficult to walk along the decks as there were

19. Motoring through the canals

so many of them. At the first opportunity to fill the water tanks I took the decision to flood the bilges as much as was practical to lower the boat in the water still more.

Fortunately, the weather was kind for most of the trip. When it did rain, we had no protection and just had to stand steering the boat and get wet, but the pleasure of travelling along the lovely canals and seeing the sites made up for any adversities. We'd been motoring along for as long as we could before nightfall and hadn't found a suitable town where we could moor up, so I decided that I'd forget about looking for civilisation and moor alongside the canal bank before it got too dark. Sophie and Tim stood by on the foredeck and I nosed the yacht into the bank until we ran aground so that they could jump ashore. Jill was on the foredeck acting as my lookout. We bumped gently into the edge and Tim and Sophie leapt the distance to the grassy bank. Jill threw them the ropes. Sophie took one of them and fastened it to a tree and Jill made it fast on the forward cleat. Tim made the stern rope fast to another tree as I swung us alongside. I couldn't get the boat alongside completely because of the slightly sloping bank so asked Tim and Sophie to find a long, sturdy log with as large a diameter as practical so that we could place one end on the bank and the other against the hull. That would allow me to tighten up on the bow and stern ropes, securing the yacht in position just clear of the canal bank. They could get back aboard by walking along the log and we would be held away from the slope of the embankment for the night. It all went surprisingly well as there were plenty of fallen trees and they returned quite quickly, carrying a perfect section of trunk that was placed in position and the boat secured. It was a good system and the log served us well throughout the trip. Jill and I stood by to help them back on board in case they needed it. Tim was reluctant. He hesitated, eyeing the route back aboard with scepticism. Sophie jumped onto the log and walked confidently to us with no problem showing an uncertain Tim how it was done. He nervously placed one foot on the log and wavering, placed the other foot in front and in a few quick wobbly strides made his way safely on board. It wasn't the perfect way to moor and spend the night but there was no danger providing we set off very early in the morning before the barges started motoring past us, creating a swell.

Tim was so confident having mastered the balancing act that he decided to go for a stroll with Sophie to see if there was any habitation nearby before it got too dark. It seemed like a good idea. Sophie walked back across the log first, glad to be on terra firma for a while and Tim briskly followed. Well, he almost did. Something happened at the halfway mark because he suddenly stopped and began swaying from side to side with his arms outstretched as he tried to maintain his balance. It very soon became obvious that the force of gravity would win. His swaying became more erratic. He twisted from side to side in desperation as he tried to stay upright, to no avail. He swayed too far to the left and tumbled headfirst into the murky water. He needed help and would have got it had we been able to stop laughing. Sophie had collapsed in a hysterical heap on the grassy bank. Jill leant up against the casing to stop herself from falling because she was so weak from laughter and I had to squat down on deck before I fell over from laughing so much. Through tears of laughter, we watched the spectacle of Tim covered in mud and green slime, trying to scramble up the bank only to slide back down again, which just made us laugh even more. Sophie was totally out of control and try as she might she couldn't stop laughing and as for Jill, well, I'd never seen her in such a state. She lost complete control of all of her faculties and decided she'd better leave, so, doubled over, she rushed off down to our foc'sle. I didn't fare any better. Tim made it to safety and stood on the grassy bank dripping filthy water and looking furious. Looking at him just made Sophie and me laugh all the harder. "Laughter is pleasant, but the exertion is too much for me." Thomas Love Peacock 1785 - 1866.

The longest aqueduct

At Nemours, the canal narrowed and curved around the town. The name Nemours supposedly is derived from the woods (nemora). The next towns were Souppes-sur-Loing, Neronville, Nargis, Cepoy and Buges where two other canals joined our Canal du Loing, the Canal d'Orléans and the Canal de Briare, one of the oldest canals in France, and the one that we took. Construction on the Canal de Briare began in 1604 and was completed in 1642. It is a summit level canal, which means that it rises then falls connecting two river valleys. Summit level canals were a means of connecting different areas of the country prior to the construction of railways. Navigating the Briare along its length of 54 kilometres, the first 12 locks raised us 41 metres higher and then we dropped 85 metres through the final 24 locks. We passed through Montargis, sometimes called the Venice of the Gatinais due to its network of canals and bridges, Chatillon-Coligny and then Rogny-les-Sept-Ecluses. The original Sept Ecluses (seven locks) are no longer operational, so we entered the modern alternative, an impressive flight of automated locks. The first flight of six raised us 24 metres and after a short distance further on we descended 28 metres via a flight of seven locks. From the beginning to the end of that section, the total distance was 14 kilometres. We motored on through Ouzouer-sur-Trézée before reaching the town of Briare, an interesting town with three canals running through it. Thus far we had negotiated a total of 51 locks. The next section to navigate was the 196 kilometres along the Canal latéral à la Loire and its 38 locks. With the exception of the automated locks, all other locks on our journey were operated by lock keepers to keep the incessant flow of barges on the move.

20. The Briare aqueduct.

An impressive sight greeted us as we approached the aqueduct de Briare, which was designed by the canal engineer Abel Mazoyer and constructed by the Eiffel Company. It was the longest canal aqueduct in the world until 2003 and was built to carry the Canal latéral à la Loire over the River Loire, replacing a previous river level crossing that was susceptible to flooding. Fourteen pillars support a single steel beam, which in turn supports a steel channel holding 13000 tonnes of water. It is 663 metres long and just 6 metres wide with a

183

towpath on each side bringing the total width to 11.5 metres. I throttled back on the engines and approached slowly, easing our way in with not much room to spare on either side. The wind wasn't especially strong but being so high up and exposed, what little there was, was enough to blow us against the side of the construction if I lost concentration on the steering. It felt strange peering down onto the river below us and it seemed to take a long time getting across. It was a relief once we'd reached the other end.

Don't mess with us

The Canal latéral à la Loire was built between 1827 and 1838 to connect the Canal du Briare with the Canal du Centre and replace the use of the River Loire, which flooded in the winter and dried up in the summer, making navigation difficult, if not impossible. It was a relatively level canal running for a distance of 196 kilometres with 38 locks. At Marseille-les-Aubigny, it joins with the Canal du Berry and further on at Decize it meets the Canal de Nivernais. After going through double locks at Guétin, we had a long 20-kilometre stretch before the next lock. We followed this canal to Digoin, where we took the Canal du Centre for Chalon-sur-Saône.

One night I decided to moor alongside a barge tied up to the canal bank, which we had done on previous occasions. I went alongside gently and we made fast fore and aft. As we were about to go down to the saloon for our evening meal, we were startled when a horse stuck its head out of the top half of a door right by where we stood. The barge was horse drawn and the power source had been housed for the night. We were in the habit of rising early but we weren't expecting to be woken quite so early the next day. Something didn't seem right. The movement and the noises weren't normal. I rushed up on deck and was aghast to see that we were drifting in the middle of the channel. The nasty little shit of a barge owner had simply cast us adrift and set off on his way, pulled along by his horse clip-clopping along on the track beside the canal. I hauled our mooring ropes aboard to avoid them getting caught around the propellers, started both engines immediately and motored into the canal bank where we moored temporarily whilst we sorted ourselves out and had a quick breakfast before we got under way. Apart from casting us adrift, the miserable swine had cleaned out his horsebox and shovelled the contents onto our rock strewn decks. The horse manure had found its way into every nook and cranny, making it very difficult to extract, so we decided to leave it where it was for the time being. We were not happy. It was not unusual in those days for the French to be nasty towards us Brits. In fact, come to think of it, they could be nasty to anybody at any time. Breakfast finished, we set off once more still fuming over the trouble the Frenchman had caused us and couldn't understand why he couldn't have just asked us politely to move so that he could leave. That's the standard procedure among civilised people but the bargemen were a different breed when it came to dealing with us. They resented us throughout our journey.

We slipped the mooring and motored along as fast as was practical and it wasn't long before we caught up with the little worm of a Frenchman standing in his cockpit being pulled slowly along by his horse. It was Tim who took the initiative as we approached. He picked up a dollop of the horse shit and hurled it straight at the Frenchman. It was a good shot. It hit him on his shoulder. That was all the encouragement the rest of us needed. I eased the throttles back and headed close to the barge. Jill and Sophie rushed out on deck emboldened by Tim's actions and joined him in picking out the pieces of shit and pelting the hell out of the sitting target. He was shouting and blaspheming at us for all he was worth as he steered his barge with one hand and with the other, tried to shield himself from the smelly missiles being hurled at him. The more he screamed at us, the more pleasure it gave us. We managed to reduce the pile of manure quite considerably and felt so good about it. When they couldn't extricate anymore from among the rocks, I pushed the throttles forward to increase our speed and we left him to wallow in the filth he deserved. That was one of the few horse drawn barges still in existence; it was certainly the only one that we encountered on the entire journey through the canals. In fact, the last one was supposedly laid up that same year, 1969, so it could be that we have the dubious honour of contributing to the demise of the very last horse-drawn barge by pelting it with its own shit. He should have been more considerate. Revenge can be sweet and as the Italian statesman, Nicollo Machiavelli said, "Men should be either treated generously or destroyed, because they take revenge for slight injuries – for heavy ones they cannot."

In the early 1800's, the barges were made of wood and since the transportation of produce was more regional, horses were used to haul the barges that were owned by the wealthy. For the poorer people, the men had to strap a harness on themselves and haul them along manually. In 1820, Louis Becquey initiated the construction of a vast network of navigable canals and as more were constructed, linking more waterways, the voyages took much longer over much longer distances. Haulage then became more of a family affair, with the women hauling the barges whilst the men steered. When the construction of railways began around the middle of the 19th century, they began to take preference over the canals. There was a lot of competition and the French transport minister intervened to prevent the rail companies from having a monopoly. Regrettably, the British transport minister decided differently and the British canals went into decline after the construction of the railways.

In 1879, the Minister of Public Works, the Baron de Freycinet sought to improve the working conditions of those transporting heavy goods, especially coal. He instigated the construction of 468 kilometres of new canals and the improvement of 2453 kilometres of the existing ones, which helped industry, the military, and especially helped the barge industry (Batellerie). The dimensions of the canals were standardised, based on a type of boat typical of the northern regions called a "Peniche Flamande," and the subsequent barges of 38 metres in length were called "Freycinets". The Baron de Freycinet was also keen to introduce mechanical propulsion and finally prohibited manual haulage. In the 20th century, the wooden horse drawn or manually hauled barges were abandoned for metal ones that were propelled by engines. During the sixties, road haulage became the preferred means of transportation and the canal network and locks were neglected making navigation more difficult. This had an adverse effect on the livelihood of the Batelliers. In 1960, the barges began to be replaced by larger vessels and the smaller ones that remained were either scrapped or were converted into houseboats.

We still encountered a substantial number of them on our journey and taking into consideration the current state of affairs in France at that time, with the Bargees (Batelliers) striving to compete with the ever expanding road haulage system, the virtual revolution of 1968, and the strong support for communism, it partly explains their lack of consideration and their hostility towards us. They seemed to resent us using their canals and made no allowances for the fact that we were not a commercial vessel and we were not the capitalist owners. We struggled constantly to keep our boat from getting damaged in the locks as we bumped into the barges and concrete sides of the locks when they were either being drained or filled.

21. *Coaxing us through one of the locks.*

Some locks had concrete sills underwater and it wasn't easy to avoid landing on them if there was more than one boat in the lock. The French were generally very rude and it seemed that they deliberately increased speed past us when we were moored, just to make things uncomfortable. In spite of all of that, the days were a delight and I couldn't help thinking how lucky we were to have the opportunity of navigating the length of France's inland waterways to the Mediterranean. The small villages and ancient towns that we passed through were stunningly attractive and the canals themselves delightful, set in mile after mile of beautiful countryside.

We suffered the occasional verbal abuse from fishermen hidden in the bushes on the canal bank if we swamped them as we went by. We needed to get to Chalon-sur-Saône as soon as possible so I motored along as fast as I could in the circumstances, considering how restricted we were in the confines of the canal. If I spied a fishing rod in time, I'd ease up the throttles and glide gently past but mostly the fishermen and their rods were hidden by the reeds. It wasn't until we heard the shouts as the fishing gear was abandoned in the haste to reach the safety of the bank that we realised that another unfortunate had been drenched.

"Salaud!" they'd scream, "Espèce de Con!" others would yell as their irate heads popped up above the reeds. Two of them in particular, fishing together and invisible among the reeds, became markedly enraged when they endured a jolly good soaking. They tried to escape our wash by scrambling up the steep bank only to collide with each other in their panic and fall to their knees in the canal. Their shouts of "Putain de merde!" and other equally unpleasant expletives were still audible as we receded into the distance and it's probably a good thing that at the time, we couldn't understand them. I genuinely tried not to disturb or offend them but it wasn't easy when they were out of sight and hidden by the reeds.

The man in the beret

Some of the bridges had been creating difficulties for us despite my efforts to sink the boat as low as possible. What I'd feared all through the canals happened. A bridge looked too low for us to pass underneath. I motored up to it gently and when we reached it my suspicions were confirmed, we were too high. I moored up to the canal bank and sent Sophie ashore to walk along the canal towpath to the next lock and ask the lock keeper to open the lock gates. Each lock contains around 2000 cubic metres of water and I'd hoped that by releasing that quantity of water it would enable us to squeeze our way under the bridge. After she left, I motored to the bridge again and waited and sure enough, the water level dropped just enough for us to squeeze our way underneath. Little by little, with Jill and Tim standing on the rocks on deck with their hands above their heads, pushing upwards onto the underside of the bridge, I gently pushed the throttles forward a bit at a time and we bumped our way through before the water level rose once more as more locks were opened further upstream. We'd made it and went on to meet Sophie and the obliging lock keeper waiting for us at the next lock. I noticed some old rubber tyres close by and asked him if we could take them if they were not being used for anything. He was pleased to get rid of them so we cut off some lengths of rope and lashed the tyres alongside the hull to help protect it from damage when in the locks.

Night moorings were always welcome and very much appreciated after the long, nonstop days. We were then able to sit around and enjoy a relaxing supper in a civilised manner and look back over the numerous incidents that had arisen, some humorous, some miserable but whatever, we were having an unforgettable experience together. During the days, we didn't stop to eat, managing as best we could by relieving each other for breaks but it was never a hardship, apart from the odd few days when it rained. I always had in mind the urgent need to get to Chalon-sur-Saône to have the vessel dry docked and the wheel house and mast fitted. The constant nagging thought of precious time slipping away influenced my decision making and I regretted not stopping to fill the water tanks often enough.

At one stage, the fresh water was running low and I started to get concerned that we'd be unable to find a convenient filling point soon enough. It was a beautiful sunny day and we were in the cockpit together appreciating the warmth and serenity of the journey when a pretty hamlet came into view on our starboard side. As we got nearer, we could see an elderly couple tending their garden, which ran down to the canal bank where there was a gate. I slowed down and decided to moor up at their gate to ask if they knew where the next town was with fresh water available to top up our tanks. They didn't seem to object to us invading their space, in fact, I think they were delighted that such an unusual event was taking place.

"Good day, Do you know where we can fill the water tanks," I called to him in my limited and imperfect French.

The old man looked at us bewildered and sauntered up to the side of the boat. He was fascinated that we'd stopped at his garden to ask him. He had a wonderful, kindly, weather-beaten face with a day's stubble at least and watery dark eyes. He was dressed in a pair of baggy blue working trousers and a tatty red checked shirt with a typical black beret perched on the back of his head with his grey hair visible at the front and sides. A two-way conversation continued for a while and then his wife came to join in. She was equally friendly, beaming as she approached us to find out what we wanted. She wore a floral pinafore with a floral headscarf hiding her own greying hair. They both had lovely smiling faces. After pleasantries were exchanged for a while, he ended up shaking his head. No, he didn't know where we could take on water. I doubt that they had ever travelled far from their home. Many of the French country folk never strayed far from their home towns in those days. What happened next surprised us. The delightful couple offered to supply us with water.

"We can give you water," he said.

"Thank you, you are very kind, where is the tap?" I said.

"Inside the house," he replied.

I told Tim to fetch our hose from the lazarette and Jill, Sophie and I jumped ashore and went to the house to look for the tap. The house obviously hadn't had any TLC for many years, not at all unusual back in 1969, especially for the elderly peasantry (paysans). The large, long garden was very well tended, with a huge variety of plants, vegetables, flowers, shrubs and fruit trees. The house was remarkably attractive on the outside but very old and basic inside. The amiable old couple led us through the open door into their kitchen. It was a good size and undeniably well used with signs of lots of activity. The table was covered with a blue patterned plastic cloth and on it were cooking utensils, bowls and pans. We were led to a curtain-less window overlooking the canal, beneath which was an old stone sink. At the edge of the sink was a tall, ornate cast iron hand pump with an equally ornate, long, curved handle. Jill and I looked at each other in disbelief that such a primitive system was still in use. We were in a dilemma. We needed water but this was not what we expected. We couldn't fasten the hose to the pump and even if we could it would take hours to fill our tanks and it would be exhausting pumping away for that length of time. I didn't want to offend this lovely, kind couple so I thanked them, then we went back to the boat and took out the only two twenty litre plastic jerry cans that we had. We marched back to the kitchen and over to the sink expecting to have to pump away to fill the cans. The charming Frenchman insisted that he do the pumping and when he got tired, beckoned his wife to take over. Tim and I carried the cans to the boat and poured the contents into the water tank through the deck fitting. We did this several more times and then I decided that it was a pointless task. We needed far too much water but at least we wouldn't find ourselves in the emergency situation of running out completely. We thanked our hosts profusely once again, bid them farewell, cast off, and proceeded to the next lock waving goodbye to them. They stood waving back to us until we were almost out of sight. Their act of kindness taught us that not all the French population was as unpleasant as the barge operators or the Parisians we had met.

Like a cork from a bottle

Digoin is located on the river Loire and because of a large number of waterways, the town centre cannot be reached without crossing a bridge and for us to join the next canal, we also had to cross over the River Loire on a beautiful 243 metre long, cut stone canal bridge with eleven arches. Four kilometres further on we took the 112 kilometres long Canal du Centre, originally known as the Canal de Charolais, which, after passing through its 61 locks would take us to Chalon-sur-Saône. Work began on the construction of this canal in 1784 and it was completed in 1792. It is a narrow, winding, picturesque canal linking the Canal Lateral du Loing to the River Saône and the valleys of the Loire and the Saône. The longest run free of locks on this canal was 11 kilometres and there was a short 400 metres distance between three of them. The lock with the highest elevation was at Montchanin, raising us up 10.7 metres.

We had managed with difficulty to pass under hundreds of low bridges and finally what I feared all the way through the canals, happened. We arrived at a village and as usual, I dropped the engine speed to slowly approach the bridge. We were too high. In addition to the boulders and flooding the bilges, I'd also collected some old 50-gallon oil drums en route, placed them on deck and filled them with water to help lower us further but alas, as it says in the bible "What I fear has come upon me; what I dreaded has happened to me." – Job 3:25. The metal mast step fixed to the coach roof was butting up against the bridge, making us about 20 centimetres too high. I could see no way for us to proceed and we clearly couldn't stay where we were so I took the drastic decision to cut off the mast step. I couldn't see any other alternative. With the engines ticking over in neutral and Jill, Sophie and Tim holding onto the bridge, I went and got a hacksaw and started to cut through the mast step. I managed to cut through about two centimetres on one side before it became obvious that it would take hours to accomplish it. We had a problem. I switched off the engines and sent Sophie on ahead to the lock keeper to ask him to open the lock gates, hoping it would produce a sufficient drop in the water level for us to work our way through. She had a long walk, two kilometres in fact, so we waited and eventually, the water level dropped. It looked as if we might just make it if we were quick enough. I started the engines and with Jill and Tim pushing upwards from underneath the bridge, we made some slight headway, then disaster struck. The water level rose and we were jammed. The mast step stopped our progress and we were only a fraction of the way under the bridge. The three of us sat in the steering area where the wheel house should have been and discussed how we could get out of the predicament. I was concerned about the pressure on the coach roof if the water level rose any more. A young man came from the village and lumbered onto the bridge. He was an unkempt looking individual. We looked up at him forlornly and it wasn't too long before we realised that he was most likely cerebrally challenged. He stood above, pointing down at us, laughing and making weird, unintelligible noises, wiggling his finger with an idiotic look on his face. We felt very exposed and useless as he attracted attention to us and a couple more people arrived to gawk at the three of us standing embarrassed on the deck.

I told Tim to go into town and see if he could muster up a crowd of people to come aboard and bring anything they could to help lower the boat down even more. He scrambled up over the railings of the bridge and disappeared off to the right where the town centre lay, leaving Jill and me to sit out the stares of the gongoozlers and the incessant guffawing arising from what was presumably the village idiot. Surprisingly, it wasn't long before Tim appeared ahead of a small army of villagers in high spirits. Contrary to the average Frenchmen we'd met on the journey, they were positively friendly. It was without doubt a highly unusual situation and most probably had never happened before. Amid shouts and laughter, each of the men followed Tim as he climbed over the railings and dropped down onto the deck amid the boulders and oil drums. There were twelve of them in total and they were visibly enjoying this little distraction, which would no doubt be talked about over glasses of pastis for many a year. With a great deal of grunting and animated joviality, they pushed up with their hands onto the underside of the bridge in synchronisation and we inched forward. They rested and repeated the process and bit by bit we moved further under the bridge. Each time they released the pressure, the boat floated upwards and the pressure on the coach roof alarmed me. We reached the final stage with just inches to go and with the last push we shot out from under the bridge like a cork from a bottle. The panicking villagers jumped up to grab hold of the railings, knocking into each other as they tried to pull themselves up over the railing and back onto the bridge before we took off with them on board. I rapidly put the engines into astern and backed up to allow the remaining few to get safely back to their village. They lined up on the bridge cheering and waving goodbye as we left.

"Au revoir. Bon courage," they cried.

"Merci, merci mille fois," we shouted out our gratitude and waved as I increased our speed to get us to the next lock and the impatiently waiting Sophie.

When we stopped for the night, we moored on the canal bank using the log that we'd kept. It had served us well on many occasions and Tim had mastered the art of staying upright and walking the length of it to get ashore. It was getting late and we needed provisions so I sent Sophie ashore to walk into the village to buy whatever was available with our diminishing funds before it was too dark. It looked as if it would be a lengthy walk along the edge of woodland so I told the hefty Tim to accompany her so she'd feel more secure. They set off together and shortly afterwards Tim came running back, scurrying along the pole and back on board, pale-faced and panting.

"What's wrong?" I asked.

"I'm not sure," he replied.

"Well, where's Sophie?"

"I think she's coming."

"What do you mean, you think she's coming, where is she?"

He shrugged and looked back in the direction he'd come from. He had a strange expression on his face, sort of a mixture of both fear and shame. Sophie came sauntering back to the boat very soon afterwards, looking angry.

"What happened?" I asked her.

She glowered at Tim and it was plain to see by her expression and the colour of her face that she was not happy.

"He heard something rustle in the bushes and ran and left me," she said.

Tim seemed to shrink before us. He was clearly ashamed but still refused to go back along the track with Sophie. From that moment on my opinion of him changed. I offered to go with Sophie but she insisted that she would be fine. Perhaps it was just as well as I hadn't forgotten her erotic advances on her first night aboard without Hervé and I could well imagine what she may have done if she'd got me alone in the bushes on a dark night! She'd decided that it was probably just a small animal that scared the living daylights out of the mighty Tim, so set off confidently by herself and returned within an hour with some food to add to our meagre stores. We laughed over Tim's reaction during the meal and teased him but we secretly weren't happy with him.

The next morning, one of the engines wouldn't start and we realised that Tim was not much of an engineer either, because he couldn't get it going and didn't seem to know where to begin. I set off on one engine and asked him to get the other fixed as soon as possible. He never succeeded and we did the rest of the trip on just one engine. I constantly asked him to do his job and get the second engine working but he was utterly useless. It wasn't easy maneuvering a twin engine vessel with only one of them working. One day I'd had enough and demanded that he do something straight away. His only response was to make the utterly ridiculous suggestion that we try to bump start it. I was flabbergasted when I realised that he actually meant it and even attempted to do so. He turned on the ignition and pushed the combined gear and throttle lever forward. Whatever he was, he was not an engineer and I don't know how he ever managed to convince anybody to employ him as such. I suppose we should have realised his limitations earlier when he made ludicrous attempts to catch ducks for our dinner with the boat hook. Whenever he saw a duck floating anywhere nearby he'd lunge at it with the boat hook and they'd just turn and quack at him, thumbing their little beaks at his futile attempts as they floated on past.

Despite the unpleasant episodes, the entire cruise had been a delight and it felt good to be on the final leg to Chalon-sur-Saône. The days throughout the length of the canals were long and it was often difficult to moor at suitable stops to replenish our stores so we had to make do with what provisions we had. From early morning until dark we motored along and worked the locks, squeezing ourselves under bridges and protecting our vessel from damage both in the locks and from the careless and aggressive bargees but it was an incredible experience that none of us would have missed. We had seen some amazing sites, passed through some enchanting towns, enjoyed some beautiful countryside and had had so many laughs.

CHAPTER 8
THE HEADBANGER

Minnie Mouse

More than a month after leaving Ostend, we arrived in Chalon-sur-Saône where we cleared the deck of the boulders and oil drums, discarded the remaining horse shit and emptied the water from the bilges. We then took advantage of a week-long rest whilst the wheelhouse and mast were fitted. Tim was fired when Hervé arrived and he told us he'd find a replacement engineer to join us in Cannes. I didn't see a great deal of Chalon as I was on call throughout the week. As Captain, I could hardly just disappear and leave them to it. Hervé announced that he would be accompanying us on the ten day trip to Port Saint Louis and then onwards to Cannes.

Chalon-sur-Saône is where photography originated. The French inventor Nicéphore Niépce made the first photographic print there in 1826 and the museum contains around two million photographs, plus old and new photographic equipment. In 1807, Nicéphore Niépce and his brother Claude also invented what is thought to be the world's first internal combustion engine, which ran on a mixture of crushed coal dust and resin and after triumphantly powering a boat upstream on the River Saône, he was granted a patent by Napoleon Bonaparte. The machine, a pyréolophore, is on display in the same museum.

22. On the slip at Chalon.

The work on Passing Fancy progressed, though not without problems, although after the canal journey we'd now come to expect things not to work out too well. The engine was fixed and the mast was stepped into the fitting that I'd sawn into during the bridge fiasco. The wheelhouse was eventually set over the cockpit area and we were surprised and disappointed that it was so huge. The windows were large with wide, unsightly, thick black rubber seals around them and no possibility of opening them. The Dutch hull was without fault and apart from the slight hiccup on one of the engines on the canals; the Vosper Thornycroft engines were fine. However, the fitting out by the coach company left an enormous amount to be desired. There were no teak decks, just bare metal. The saloon and aft cabin casings were much higher than they would normally have been on a professionally designed and constructed yacht and with the oversized wheelhouse on top of everything else it was not a very attractive motor yacht. Neither had any thought been given to practicalities. Everything was intended to give an impression of luxury and equipment had been added where and when it seemed appropriate as if it were one of Hervé's fleet of coaches. Far too much weight had been added to the starboard side which gave us a permanent list. There was no chart table and nowhere to store the charts. However, Jill and I had our first real command and the Mediterranean cruises that had been planned would give us the experience we needed to be able to apply for any future jobs. The wisdom and the practical experience of having cruised the entire length of the French inland waterways were invaluable and the memories would remain with us forever.

The next stage was to follow the River Saône along its 255 kilometres length to Lyon where it joins the River Rhône. It was a rather uneventful but pleasurable cruise along this charming, winding river with its attractive towns. Living in close confinement with Hervé gave us the opportunity to get to know him better. He was a happy, easy going fellow with big ideas but sadly not enough nautical knowledge to successfully achieve what he had envisioned as a luxury motor yacht. We discussed the prospects of the coming season. It all sounded very exciting reeling off the names of the places we would be visiting - Sorrento, Capri, Rome, La Spezia, Monaco, Cannes, St Tropez, Ajaccio etc. We got along famously and we became more like members of the same family rather than employer/employees. We approached Lyon in the rain but this time it didn't matter because we had the shelter of the oversized wheelhouse. Lyon is the third largest French city after Paris and Marseille and has a reputation as a centre of gastronomy. As its cuisine developed, it became a huge success nationwide, much appreciated by the wealthy French. The accomplishments of the chef Paul Bocuse later turned it into a worldwide success. For 5 kilometres, the river, with its many twists and turns, snakes its way through the city and it was a relief to see mooring spaces all along the quaysides. Despite the rain, the whole experience was quite remarkable. We saw a convenient mooring in the city centre, so I slowed the engines and eased the boat alongside the quay. Jill and Sophie secured the mooring lines and we settled down for a well-earned rest.

We were obliged to take a pilot on board to take us down the fast running River Rhône to the gorgeous city of Arles, over 300 kilometres away. The wide, deep River Rhône is 800 kilometres long and had a notorious reputation as a navigational nightmare because of the shallows and its eight knot current. It originates in Switzerland and flows down to join with the River Saône, picking up waters from other rivers en route and it is the only major European River that flows directly into the Mediterranean Sea. It often floods in spring and early summer when it is swollen by melting ice from the Alps. Only its southern half is navigable and since we were there it has been tamed with a series of locks and canals so that pilots are no longer obligatory. Our pilot stepped aboard and shook hands with me looking up at the overcast sky.

"Bonjour Capitaine, there'll be a Mistral tomorrow," he announced, "We'll have to wait until it dies down before we set off."

"How long will we need to wait?" Hervé enquired.

"Could be a day, could be two or three." We shook hands once more, said our "au revoirs" and he stepped off the deck onto the quay and disappeared into the rainy distance.

I remembered learning about the Mistral in my meteorological training at the Warsash Navigation School. It is a wind that often develops after a cold, rainy front has passed through Southern France. We were to learn to fear this violent, dangerous wind that can suddenly materialise from flat calm conditions. It is usually accompanied by a crystal clear sky, which is often a warning of its coming. It is a katabatic wind; on clear nights, dense, cold air descends from the mountain slopes and as the ground radiates its heat away, the cooling air comes into contact with the descending cold air causing it to gather speed and strength as it comes screaming through the long, narrow Rhône valley, affecting the whole of Provence, the Languedoc, the Cote d'Azur and as far south as Corsica and Sardinia. Its effect is heightened significantly if the mountains are snow covered. It is not a good idea to be at sea in a Mistral. My father spent a large part of his life at sea and he told me that one of the worst experiences he'd had in all those years was in the Golfe de Lyons where the Mistral can be treacherous. That evening the rain stopped and the next day the sun was fierce in a cloudless, intense blue sky and the wind had already started to blow.

Jill and I stood on deck soaking up the sunshine and appreciating the fact that we had got that far. Lyon was vibrant, noisy, hot, stimulating and looked magnificent in the sunshine. We were waiting for Sophie to emerge from her cabin as we needed to stock up on provisions to get us as far as Arles and Jill and Sophie had decided to go shopping together. A strange apparition appeared. Jill and I looked at each other in disbelief and grabbed each other by the arm as we struggled to contain our laughter. There before us stood Sophie looking like a brightly coloured caricature that for some reason reminded us of Minnie Mouse. She looked utterly ridiculous, having metamorphosed from her usual self into something resembling a grotesque circus clown. She had, for some inexplicable reason decided to wear a pair of shiny, heavy, black leather shoes, a pair of knee high, red and white striped woollen socks, a minuscule pair of exceedingly tight, dark blue shorts and a strange and revealing, billowing, multicoloured top.

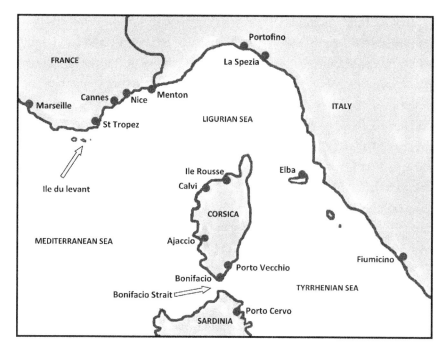

23. Italy and Corsica

Her shortish blonde hair was tied in bunches that poked out horizontally from the sides of her head and her excessively made up face reminded me of a cartoon depiction of an over the top burlesque personality. The only thing missing was the bright red cheeks. On stage in a French farce, she would have brought the house down but my heart sank for Jill who was in the unfortunate and embarrassing position of having to accompany this outlandish creature into town. We never understood what had possessed her to materialise into this strange, laughable person and in a busy city of all places. Whatever statement she intended to make, I hope she felt that she'd succeeded. It goes without saying that, as expected, heads turned in amazement as she marched through the streets with Jill.

"Oh look," she said to Jill, "Everybody's staring at you." Perception can be a peculiar thing.

By the time they returned with the shopping, the wind had increased and it howled and howled for three days. When it finally stopped the pilot reappeared. It was a calm, hot, sunny day when we cast off the mooring lines and he took command of the boat until we reached Arles. It was a treat for me to hand over responsibility to someone else and be a passenger. We were able to run at high revs and with the raging current carrying us along we were doing close to the 16 knots that Hervé had said the yacht was capable of. He was beaming and couldn't contain himself.

"Ha ha, we're doing the 16 knots I said we would do," he cried.

"Well, not exactly," I corrected him; "We have an eight knot current behind us that's pushing us along so it only seems that the boat is doing sixteen knots."

"No, no, that's not true, look at us go, ha ha," he laughed.

I couldn't convince him no matter what I said. He was in a little fantasy world of his own. The pilot had his regular spots where he stayed when we stopped for the night and when we reached Arles, he disembarked, leaving me to continue navigating the journey to Port-St-Louis on the Mediterranean coast. We stayed the night in Port-St-Louis and the next day passed through the final canal of the journey that allowed us to pass from the River Rhône into the blue Mediterranean Sea of the Golfe du Fos. The canal was built in 1871 because the Rhône delta is unnavigable due to constant silting. It was thrilling to burst forth at last into the open sea after all those weeks travelling the entire length of inland France. Our emotions were running high; we were overjoyed and I opened up the throttles and set course for Marseille, a mere 36 nautical miles away.

The melting pot

The sight of Marseille was impressive as we got ever closer. Inside the port, having passed between the two forts at the entrance, Fort St Pierre to the north and Fort St Nicholas to the south, we saw a convenient mooring with an excellent view of the city and wasted no time in seizing it. Vessels moor up stern to in Mediterranean harbours, so the twin engines made the maneuver easy. I pushed the port throttle forward and the starboard throttle into astern to spin the yacht around and dropped the anchor before putting both engines into astern to back up to the quay as the anchor chain rattled out. At a short distance away from the quay, Jill secured the anchor brake and Sophie threw the stern ropes to waiting helpers. When the ropes were slipped onto the mooring posts, Sophie took up the slack and made them fast to the cleats on each quarter of the aft deck. The engines were shut down and the gangplank put in position. It felt wonderful to be safely settled in this exciting port with glorious sunshine scorching us from a clear blue sky. It was the best we'd felt since leaving Kortrijk in Belgium almost two months previously. Hervé and Sophie wasted no time; they set off down the gangplank with Hervé leading.

"Merde!" (Shit).

We heard an anguished cry, turned and saw him squatting on the gangplank holding his forehead with Sophie kneeling beside him, comforting him. We had never before needed to disembark from the gangplank so it hadn't occurred to us that a horizontal bar spanning the distance between the davits, would be in the direct line of the head of anybody descending the sloping gangplank. Yet another folly when the yacht was fitted out without sufficient knowledge of yachting. After a few kisses and cuddles from Sophie, he recovered sufficiently to wobble his way down to the quay, still holding his head and remembering to duck under the useless bar.

Jill and I celebrated our arrival by opening a fine bottle of Châteauneuf-du-Pape, which remained from the shopping trip in Lyon. We sat on the foredeck gazing at the view of the city, appreciating the warmth, the colours, the smells and the noise of all the activity in this bustling port. Marseille is France's second largest city and has been an important port since Greek and Roman times. It was founded by Greeks from Phocaea (now Foça in modern day Turkey) in 600 BC when they established their first settlement there, known as Massalia. Around 325 BC Massalia's most famous inhabitant, Pytheas, organised a voyage into the Atlantic Ocean, visiting England, Iceland, Shetland and Norway and was the first scientist to describe drift ice and the midnight sun. He was also the first person to discover that the phases of the moon affected the tides and established the city's latitude using mathematical instruments that he had developed himself.

Massalia came under the control of the Romans around 49 BC and it prospered throughout the centuries under their occupation and then under the Visigoths from the 5th to the 8th century. In the first century, during the Roman period, it is thought that Mary Magdalen and her brother, Lazarus, evangelised the city and established the Christian administration. Legend has it that they landed at Les Saintes Maries de la Mer, a few kilometres to the West. Massalia's economic success collapsed in the 8th century when Charles Martel, ruler of the Francs, attacked it because it had rejected the governor he'd installed a few years earlier. The town didn't recover until the 10th century when it was governed by the Counts of Provence. In the mid-13th century, there were two rebellions, the last one finally being quashed in 1263 enabling Marseille to prosper once more. The prosperity was short lived, however, as in 1348, the bubonic plague arrived and 15,000 of its 25,000 inhabitants perished. In the 16th century, it suffered another plague and again in 1720 when 100,000 people perished. In 1792, 500 Marseillais were dispatched to Paris in support of the French Revolution and on their march there, they sang their rallying cry, the Marseillaise, which has become the French national anthem.

In the 19th and early 20th centuries when France colonised Tunisia, Morocco and Algeria to create part of their empire, Marseille became known as the port of the empire. Greeks and Italians began arriving to escape from political and economic unrest in their countries, and by the early 20th century no less than 40% of the population was Italian. In 1915 Armenians arrived and in 1917, it was the Russians. From 1936 onwards, it was the Vietnamese and Corsicans. Between 1935 and 1945, the Spanish came to escape the civil war and General Franco, then North Africans, followed by sub-Saharan Africans. In 1940, during World War II, the city was heavily bombed by the Germans and Italians and it fell under German occupation in 1942. Two years later, the Allies bombed the port in preparation for its liberation, which took place in August with the combined effort of the allies and 130,000 French troops. In the 1950's, the city was rebuilt with the damages paid by the governments of East and West Germany and Italy and then over a million immigrants arrived from the colonies. After Algerian independence in 1962, there was an additional mass immigration that included 150,000 former ex-pats, known as pieds noirs (black feet). So Marseille is, without doubt, a veritable cosmopolitan melting pot if ever there was one.

The principal commercial port is the Port de Joliette. The old port, which is where we moored, is reserved mainly for leisure craft and fishing boats, fishing being a major industry. The daily catch is landed and sold on the Quay des Belges and Jill and I couldn't resist taking a stroll there to soak up the atmosphere and wonder at the wonderful variety of fish on display. There are many bars, restaurants, hotels and shops around the old harbour making it a bustling and fascinating place to be with its teeming life, colours, smells of the sea, fish, spices and food and Jill and I felt on top of the world. Apart from Marseille's history, its architecture, and its culture, its beaches and the surrounding areas are also major tourist attractions. It is in close proximity to the Calanques, a 20 kilometre long stretch of coast containing many steep, narrow, picturesque inlets. There is also the Camargue, a 930 square kilometre plain between the two arms of the Rhône delta, the largest delta in Europe, a third of which consists of reed covered marshland and lakes separated from the sea by sandbars. It is renowned for its free roaming semi-wild white horses and black fighting bulls that are bred to be sent to Spain. It is also Europe's largest habitat for pink flamingos.

The reason for stopping at Marseille was to have our compass fitted and adjusted, ready for our forthcoming cruises. It would have been so nice to have spent longer there than the one night but we were employed to make money for Hervé and we couldn't do that in Marseille. The harbour became alive early in the morning. It was another hot, sunny day with a cloudless blue sky. After breakfast, Hervé went ashore and returned later with the compass adjuster. They walked up the gangplank and the adjuster immediately went to work installing the compass on the binnacle. Wasting no time, as soon as that was done, I started up the engines. They had a satisfying roar as they burst into life.

"Cast off," I ordered Sophie and she hauled in the stern ropes that had been slipped by a kindly fellow yachtsman on the quay.

"Heave away," I called out to Jill; she switched on the power to the windlass and heaved in the anchor. We cruised gently out of the harbour heading for the Chateau d'If. ('If' being French for yew tree). The island lies 1.6 nautical miles west of the old harbour of Marseille and half a nautical mile offshore. It is actually a fortress with high ramparts and gun platforms rising steeply from the sea. King Francis 1 had it built in 1524 - 1531 as a strategic defence against attacks from the sea. It was never actually used as such but it did serve as a deterrent. Because of the strong surrounding currents and its isolated position, it was once used as an escape proof prison until the end of the 19th century and was dreaded by those unfortunate enough to be sent there. In the Alexander Dumas novel, the Count of Monte Cristo was imprisoned there. It is now uninhabited, has been open to the public since 1890 and its dungeon is now a tourist attraction.

When we were offshore of the Chateau d'If, we lined up two prominent markers on the island. A compass needle ordinarily points to the magnetic North Pole but is deviated away by the magnetic fields of the vessel. I kept the yacht steady on the two markers whilst I swung her around the eight cardinal points of the compass so that any deviation from the magnetic north could be noted by the adjustor. He then eliminated them as far as was practical by placing corrector magnets with opposing magnetic fields around the compass. Any deviation that remains after the correction is recorded on a deviation card, which I had to allow for when plotting a course on the navigation chart.

Deviation became a more pronounced problem when iron started to be used in shipbuilding and numerous accidents occurred that were blamed on the exceedingly complex problem of deviation. It was even suggested that iron ships would never be safe. Magnetism is an invisible force that changes as the ships location changes, a fact that was little understood and therefore very difficult to teach until 1886, when Captain George Beal produced a Deviascope, which provided a means of teaching the calculation and elimination of deviation. A Deviascope is a wooden, ship shaped platform with a compass at its centre and grooves on its upper surface into which magnetic bars can be placed. The training for my Yacht Masters Certificate required me to be able to satisfy the Board of Trade examiner that I fully understood and was able to calculate, with trigonometry, how a ship's magnetic field affected the compass needle. I had to be able to calculate the type, strength and position of the corrector magnets, apply them and make up a deviation card. The examiner inserted magnetic bars into the grooves, throwing the compass needle out and gave me an hour to correct it. I did well with my calculations and felt very pleased with myself having finished with 15 minutes to spare. Then, shock, horror, I realised that I'd done it wrong. I went into a panic and scrambled to recalculate. Sweating and fearing that I would fail my exams on that, I frantically recalculated and with a tremendous sigh of relief, finished everything at the moment the examiner walked through the door. I have never forgotten the despair I felt when I'd discovered my mistake. But, hey, I was now Captain of a yacht off the shore of Chateau d'If and relying on somebody else to correct the compass for me.

In addition to deviation, there is a variation between the magnetic North Pole and the geographic North Pole that has to be taken into account. The angle between the two poles varies according to the position of the vessel on the earth's surface on a horizontal plane and the passage of time. The distance between the two increases each year by about 40 miles and is due to the earth's magnetic lines of force not running in a straight line from north to south but instead spreading out in easterly and westerly directions. In some places, the variation can be more than 30° and in others 0°. After the deviation and variation have been applied to the true compass heading, the strength and direction of the tides are extrapolated from tide tables and finally, the wind strength and direction must be taken into account. When all this information has been ascertained and applied, the final course to steer can be arrived at. Navigation in the Mediterranean is simplified because the tidal flows and height variations are minimal and for the most part need not be considered.

With the compass adjustment finished, I pushed the throttles forward and headed back to the old port of Marseille. It was getting late in the day and I was anxious to get to our destination in Cannes. We repeated the mooring procedure, lowered the gangplank once more and Hervé and the adjuster went ashore to conclude their business so that we could cast off and start our journey to Cannes.

"MERDE!" I heard as the compass adjuster smashed his head on the bar and then staggered half dazed to the quay.

By the time the business was concluded and Hervé was back on board it was late afternoon but we cast off and motored out of Marseille for Cannes. We didn't get very far but at least we'd got away. We moored up and spent the night in La Ciotat at Hervé's request. La Ciotat is situated more or less equidistant between Marseille and Toulon. In 1895, this pretty town and harbour was the setting for one of the very first moving films, "L'arrivé d'un train en gare de La Ciotat" (The arrival of a train at La Ciotat station). Lasting for just 57 seconds, the film was shown in Paris on 28 December, the first ever public showing of a moving picture. It was made by the Lumiére brothers who made a further three films in La Ciotat that same year and in 1904, they developed the world's first colour photographs. The game of pétanque was also invented in La Ciotat in 1907 by a café owner named Ernest Pitiot, whose objective was to help a keen ball player called Jules Lenoir, whose rheumatism prevented him from running and throwing a ball. Ernest Pitiot's partner in the café was his brother Joseph, and between them, they organised the first pétanque tournament, which took place in La Ciotat in 1910.

All worth while

I woke bright and early the next morning and climbed the ladder from the cabin that Jill and I shared. I stood on the foredeck absorbing the beauty of it all. The attractive harbour and its cluster of pleasure boats and the lovely town bathed in sunlight. The sea was flat calm, the sky was cloudless and a beautiful colour blue. The sun had risen and it was already getting hot. Jill came up on deck to join me and we felt so privileged to be there, doing what we wanted to do and getting paid for it. It could hardly be considered work. I walked to the aft deck and hoisted the Panamanian ensign. It was customary to lower the ensign at sunset and hoist it at sunrise; a routine adhered to by all British Skippers in those days. We had all slept well knowing that we would soon be in Cannes and the long journey would be over. The others woke and joined us on deck. We were happy and went down into the saloon and had breakfast. The town and harbour had started coming to life with boats of all descriptions already leaving harbour, their engines chugging away as they passed us. When we'd finished and cleared away, I got out the relevant chart, spread it out on the only practical available space which was at chest height between the steering wheel and the wheelhouse windows. Climbing up there wasn't easy because there was an instrument console on the starboard side of the wheel, so I had to get up on the port side which required considerable agility because below it there was an open hatch leading down to the saloon. When I'd got up there I had to squat down on my hands and knees with the chart spread out in front of me. After this feat of gymnastics, I was concerned about how I would manage in a rough sea when I would be sliding from one side to the other.

I set the course for Cannes. We slipped our moorings, hauled in the anchor and headed out into the calm, blue sea. The trip was captivating along the beautiful coastline. We passed the enchanting Iles d'Hyeres, having not the slightest idea then, how prominent a role these islands were to play in the not too distant future and how the events that took place there would become indelibly etched in our memories. We continued on and half way through the trip we were accompanied by a pod of dolphins playing in our wash. They swam alongside us, crisscrossed our bows and put on a spectacular aquatic display for us, leaping out of the water in numbers. They stayed with us for a while before disappearing into the distance. In the bay of Cannes, a short distance from its two harbours, Sophie shouted,

"Look!" and pointed excitedly off to our port bow. We saw a huge swordfish leap out of the water and splash back down again.
I headed for the eastern harbour, Port Pierre-Canto, the first ever yacht marina in France. It had only been open for business since 19 July 1965, so there were still berths available and we were fortunate to find one directly in front of the yacht agency. It was to prove very useful in finding

clients to charter our strange looking yacht, which seemed even stranger among the impressive, exceedingly expensive luxury yachts already berthed there. I backed the yacht in stern to between two immaculately maintained floating gin palaces. For some strange reason, two stainless steel cosmetic protuberances had been stuck onto our exhaust outlets. They served no useful purpose other than to make me aware not to back up too close to the quay each time we moored up stern to, for fear of crunching them into nothingness. After we left Passing Fancy, the first thing the replacement Captain did was just that. On his very first day in command, he went too close to the quay too quickly and smashed the useless exhaust outlets into concertina shaped lumps.

It was a marvelous feeling when I'd shut down the engines for the last time, or at least until our first charter. It had taken us two awesome months to complete the journey. We'd arrived! To quote Christopher Columbus, "By prevailing over all obstacles and distractions, one may unfailingly arrive at his chosen goal or destination."

It was getting hotter and we stood on deck taking it all in; Cannes - at last. Knowing that we were nicely settled in for the duration of the season and able to relax for a while, Hervé invited us for an ice cream as a little celebration. We tidied the boat up and then, in our shorts, sandals, shirts and sunglasses, we walked down the gangplank, looking forward to seeing more of Cannes and the promised ice cream.

"Ouch," I cried as I smashed my head on the transverse bar. Jill, Sophie and Hervé followed, ducking under it.

Port Pierre-Canto is a fairly large marina with yachts of all sizes and descriptions. It lies at one end of the two kilometre long Croisette, which runs along the shoreline, with the old harbour of Cannes at the other end. We exited the marina and strolled into the centre of Cannes along the Croisette with its expensive designer shops, plush hotels, restaurants, palm trees and a dazzling display of colourful flowers. Cannes was once just a small fishing village lying in swamp land, under the control of the monks of St. Honorat and was used as a port of call for both the offshore islands, Ile St Marguerite and Ile St Honorat, where most of Cannes history lies. In the 10th century, it was called Canua, a derivation from Canna, meaning reed or cane. In the 11th century, it was fortified with the construction of a castle and henceforth became known as Cannes. It gained its independence from the monks in 1530. The small fishing village was sometimes visited by ships from the Orient and on 15 October 1579, a sick woman disembarked from one of them. It is suspected that she was a victim of the plague but in those days very little, if any controls were carried out. By 25 November, 400 people had died. The lack of hygiene compounded the situation which rapidly escalated, overwhelming the population so much that corpses were left lying in the streets. Two thousand Cannois, (Cannes residents), three-quarters of the population, had succumbed to the disease by 1580, when it began to abate. Only three hundred remained alive, mainly in the old town of Le Suquet.

In 1834, the politician and author, Lord Henry Brougham, visited Nice, which at that time was the frontier between France and Italy. He discovered that it was suffering from a cholera outbreak, so he returned to Cannes where he had spent the previous night. He ended up buying a plot of land in La Croix des Gardes, which lies to the west of Cannes, between La Bocca and Le Suquet, and built a villa there. He set about improving the living conditions in Cannes and as a consequence, other members of the British Aristocracy became captivated and began to arrive. As more and more of their winter residences were built, Cannes became a popular seaside resort for the privileged and wealthy, with La Croix des Gardes, the oldest residential area of Cannes, becoming known as the English Quarter. Many of the luxury residences, which still exist, were built in the style of Roman villas and castles reflecting the wealth of the proprietors. At the end of the 19th century, railways were built and trams were introduced. In the 20th century, Cannes was modernised and luxury hotels were constructed to cater for the demands of the wealthy clientele. After World War I, the number of British and German visitors went into decline and it was when the Americans began arriving that Cannes went from a winter resort to a summer one and has remained so ever since. The first international film festival, now a major yearly event, took place in September 1946. The thriving tourism industry and the many festivals and business events that take place throughout the year are now the major contributors to Cannes economy.

We strolled along the magnificent pedestrian promenade, the

Croisette, with its hordes of tourists and celebrities. When we reached the Festival Bar, Hervé saw the only table available for four people so nipped in and sat down before it was taken by anybody else. We joined him and there we enjoyed the most expensive and largest ice cream we'd ever had. The next day, Hervé returned to Belgium but before leaving, he bought some cheap, folding camping chairs for the aft deck. We couldn't help noticing the contrast between our chairs and the luxurious ones on the other yachts. He told us that he would find and send out an engineer to replace the hapless and hopeless Tim and then he said goodbye and set off, leaving behind a sad looking Sophie but she didn't stay sad for long. The atmosphere of Cannes in the summer was too intoxicating for that. Although Passing Fancy was a little disappointing to us when we compared her to the expensive floating gin palaces around us, we were very happy and Hervé was a likeable man.

Sophie's choice

The hull was filthy after the canal trip, from entering and exiting the slimy locks and rubbing up against barges, so our first job was to get it clean again. I saw a floating platform tied to one of the quays and after a few enquiries was told that it was shared around by the yacht crews for maintenance duties. We paddled it around alongside Passing Fancy so that we could stand on it and move it around the hull whilst we scrubbed away the grime. It took the whole day before we had a clean, shining hull. That accomplished, we made the most of having the boat to ourselves with nothing much to do and no cruises planned. We spent our time sunbathing, dining in the local restaurants, drinking in the local bars, visiting places of interest and getting to know Cannes and the other nearby towns. We chatted to and got to know other yacht crews and some of the owners and it wasn't long before the seductive Sophie began to attract the attention of male crew members in both harbours. She returned their lascivious glares with a naughty twinkle in her eye that encouraged them even more.

It was glaringly obvious that a certain Skipper, Peter, from a yacht nearby, befriended us with the specific intention of getting to know

Sophie more intimately. He was married, with a family in the U.K. and had been in Cannes by himself for some time; from the tales he told us, he hadn't lacked sexual encounters. He confided to us that he would dress in the finest clothes he had and stand with a drink at the bars of the opulent hotels on the Croisette in the expectation of catching the eye of a wealthy, lonely woman or a woman who just happened to be there for the same reason as himself. Sophie, for him, was an easy and far less expensive conquest, if he played his cards right. He knew Cannes very well and we had a good time as he took us to the best night clubs, bars and any parties that were taking place. After one particularly boozy evening in a restaurant, we went back to Passing Fancy for a few more drinks and later, well after midnight, decided to go for a night time swim. We staggered drunkenly and noisily to Peter's yacht so that we could use his rubber dinghy to transport us to a convenient spot, relying totally on his local knowledge. We clambered, or more accurately, fell into it one at a time. Sophie went first. She leapt from the quay and as she landed in the inflatable dinghy it shot forward so that she landed on her back laughing hysterically. Once she'd managed to sit up, I leapt in and the same thing happened and I fell against Sophie knocking her over again. Then Jill jumped in, followed by Peter with similar results. We were convulsed with laughter. Jill, Sophie and I had no idea what happened next until we ran aground on a beach, which we thought was on one of the offshore islands. Giggling like crazy, we stripped off, leapt into the sea and had a riotous time. The next morning, feeling absolutely dreadful from a hangover, we sat around trying to piece together the previous night's events. In the ensuing conversation, we discovered from Peter that we hadn't been to the islands at all but on the beach of the Croisette in full view of anybody who happened to be still around in the middle of the night. It was a miracle that we hadn't been arrested. From then on we were more prudent.

One night in a bar in Juan-les-Pins, Peter decided it was time to make his play for Sophie. He told her that he wouldn't mind getting to know her better. His chat up line wasn't particularly remarkable or complimentary but it was memorable because of its lack of subtlety.

"What I like to do," he said, "Is sit on the aft deck of my boat in the evening with a drink and a beautiful girl."

Sophie looked at him coquettishly.

"You'll do," he said, leering at her.

It was a couple of nights later aboard Peter's yacht where the inevitable happened. He'd invited us to supper, and we turned up carrying some bottles of fine wine. The evening went well until the end of the meal when Jill and I were expecting to be offered coffee and cognac. It wasn't to be because Peter intended offering Sophie something else that didn't include Jill and me. Leaving the two of us sitting on our own in the saloon, he led her to the forward cabin after leaning close and whispering something in her ear. Sophie giggled and offering no resistance, followed him. Well, a few hesitant steps perhaps but she knew and he knew and we knew what the finale would be. They closed the door but we could still hear them whispering - at least Peter was whispering.

"No," Sophie said forcibly, then less forcibly "No," and the next time a quiet murmuring "No," then an indecipherable whisper and finally there was no more conversation so Jill and I slipped away back to Passing Fancy.

With the exception of some fibreglass yachts, all others had immaculately kept teak decks and it was customary to remove shoes before going aboard any of them. Receptacles were kept either on the quay, at the bottom of the gangplanks or on the aft decks at the top of the gangplanks in which footwear was placed. Passing Fancy was an exception. We had steel decks and they became so hot in the baking sun that you could literally have cooked on them; consequently, we were most likely the only yacht in the harbour, if not in the whole of the south of France, where footwear was compulsory for fear of having scorched feet. We were also feeling the effect of being unable to open any windows in the wheelhouse.

Pierre, the engineer, arrived a week after Hervé had left us. He'd recently finished his military service in Belgium. He was young and slim with untidy ginger hair that was still cut in military style. He had blue eyes, a freckled face and an amiable, mischievous personality and thankfully, he had a good knowledge of engines. He and Sophie were able to converse in their native language and since nobody else we knew spoke Flemish, they became close but we were always slightly wary knowing that Sophie was, in theory at least, still Hervé's girlfriend. Shortly after Pierre's arrival, we took delivery of a tender sent from Belgium. Once again Hervé had not researched sufficiently. He'd sent us a hard-hulled speedboat with a powerful Johnson outboard motor. The whole thing was far too heavy and large for us to hoist on the davits so we had to tow it behind us. Fine in calm weather but dangerous, if not impossible in a rough sea.

CHAPTER 9
JIGGLY BITS

Millimetres from death

I had made it known to the agency that we were available for charter as we'd had no bookings for Hervé's irresistibly sounding cruise. With nothing to do except the odd bit of maintenance, we were lying on deck sunbathing when I was hailed from the quay by the office charter manager. She was standing with three couples peering over the transom at our strange looking yacht.

"Good morning Captain," she said, "May we come aboard?"

"Of course, please do," I replied as I tried to adjust my swimming trunks, feeling embarrassed that I wasn't dressed properly. Other crews wore smart uniforms of mainly pristine white shorts and short sleeved shirts. We had to wear what clothes we had and as it was so hot, we chose swimwear. Maybe it didn't give a very good initial impression but at that time, being new on the scene, we hadn't realised the importance of smart uniforms, something else that Hervé had overlooked. As it happened, it made no difference; we managed to get enough charters regardless.

They removed their shoes and climbed the gangplank, ducking under the lethal transverse bar. Once they placed their bare feet on the scorching hot steel decks they regretted having no shoes and they started to hop for the shelter of the wheelhouse. They didn't make it, the decks were far too hot so they scurried back down to the quay for their shoes, the first in line staggering backwards with a curse as he smashed his head on the bar.

"These people are thinking of chartering you for a week, are you available?" She asked when they'd re-boarded. It was an unnecessary question. We hadn't been in Cannes long and we were already eager to go to sea again and would have accepted almost anything. I say almost anything because had I known what was in store for us I would never have accepted what was offered that day; I suspect the only reason that they came to us was that no experienced Captain would have accepted them either, for reasons that will become clear.

"They are a party of six and would like to set sail tomorrow for the Iles d'Hyères, would that be possible?"

"Yes, that's no problem," I said trying to hide my delight at the prospect of getting under way and visiting somewhere new.

They went below decks to check out the cabins, had a look around the saloon and the decks, chatted to the office manager and confirmed that they would like to book us.

"They would like to go ahead and want to know if they could pay you at the end of the week's charter," she said.

I looked at the six of them. They seemed pretty much like anybody else enjoying the pleasures of Cannes, except I didn't realise at that moment what constituted pleasure for them. Nobody would ordinarily agree to accept payment at the end of a charter but I didn't know that then. They seemed pleasant enough and had the appearance of being wealthy with their fine clothes and jewellery.

"Yes, that will be OK," I agreed. I was about to learn some valuable lessons.

"Tomorrow morning then at around nine o'clock, we'll be here," said the main character, a large, overweight, hairy, grinning American. The other five were French, three of them attractive, beautifully dressed, bronzed girls.

They left with the first in line, the American, striking his head on the bar.

"Shit!" he cried.

The next morning, we prepared the yacht for sea, lashing down anything that might move and stood on the aft deck waiting for the arrivals. We saw the American approaching from the harbour entrance in a speedboat. He moored it out of sight and shortly afterwards, walked up the gangplank accompanied by his female companion.

"Good morning," he said, smiling and came and shook hands with us.

I noticed that he spent a little longer holding on to the hands of Jill and Sophie as he leered at them both. His companion shook hands with us and almost immediately afterwards the other two couples arrived at the bottom of the gangplank. We greeted each other in the same traditional French way, with the inevitable handshakes. The American appeared to be the negotiator and the main decision maker.

"We want to go to St Tropez," he said as his companions took what little luggage they had down to the aft cabins. It seemed strange that there were no suitcases, just small bags.

"OK," I said, "I'll set a course and we'll leave when you're ready."

"We're ready now," he said.

Standing alongside the steering wheel, I contorted myself to reach over to where I'd spread the navigation chart on the space under the wheelhouse windows. It was already getting hot and uncomfortable because of the inability to open any of the windows. I started the engines and it felt so good to hear the gratifying sound again as they burst into life. We kept the speedboat at our stern under the gangplank and I sent Pierre down to tie a tow rope to it, tilt the outboard motor to lift the propeller out of the water and lock it in position. That done he climbed back aboard and we hoisted the gangplank. Pierre and Sophie each cast off one of the two stern lines, Jill hauled in the anchor, I pushed the throttles forward to slow ahead and we motored out of the harbour. We were jubilant to be at sea again and enthusiastic about seeing St Tropez that we'd heard so much about. When we'd cleared the port entrance it felt good to be freed from the blistering heat in the harbour and to be cooled by the sea breeze. The day, like all the others, was hot and sunny with the clear blue sky that we'd become accustomed to. The sea was kind to us. It was a beautiful blue colour, sparkling in the sunshine and both crew and charterers were eagerly looking forward to the coming week. From Cannes to St Tropez is 25 nautical miles and ordinarily it would not take long for the average motor yacht to cover that distance. We, however, being able to do no more than eight knots were in for a longer than average voyage.

It wasn't long before the champagne corks were flying through the air as our charterers started their celebrations. The jovial atmosphere was contagious and Jill, Sophie, Pierre and I were happy as we motored along. What happened next took us by surprise. They stripped off completely. Somebody produced some bongo drums and began hammering out a tuneless staccato rhythm as the others danced around rowdily along the decks with their appendages bouncing up and down. We were a little shocked but smiled at their antics. We stopped smiling when the American appeared on deck carrying a revolver and started firing into the air. I began to realise that maybe our charterers weren't quite the pleasant individuals I'd thought they were when they first came aboard. We'd never towed the speedboat before so I checked from time to time that all was well and noticed that the outboard motor had dropped back down into the upright position, creating a drag. I stopped the engines leaving them to tick over in neutral. We pulled in the speedboat and I sent Pierre down into it and told him that he must make sure that the outboard motor was locked properly in the tilted position. To do that, he descended the metal rungs on the transom that had been attached for swimming purposes. The charterers seemed unaware of what was happening as they danced and sang between guzzling mouthfuls of champagne. The inebriated American snatched up the bongos and threw them over the stern, shouting out some unintelligible babble. Pierre, having secured the outboard motor as directed, was in the process of clambering back on board and popped his head up over the stern at the precise moment that the American took aim, or rather, pointed the revolver roughly in the direction of the drifting bongos and fired at them, laughing as he did so. The bullet whistled towards the doomed bongos, visibly parting Pierre's hair on the top of his head, having missed him, literally by millimetres. I doubt that his military training had prepared him for anything quite like that because his face changed instantly from the normally tanned, smiling Pierre we'd come to know to a deathly white as he clung quivering to the transom with his eyes transfixed in terror and his mouth agape.

Jill, Sophie and I stood horrified. Pierre had been millimetres from certain death. We had to wait for him to compose himself enough to be able to release his grip on the rails and climb aboard and stop quivering. His face regained its usual bronzed colour eventually and the frivolities died down after that, but not completely. I was on my first ever charter and I had no idea what to expect, but what had just happened was a little unsettling! If such an occurrence had happened at a later date, I would have instantly returned to harbour and refused to continue with the charter.

The tow rope to the speedboat was paid out, I opened up the throttles once more and we continued towards St Tropez, or so I thought.

"Where are we going?" asked the American after a while.

"What do you mean?" I replied.

"St Tropez is over there," he gestured, pointing his finger way off to starboard.

"Not according to my calculations," I said

"I promise you it is, I've been there many times and I'm telling you it's over there," he insisted.

"Well, I've laid off my course on the chart and I can assure you that I'm on the right heading," I said.

He continued to argue. I took up the chart, showed him where St Tropez was, showed him the correct course I'd plotted and showed him that our compass heading was correct. It did not convince him. He went down to his cabin and returned with a small pocket compass, held it up and convinced himself that he was correct and that I was wrong. I carried on following the course I'd plotted correctly.

"Look," he said, "There is the correct course and I'm telling you that St Tropez is over there."

We were getting nowhere, so on his insistence, I looked at his compass and it showed the bearing I'd plotted. I looked at my compass and it showed the bearing I'd plotted - yet Passing Fancy was pointing away from where the American assured me was the direction of St Tropez. How could both compasses be showing the same heading and yet have such a huge difference in where the needles pointed? I was in an awkward situation. I checked everything again and it did seem that if we continued to go in the direction we were heading it would take us a long time to get there. In fact, had we continued, we'd have finished up in North Africa at some unspecified date. The brand new compass that we'd had fitted in Marseille had lost most of its fluid and although the heading I was following was the one I'd plotted, there was a difference of 40° between his compass and mine. I trusted his knowledge, turned to starboard and for the rest of the voyage used his pocket compass, which he then offered to sell me for "Five bucks". I declined.

After both rudders had snapped off in the English Channel, the unlagged exhaust pipes had melted the hose for filling the water tanks and caused the cabin soles to become hot, the lack of a navigation area, being too high to pass under the canal bridges, the wheelhouse with windows that wouldn't open, bare metal decks that we couldn't stand on, the dangerous and useless bar between the davits, a tender that was too big and heavy to hoist on the davits, a permanent list to starboard, an eight knot maximum speed instead of the sixteen promised and now a malfunctioning compass, Jill and I wondered what else could possibly go wrong. Plenty was the answer, but we didn't know that then.

The name St Tropez is derived from St Torpes, a legendary martyr beheaded by the Roman Emperor Nero. His body was allegedly cast adrift in a boat that landed up in what is now known as St Tropez. At one time it was a Muslim colony which was finally expelled by the Counts of Provence. In 1436, sixty Genoese families arrived there at the request of Count René I, who wished to repopulate the area. As an enticement, they were granted tax exemption, a privilege which they retained until Louis XIV annulled the agreement when he established French jurisdiction in 1672. In 1470, the Genoese were granted permission to build the city walls and the two towers that still stand, one at the end of the Grand Môle and the other at the entrance to La Ponche, (from the Provençale word Poncho, meaning point and relating to a pinnacle of rock). St Tropez was an unpretentious fishing village until famous people in the world of fashion began to visit in the early 20th century. On 15 August 1944, during the invasion of Southern France, the Allies landed at St Tropez, making it the first town on that section of the coast to be liberated. In 1956, Roger Vadim made the film "And God Created Woman" there, which catapulted its female star, Brigitte Bardot to international stardom, cementing her persona as a "sex kitten" and contributing to the fame of St Tropez. In 1958, she bought a house in St Tropez, and ever since then the town has become a magnet for celebrities of all nationalities and descriptions and tourism is now its principal source of income. The beaches are located south of St Tropez in Pampelonne Bay, a popular anchorage for visiting yachts, which we came to know very well. The most famous beach is Tahiti Beach, featured in the Brigitte Bardot film and where clothing is optional.

The town and harbour were an exquisite sight as we approached from the sea and it was a wonderful feeling to be there after all that we'd heard about it. I instructed Pierre to get into the speedboat and motor in ahead of us, otherwise maneuvering into position with it swinging behind us would have been very difficult. This had the additional advantage of allowing him to locate a suitable mooring in the crowded port by the time we arrived with Passing Fancy. The charterers donned the minimum attire that they could respectably get away with and I motored in through the harbour entrance. We dropped anchor in the middle of the port, backed up to the quay, lowered the gangplank, and settled in for the rest of the day and night. St Tropez is an exhilarating place to be in the season and especially at night when it is teeming with life. There are restaurants and bars around the harbour, and street artists and vendors exhibiting their works. There is live music, and all sorts of street entertainment taking place - acrobats, fire eaters, magicians and so on, all hoping to make money from the tourists. We had a wonderful time there wandering the streets and sitting drinking coffee in La Gorille, one of the most renowned bars on the quay, while we watched the activities and the posers. Some of them, especially the girls, wore outlandish and sometimes very revealing, eye-popping clothes.

We were backed onto the quay that was brimming with tourists gawking in awe at all the impressive yachts moored up with their wealthy owners posing on the aft decks for the "ordinary people". When the gawkers reached us, Jill unintentionally put on a performance for them to equal the street entertainers judging by the crowd that gathered at the bottom of our gangplank. In the thirty degree heat, she had the unfortunate job of trying to light a barbeque that defied all her attempts. It was slung over the stern rail to protect the decks. There were no firelighters so she rolled up pieces of paper, placed the charcoal on top, squirted it all with methylated spirit then pumped away with a pair of bellows. Each time she lit the paper and blew it with the bellows, the flames went out, much to the amusement of the gathering crowd, which encouraged more tourists to come and find out what was going on. Sweating, cursing, red-faced and speckled with charcoal dust, she lit match after match and blew and blew with the bellows, urged on by the eager bystanders.

"Oooh," they murmured in chorus each time she struck a match and pumped away with increasing rapidity.

"Aaah," they cried as once more the flames died and another cloud of dust was blown over her.

"Hooray," they cheered and clapped when eventually, Jill broke the spell on the voodooed charcoal and it grudgingly started to glow. Triumphant, she took a bow to the accompanying applause.

The most outlandish activity of all, however, took place in the wheelhouse of Passing Fancy. Our charterers had invited some guests aboard for drinks and to share in the feast that Jill was preparing on the aft deck and some of their antics gave us an insight of what was to come. I stood alongside Jill and behind me, hidden from the view of the passing crowds, they stood around drinking champagne. I turned and walked forward to see where Sophie and Pierre were and when I peered into the wheelhouse I saw one of the girls shove her hand inside the minuscule trunks of the man standing next to her, pull out his flaccid penis, dip it in her champagne glass and swirl it around. She then squatted down and put the dripping member in her mouth and licked it clean. It beggars belief that nobody else saw what happened. Jill and I were stunned and it was a relief when we left the next morning before anything else untoward happened; it made us wonder what else was in store for us; we didn't have long to wait!

Full nakedness

The Iles d'Hyeres were the next port of call, in particular, Ile du Levant. There are three islands lying off the coast of Hyeres, known also as the Iles d'Or (Golden Islands) because of the way the mica and quartz in the rocks sparkle in the sunshine. The largest and westernmost, Porquerolles, is seven kilometres long and three wide with a small village that was established in 1820. It was privately owned for over seven hundred years, being sold and resold numerous times. In 1912 Francois Georges Fournier bought it for one million, one hundred francs. His father had been a Belgian bargeman who delivered coal but Francois was an adventurer who made his fortune prospecting for gold in Mexico. He later travelled to Panama, California and Canada, adding to his wealth in the process. In 1914 he became a French national and planted a vineyard of 200 hectares. His wine was the first to become established as the Cote de Provence Appellation. In 1970, the state purchased eighty percent of the island to prevent any development taking place and it is now mostly a national park.

Port Cros, at four and a half kilometres in length and two kilometres wide, is the smallest of the three islands. It had also been in private hands for centuries until the last proprietor, Madame Henry, died in 1966, bequeathing it to the state on condition that it would remain a national park. I have cruised the Mediterranean Sea extensively over the years, visiting its large and small islands and the Iles d'Hyéres still remain my favourite islands.

Ile du Levant, our destination, was well known for a different reason. It is approximately the same size as Porquerolles, being eight kilometres long and two kilometres wide. In 1860, a prison was created for young offenders and orphans with the first unfortunate souls arriving the following year. Napoleon III, in a desire to rid the towns of orphans and delinquents, sent them to the island where they were sentenced to hard labour. During the seventeen years that it was used as a prison, one hundred of the youths that were sent there died. In 1892, the state took possession of ninety percent of the island, reserving it for the military, leaving the remaining ten percent in the hands of the descendants of the family that had previously owned it. An estate agency bought it from them in 1928, and later, in 1931, it was taken over by two doctors, Gaston and Henry Durville, who created the first naturist village in Europe, which became increasingly popular between 1950 and 1970. The village, Heliopolis, has a small school, a chapel, a police station, a village hall, a post office, a bakery, hotels, B&B's, restaurants and a food shop. There is also a clothes shop selling "minimums", the only clothing necessary, which is generally obligatory in the harbour, the village square and shops and optional in restaurants. Minimums are, as the name suggests, tiny pouches to fit over the male genitalia and minute triangular patches for the females, otherwise, nudity is expected, if not obligatory. One wonders how many designs there can be on offer for such minuscule garments. The only way to reach the island is by boat and no cars are allowed. When Jill and I were there, there was no electricity, which allowed the nature lovers to benefit from the clear skies and the myriad of stars. It was a good thing that some of us had torches. "Full nakedness! All my joys are due to thee, as souls unbodied, bodies unclothed must be, to taste whole

24. *At anchor off Corsica.*

joys." - John Donne.

We hadn't realised when we went there that our charterers were expecting and openly looking for more than naturism. They wanted to profit in as many ways as possible from the abundant offerings of naked flesh. We motored in as close to the shore as safety permitted and dropped anchor a short distance from the small port among the other anchored craft, naked swimmers and smaller boats flitting to and fro. Our party wasted no time. Divested of everything except a thick coating of sun tan lotion and a small bag in which to carry a few items, the two French couples, Marco and Celine and Didier and Myriam, climbed over the stern and into the speedboat. Jill, dressed in her bikini, followed them, started the engine and took the four naked, animated guests ashore, leaving the American, Clyde and his French girlfriend Marie on board. They both disappeared down to their cabin. Whilst they were away, Sophie, Pierre and I profited from the little free time we had in such an idyllic place. We jumped into the sea and enjoyed a quick swim in the clear, blue, warm water. Accompanied by a curious Jill, It didn't take our guests long to meet up with a couple of their nature loving friends on the shore.

"Bonjour," each one said to the other as they exchanged the habitual kisses on both cheeks.

"How are you?"

"I'm fine thanks and how are you?"

After the usual greetings and kisses, the conversation focused on the mammary glands of their female friend who had, a few days prior to the meeting, suffered from fairly severe sunburn.

"Oh, what happened to your boobies?" Celine asked

"Sunburn," she said.

"Oh what a shame, how are they now?"

"On the mend but still sore," she replied, stroking them.

"Oh, what a pity, a poor sunburned titty," Marco said cupping them both in his hands and lifting them up, whilst Didier stroked them. Our two French men felt it vital that they carry out a closer inspection by feeling around the two flopping bosoms, lifting them up and scrutinizing them thoroughly as Celine and Myriam, amused, watched the inspection that took longer than was warranted. Feeling satisfied that they'd accomplished all that they'd wanted to, they said goodbye, agreeing to meet up again later. The woman walked off with a smile on her face and Jill marched off to the shop with our four guests. The shop supplied all that was needed and I emphasise that I'm only talking groceries. Two young, tanned girls, clad only in the minimum of minimums, asked how they could help. It was obvious to Jill, that the two Frenchmen were deliberately requesting more than was necessary from the top shelves so that they could get a good eyeful of raw flesh as the girls climbed and stretched to reach the mostly unwanted goods. Celine and Myriam seemed equally enamoured with the display. With the shopping done, they headed back to the speedboat that had been left alongside the landing stage. Jill jumped in and started the engine. Marco and Didier passed her the bags of shopping and then each lit a cigarette before boarding. Celine and Myriam were ogling the unattired passers-by. A few puffs of the Gauloise later and with it still stuck in his mouth, Didier placed a foot on the side of the speedboat so that he could spring in alongside Jill. He hadn't taken into consideration that boats are not static in the water and the speedboat drifted from the landing stage, leaving him straddled with one foot on the quay and the other on the speedboat. His legs parted to an alarming degree until finally, almost split in two; he plunged into the sea, still with the Gaulloise in his mouth. He emerged spluttering and coughing, spat out the soggy cigarette and grabbed the side of the boat to avoid sinking back down again. Jill was doubled over with laughter as were the other three on the quay. As Marco exploded with laughter, his Gaulloise flew into the sea. The two girls, guffawing and snorting like crazy, had their arms around each other for support. It wasn't long before a few spectators joined in the hilarity. Nobody was in a fit state to aid the hapless Didier as he struggled to pull himself into the speedboat. To quote Charlie Chaplin, "A day without laughter is a day wasted."

Meanwhile, back on Passing Fancy, Clyde and Marie were still locked in their cabin. It was only when the speedboat arrived with the occupants still in fits of giggles that they emerged. The shopping was unloaded and after scoffing on more champagne and food, they went ashore again for the evening where they met up with fellow revelers. This was convenient because they would sometimes arrange for their new found friends to collect them and bring them back to Passing Fancy in a boat so that Jill, Pierre or I didn't need to keep running them backwards and forwards in the speedboat. It was quite an eye opener being there and our eyes were to be opened far wider. They returned in the early hours of the morning drunk and in high spirits.

Much later that morning, after they'd all slept off the effects of the previous night's revelries, the American came up from his cabin and into the saloon where Jill, Sophie and I were standing chatting. He approached us, beaming, with perspiration glistening on his naked, hairy body that showed the unmistakable results of an indolent life of excess.

"Good morning, "he said pleasantly.

"Good morning," we replied.

"You sleep well?" Sophie inquired in her broken English.

He came up close to her and mumbled something inaudible but we made out two words, "tac-tac".

"What's tac-tac?" asked Sophie innocently. Jill and I had never heard the expression either but we gathered from his actions what he meant. We were beginning to dislike this crude creature. He put his arms in front of himself and thrust his hips at Sophie in a suggestive manner.

"That's tac-tac," he grinned.

Sophie blushed.

"You can take your clothes off too if you want," he suggested with a look of anticipation in his eyes at the thought, no doubt, of seeing Jill and Sophie "au naturel".

They declined. We, of course, as professional crew, had to adhere to a proper code of behaviour but an irresistible temptation to indulge in a little voyeurism overcame the young, aroused Pierre. One afternoon, with our randy charterers ashore mingling with the plenitude of reciprocating nudists that were scattered over the beaches and hidden among the bushes in the spaces officially allocated to them, Jill, Sophie and I were sunbathing on the coach roof in front of the wheelhouse.

"Where's Pierre?" Jill asked after a while.

"Oh, that's a good question, I haven't seen him since lunch," I answered.

Jill turned to Sophie.

"How about you, Sophie, is he in the cabin?" she said. (Sophie and Pierre shared a cabin).

"I not see him there," said Sophie. "Maybe he sleep now."

"Better let him rest," I said and we thought no more of it as we soaked up the sunshine and relaxed.

A little later, taking advantage of the free time we had, Jill suggested we have a snack before the unruly guests returned. We left Sophie to bronze her voluptuous body a little more and went into the saloon to see what was available to eat. The floor to ceiling curtain on one side was misshapen. There was a bulge that caused it to rise from the floor, revealing two bare heels at the bottom. I pulled the curtain back and there was Pierre, bent over, peering out of the window with the ship's binoculars glued to his eyes. He spun around red faced and shoved his hands behind his back in an ineffective attempt to hide the binoculars from our view.

"Pierre, what are you up to?" I said, an absurd question as it was obvious what he'd been doing.

He looked first at me, then at Jill, then back to me and then cast his gaze downwards. He was so embarrassed and I couldn't help feeling a little sorry for him as he stood in front of us with a stupid smirk on his blushing face.

"Give me those binoculars. These charterers are paying a fortune to hire the boat and us and they expect privacy, what do you think would happen if they saw you spying on them?"

He handed them to me sheepishly.

"What did you see there anyway?" I asked. He looked at me and his smile broadened.

"Don't let me see you doing that again, it's not allowed," I told him as I went behind the curtain and peered through the binoculars myself. Pierre and Jill giggled.

Where the sun don't shine

As the days progressed and the six charterers spent more time on the island, they met a number of other nudists that they invited back to Passing Fancy and the goings on became more debauched and the crude American, who appeared to be the main instigator, became more obnoxious. It was difficult to remain pleasant to him but we had to for the sake of the charter. Sundry naked, promiscuous guests were invited back to Passing Fancy and I wonder if they were cognizant of Clyde's debased agenda at the time - but judging by the enthusiasm with which they climbed aboard, the answer, I think it fairly safe to assume, was in the affirmative. They leapt barefoot from the boats straight onto the piping hot steel decks. With much squealing they began hopping up and down, bumping into each other with their assorted appendages jiggling as they rushed to find a place where they could stand without getting their feet scorched. There was nowhere that could be safely reached in time so they leapt back into the boats for their flip flops. Once the mayhem had subsided, we heard the familiar sound of champagne bottles being opened, accompanied by lively chatter and a fair amount of stroking and groping of each other's various body parts. The barbeque was set up, suspended over the stern rail, and Jill performed her usual ritual of puffing away with the bellows to get the charcoal glowing whilst the frivolous crowd guzzled champagne. It was always Clyde and Marie who instigated the obscenities but the others wasted no time in joining in. Marie was a slim, tanned, very pretty girl with long blonde hair and she would perform her usual outrageous party trick of dipping the odd penis in her champagne and then squatting down to suck it dry. Not all of the guests were so coarse but none of the men seemed to protest when it was their turn. They stood with their hands on their hips and smiles on their faces as they looked down at her. Some of the young girls giggled and some looked on surprised but none of them were eager to emulate Marie, at least not that we were aware of. An especially provocative young girl made her way forward to climb onto the coach roof and sun bathe. She climbed the ladder and bent over to crawl onto the coach roof; it was a beguiling sight and too much for Clyde to resist. In the wink of an eye, as if from nowhere, he was behind her. He grabbed her buttocks, held her in position, parted her cheeks with his thumbs and buried his face into her rear end. Whatever he did as he wiggled his head from side to side and whichever orifice he chose to do it to made her squeal with delight. I suspect it involved the activation of one or both of the exceptions that Leonardo da Vinci mentioned when he said, "The function of a muscle is to pull and push, except in the case of the genitals and the tongue."

"Ooh," she cackled as she squirmed and wiggled her perfectly formed posterior in his face.

From where I stood, close by, I heard a sound that I recognised and saw

Clyde reel backwards with significant force, his eyes wide in surprise. He hit the handrail with his back and grabbed it with both hands to prevent himself somersaulting backwards into the sea. She'd farted into his face. Maybe it was because she got over excited or maybe it was something Clyde did but whatever it was they both erupted into intractable laughter afterwards.

There was nowhere we could escape from what was going on in the confines of the boat. Mostly we'd stay on the foredeck well clear of them, which meant sitting around in the baking sun. It wasn't so bad since there was usually a breeze that picked up each afternoon, sometimes quite strong, as the land heated up. The wheelhouse was far too hot to stand around in and the aft deck, shaded by a canvas awning was the charterers' main area as was the saloon and cabins. The best moments by far were when they were ashore and we had the boat to ourselves, often for most of the day. Then we'd laugh and joke about the goings on and we'd swim and enjoy a relaxing meal with some excellent wine. Those moments made it all worthwhile and in any case, we were having the experience of a lifetime. It certainly had to beat hands down any stuffy old office job, listening to the humdrum chatter of bored workers, probably discussing nothing better than the previous evening's TV programs. I'd had my share of that.

The six charterers had, in all probability, been establishing a reputation on the island and it wasn't long before boats were coming alongside and the occupants engaging in conversation with them. Some were invited aboard and invariably left with satisfied grins on their faces, others were put off until a later time or day. Our charterers didn't need to go ashore very much from then on because the seekers of pleasure came to them. We, that is Jill, Sophie, Pierre and I mostly kept well out of the way and preferred not to know too much of what was taking place. We only had to allow our imaginations a little freedom to come up with probable bawdy happenings, based on the performances we'd witnessed already. As the charter was approaching its end, we thought that maybe they were grateful for a little time to build up some energy after the hectic few days they'd been having. They were, for once, having a rare afternoon relaxing and behaving in a civilised manner. They lounged around in the sun, slapping sun tan lotion over each other and emptied what seemed like endless bottles of champagne. Their conversation with us and among themselves was courteous and even the insufferable Clyde could have been mistaken for a decent human being. All was well for a while and then we heard a shout.

"Bonjour," somebody called out from one of two inflatable boats that were heading our way.

Our libidinous charterers looked up, waved to the multitude of raucous, naked bodies that started calling back and waving wildly. Both boats were packed solid with persons of both sexes and they were clearly intent on having a good time and it was obvious from the determined way they headed for us that they intended for the action to take place on board Passing Fancy. The two-way conversations that were shouted out across the water were mostly unintelligible to us but no translation was needed. The body language explained everything. The two boats gently bumped alongside us, were made fast and twelve people enthusiastically clambered onto the decks before anybody had a chance to warn them.

"Ouch."

"Merde."

"Shit."

A whole load of profanities were expressed as they leapt in the air and started hopping around, bumping into each other as they scattered in every direction in the hope of finding a spot that didn't blister their feet. They never would make it to safety as the decks had had all day to heat up and so they dived back into their boats for their flip flops. Mostly they were reasonably well behaved and didn't commit any obscene acts in front of the crew. By early evening there was nobody to be seen on deck, they had somehow all squeezed into one of the aft cabins. The laughter, screams, grunts and many other thought provoking sounds were clearly audible to us, accompanied by the sound of splashing and running water. They were piled into the shower. Whatever went on down there must have been so outrageous that it even appalled the shameless Marie. She came running up to the deck in tears and sought the privacy and safety of the coach roof. Clyde, the most vulgar of them all, had no doubt been responsible for upsetting her. He appeared shortly afterwards, went to her and did his best to comfort her. He didn't seem overly concerned because all the time he was smiling as he stroked and cajoled her. She was crying and pushed him away.

"Va t'en. Laisse moi tranquil!" she screamed at him. He put his arm around her and murmured something in her ear, still smiling. He was evidently pleased with what he had done despite Marie's disgust and she struggled again but less forcefully. It took a long time for him to calm her down. The others started to appear on deck but by that time the atmosphere was much more subdued. Whatever had happened down in the shower had had a disturbing effect on everybody involved. Shortly afterwards, when Marie had composed herself, she and Clyde, with his hairy, flabby arms wrapped around her, went to talk to the others gathered on the aft deck. After a while, the guests climbed into their boats and set off for the shore, never to be seen again.

We were relieved when the time came to leave Ile du Levant. The whole adventure had been an astonishing revelation to us. The shopping trips that Jill and I made together were intriguing. We kept our bathing costumes on as was expected in the town and it was an unusual experience to be served by women wearing just a minimum. In the years that followed, our subsequent trips to Ile du Levant were enjoyable and we never again met such perverse people.

"Heave away," I called to Jill and the rattle of the anchor chain was music to my ears. We were leaving and would soon be rid of the sex crazed sextet. It was all over. Well, that's what we thought.

"We want to stop off at Cavalaire to meet some friends," said Clyde.

"OK," I said and set the course.

Encircled by two capes, Cap Cavalaire to the west and Cap Lardier to the east, Cavalaire sur Mer is a pretty little town set in a bay with a beautiful three kilometres long sandy beach at the foothills of a small mountain range called the Massif des Maures. I doubt that what was about to take place aboard the Passing Fancy that evening was a routine activity there.

It always felt good to be at sea again and delight in the wonderful scenery, the inevitable clear, blue sky and sea, the gentle breeze, the hot sun beating down and the comforting movement of the boat as we pushed our way forward to the next destination. Cavalaire sur Mer was just twenty nautical miles away so after a few hours we dropped anchor in the bay a short distance from the town. It was there that we spent the last night. The aberrant couples were taken to the harbour entrance in the speedboat and left there. Dusk brought a familiar scene, two inflatable boats filled with boisterous couples bumped alongside. The occupants clambered aboard. The men with their members barely tucked into the minuscule pouches and the topless girls wearing tiny strings of beads covering what little modesty they had left. They descended into the saloon and closed the doors. Music, laughter, thumping and shouting was soon heard. The noise went on for some time which kept us awake, so Jill and I went up onto the foredeck. Sophie and Pierre were already there. We'd heard them talking. It was worse for them because they had a cabin nearer to the saloon so they didn't even bother to attempt going in there. The four of us sat around chatting and laughing for a while. We hadn't had much sleep throughout the charter and we were happy that this was to be the last night. It was a fabulous evening. There was a crystal clear sky, a small crescent moon and countless millions of stars shining above us. The lights of the harbour and the town were scattered along the coastline in the distance, the boat very gently rocked in what little swell there was and the deck was cool enough to stand on with bare feet.

"Tomorrow, we'll be back in Cannes and it will all be over," I said.

"Thank goodness," Jill, Sophie and Pierre replied in unison.

"It hasn't been easy but this is the last night and just look at that fabulous view. We're so lucky to be here." They agreed with me.

"I'm surprised they've got any energy left after what they've been doing," said Jill. We chuckled.

"Yeah, disgusting bloody creatures," said Sophie. Her English had improved even during the charter and she'd learned a few more words, some of them of an indelicate nature. She had a gift for languages that I envied.

"Or lucky, depending on how you look at it," I said. We chuckled again.

"I wonder what they're up to in there; it's gone a bit quieter now," Jill said.

"Well, after what we've witnessed, I think we've all got a pretty good idea," I said.

Pierre had a broad grin on his tanned face and suggested he go and peer through the curtain. We were feeling mischievous as we became more relaxed, knowing that in just a few hours we'd be free of them. He stood up and tip toed along the deck and very quickly came scuttling back giggling.

"There's a crack in the curtains, so it would be possible to see in," he told us.

"I don't think we should do that," I said authoritatively.

The four of us looked at each other inquiringly. Curiosity overcame all other sentiments. I stood up and went to see if there was indeed an opening in the curtains. There was but I decided that it was not a good idea to proceed so turned to go back to the foredeck. I bumped into a tittering Pierre who'd crept up behind me, encouraged by Jill and Sophie. His eyes said it all. He nodded his head in the direction of the opening in the curtains as he tried to stifle his giggles. I felt that I was committed then. We both crouched down and crept to the opening, holding on to each other as we tried to make ourselves less conspicuous. We peered through. What we saw wasn't what we'd expected to see. A startled and unknown face stared back at us. In an instant, the curtains were abruptly drawn and we scuttled back giggling to join the two girls. After a further half hour, we decided we'd better try to get some sleep and we went off to our respective cabins. The noise went on well into the night. We awoke early as we did every morning and what we saw when we entered the saloon had us wondering how our charterers' guests got home because the strings of beads and minimums were lying around on the floor and some were piled into ashtrays. The most intriguing item though was a wooden handled, multi thronged whip. "Home is heaven and orgies are vile, but I like an orgy, once in a while." So said Ogden Nash, an American known for his humorous poetry.

Running scared

One long week after the perverts first boarded, we weighed anchor at Cavalaire and set course for the return to Cannes. It was another hot, sunny day but with a stiff breeze picking up making the sea choppy and causing the speed boat on its towrope to veer from one side to the other. It was such a stupid mistake to buy one so large that we couldn't haul it up safely on the davits and it was to be a constant concern in rough weather. Using Clyde's pocket compass to steer by we arrived in Cannes before midday and moored up in our berth outside the agency office. That was the first charter that Jill and I had ever done and what an introduction it was. We didn't know, but felt pretty certain that orgies on board weren't the norm! I'd calculated the cost of the fuel we'd used and added it to the charter fee, plus an additional amount to cover the cost of the crew's food. I presented it to Marco and Didier when they came up from below onto the hot steel deck.

"Voila, I've prepared the final bill for you and we hope you enjoyed your week with us," I said holding out the neatly written bill, which they took with them down to the cabin.

"Clyde will pay you, we've each given him our share of the charter fee," Marco said when they left fifteen minutes later. "And this is for you and the rest of the crew," he added as he handed me a bundle of francs as a tip.

"That's very nice of you, thank you," I said.

"Clyde has our contribution so he now has the full amount to pay you," he emphasised and I detected a hint of concern. It was obvious that they didn't much care anymore for the gross American and the fact that they emphasised that he'd received the full charter fee led me to believe that they didn't trust him very much either. No surprise there! I got the impression that they would be as delighted to be rid of him as Jill and I would be. Their explanation seemed reasonable enough so we shook hands and said our goodbyes. They descended the gangplank with Céline and Myriam, Marco leading the way.

"MERDE!" he shouted as he smashed his head on the transverse bar, staggering backwards into the other three. As we hadn't moored stern to since St Tropez we hadn't needed to use the gangplank so everybody had forgotten about the dangerous bar. The four of them walked away carrying their little luggage bags, with Marco rubbing his forehead. Clyde was still down below with Marie. Jill, Sophie, Pierre and I stood waiting in the sweltering wheelhouse for him to emerge and pay the bill so that we could rejoice in his departure. Eventually, he came up to us with a cunning grin on his face, followed by an overly pleasant Marie.

"Marco and Didier told me that you will be settling the bill," I said.

"Yeah, of course, that's right," he confirmed. "I'm just going to place our luggage in my boat over there," he pointed to where we'd seen him moor it not far away. "And we'll be free to sort out the finances. I'll be right back." He and Marie, remembering to duck under the bar, went with their bags to their boat and Jill and I waited, watching them and feeling uneasy.

The speedboat roared out of the harbour at full throttle with Clyde and Marie in the front seats looking straight ahead. My heart raced. My stomach sank. I stared in disbelief as the pair of confidence tricksters disappeared. I was utterly shattered as the terrible realisation of my situation hit me. Jill and I looked at each other with a sick feeling rising in our guts.

"The bastards," I shouted. "We should have known we'd get trouble from that pair."

I rushed into the agency office.

"The American you introduced me to has just run off without paying for the charter," I blurted out to Isabelle, the person who had brought him on board one week earlier.

"What?" she cried. "Do you know where he went?"

"He disappeared out of the harbour in his speedboat and I've no idea where he was heading."

"What about the others, where are they?"

"They went off earlier. They told me they'd given all the money to him." She called the office manager, Alec, and clearly concerned, explained what had happened. They immediately started making phone calls. The office staff sprang into action trying to track down any of the six that they could. After all, their commission was at stake too.

"What were they like?" Isabelle asked.

"Well, it wasn't exactly what I'd expected! We went to Ile du Levant and they turned out to be a bunch of perverts. They started stripping off as soon as we left harbour," I told her.

"You mean they stripped off completely?" She said, aghast.

"That was the mildest bit," I said and I explained the full episode in detail, much to her horror. It was obvious that she felt some responsibility and I felt that I should have been advised by her at the beginning that it was customary to be paid in advance. I was a novice. She was an experienced professional. The office staff commiserated with me and I headed back aboard Passing Fancy feeling utterly dejected. Jill was waiting for me at the top of the gangway. She put her arm around me, kissed me and offered words of reassurance. I felt a bit better.

"Don't worry; I'm sure something will work out. He can't be that far away," she said, trying her best to console me.

Sophie phoned home to Hervé to tell him all about the charter. He was not happy with the outcome but understood our difficult circumstances and was happy that we'd at least been chosen by the agency, especially as so far he'd only had one confirmed booking for the cruise he'd been advertising in America. He was not so happy when she told him how unbearable it was in the wheelhouse with no ventilation and that he should do something about it.

By mid-afternoon the following day, the agency had tracked down Marco and Didier through their numerous contacts and discovered from them that the American had his speedboat moored in the Port Pointe Croisette, a small port a short distance from Port Pierre-Canto. They somehow got the message to him demanding he settle the charter fee without delay. The next day no reply had been received so Alec came aboard to update me.

"We know he has his boat moored in the small harbour across the way," he told me. "He's had plenty of time to settle the bill by now, so I think we should go there and confront him straight away because he knows that we are on to him."

"OK, let's take my speedboat and go there now," I suggested.

"Let's go then," he agreed.

We set off down the gangplank in a hurry and I smashed my head on the bar almost knocking myself out in my haste to disembark. Feeling dizzy from the mighty crack on the head I'd received, I jumped in the speedboat followed by Alec. I started the engine and we set off for Port Pointe Croisette. I kept to the speed limit in harbour but once clear of the entrance I opened up the throttle. We wanted to reach his boat before he could escape and if necessary, seize the boat and release it only after he'd paid the charter fee. The port was in sight and we were close. A short distance from the entrance, a speedboat came slowly motoring out. The man at the controls didn't seem certain which way he wanted to go, first veering off one way then the other and then started to head towards the Iles de Lerins, a short distance off Cannes. The figure was unmistakable.

"That's him," I said.

"Good, let's collar him," said Alec and I altered course to intercept him.

"He's seen us and he's recognised me and he's heading straight for us," I said.

"I wonder what his intention is." Alec was thinking out aloud.

"He's got a gun," I informed Alec.

"HE'S GOT A GUN?" he cried in horror. "Turn around, let's go back, quick." After I'd told him how unpredictable Clyde could be and how furious he must have been that we'd foiled his plans, Alec didn't want to take any chances.

I spun the wheel hard over to starboard and pushed the throttle to maximum. The boat almost leapt out of the water as we spun around in a tight circle with the gunwhales almost at water level, then we shot forward when I brought the wheel around to midships. We looked behind us and Clyde had opened up his throttle and was roaring through the water in pursuit. We raced across the bay towards our home port. Clyde was gaining on us. His ill-gotten gains from what had likely been a lifetime of conning people had allowed him to buy a bigger and better speedboat than we had. I had the throttle opened up to maximum. Both boats were almost flying and we heeled over alarmingly as I spun the boat around the mole and into Port Pierre-Canto. I ignored the usual speed limit and headed directly to the quay where Passing Fancy was moored. When we arrived I pulled back the throttle to neutral and as we went alongside, Alec leapt ashore with the painter, quickly made it fast to the mooring ring and ran to the office. I was right behind him. We sped through the door.

"What's going on?" the secretary asked.

"It's him, Clyde, he's coming after us and he's got a gun," Alec gasped.

There were four of us, Alec, Isabelle, the secretary and myself. We were huddled together peering through the blinds, wondering what would happen next. We saw him arrive. He moored up his boat and headed towards us. He looked enormous, far bigger than I'd remembered him. We looked at each other, staying huddled together. He got closer and then the door flew open.

"I understand you want to see me," he boomed.

"Er, yes, that's right," Alec spoke first in an uncertain voice with a slight tremor. "We need to settle the amount of the charter fee."

"I know. I was going to pay, I just needed to sort out a few things," he growled.

"Ah yes, please sit down," said Isabelle in a sweet voice.

The conversation continued, sometimes politely and sometimes more heated. Nobody wanted to upset Clyde, not merely because of his unpredictability but also he did have a gun and his plan to disappear with many thousands of francs had been thwarted, so he was patently upset about that. Furthermore, he still held the money that we wanted; upsetting him would have made getting it more difficult, although I was pretty sure that the agency had contingency plans now that they knew the whereabouts of the other charterers. Clyde was in an awkward situation. He knew that we knew we had closed in on him so he had to make a hasty decision. He agreed to come back and pay within an hour or two, which he did and fortunately, I was able to report to Hervé that it had all ended satisfactorily. I had just learned a valuable lesson. Never again would I leave harbour with charterers who hadn't paid in full in advance.

CHAPTER 10
WHOSE BOAT IS IT ANYWAY?

A shame about the ice cream!

Before any more cruising could be done, I had to order a replacement compass and suggested to Hervé that he contact the supplier in Marseille who had sold him the faulty one. We could have finished up in an awkward situation had we been on a long sea passage. The new one arrived and for the adjustment, we motored out to the Iles de Lerins, specifically Ile Ste Marguerite, the largest of the group of four islands, just half a mile from Cannes. It has Europe's oldest eucalyptus forest, which is the second most visited forest in France. In Roman times, the island was called Lero after a revered Ligurian demi God, Leron, (the Ligurians were the first known inhabitants of the islands, around 600BC) and it is thought that it may have been renamed after Crusaders built a chapel in honour of Saint Margaret of Antioch. In 1612, possession of the island passed from the monks of St Honorat, who owned both islands as well as much of the mainland, to the Duke of Chevreuse. He constructed the island's fortress, which became a barracks and a state prison in the 17th century and it remained a prison until the 20th century. Its most famous prisoner was "the man in the iron mask" whose cell is now a tourist attraction. Little is known of the true identity of this prisoner. The only reliable information originates from correspondence between his jailor, Bénigne Dauvergne de Saint-Mars, and his superiors in Paris. He was supposedly born in 1640 and died in 1703 after spending 34 years incarcerated in numerous prisons in a mask of black velvet to conceal his identity. He was transferred to Ile Ste Marguerite in May 1687 and it was during this transfer that the rumour spread that he was wearing an iron mask. Instructions were issued that he be placed in a cell with multiple doors. In 1698, he was transferred again, this time to the Bastille, where he died five years later.

Ile St Honorat, the second largest island, lies one mile from Cannes. It was devastated by an earthquake and tidal wave in 410 and became uninhabited until the hermit Honorat went there shortly afterwards, intending to live alone. However, his disciples followed him and a monastic community quickly developed. The island and the monks have suffered numerous attacks over the centuries. During the French revolution, the state took control, disestablished the monastery and sold it to a wealthy actress who lived there for twenty years. The Bishop of Fréjus bought the island in 1859 and ten years later a Cistercian community was founded which exists to this day. It is now a popular tourist attraction, with free visits to the fortified monastery on the Southern tip of the island, which is visible from afar. Events, religious retreats, and tastings of the wines and liqueurs made by the Monks are on offer. The two smallest islands are uninhabited.

With the new compass swung and corrected we moored up once again in Port Pierre-Canto. The compass adjuster wasn't happy that he'd had to suffer the heat of the wheelhouse and when he gave his head a mighty crack on the bar as he left, he was fuming. It was at that time that I took out one of the signalling flags and tied it to the deadly bar between the davits as a warning to everybody to duck their heads as they disembarked. Sophie chatted to Hervé and told him that he would have to do something about providing some sort of ventilation in the hot wheelhouse, as indeed I had myself on numerous occasions. Almost as soon as Sophie had put Hervé in the picture about that, another problem emerged. Jill became aware of water on the galley floor. The refrigerator could no longer cope with the heat and the freezer compartment had defrosted leaving us a soggy, stinking mess to clear away.

We spent a few days relaxing and entertaining our friends with stories of our recent experiences. The yacht also had to be cleaned inside and out. We decided to throw away the tiny rows of multi coloured beads left behind at Cavalaire, as none of us had any desire to make use of them. However, we kept the thonged whip as a souvenir to show to any disbelieving friends. Sophie didn't waste any time parading around in her seductive manner, wearing a minuscule bikini and it wasn't long before love sick crew members from various yachts began to gather at the bottom of our gangplank once again, staring expectantly in the hope of attracting her attention.

I think that the agency may have felt responsible for offering us the last charter because it wasn't long before we were offered another. The difference between the two charters could not have been greater. The next one consisted of one solitary American male who wanted to use the yacht simply as a floating hotel room, albeit an exceedingly expensive one that was undoubtedly paid for by his company. There are many festivals and business meetings in Cannes throughout the year and yachts are often chartered for the durations. Mostly they don't leave port because the charterers spend the days at the conferences and also, the glamorous women sometimes don't want to go to sea for fear of messing up their hair! Our American restored our confidence in chartering. He was polite, charming, generous and a pleasure to talk to during what little time he spent on board. He would leave each morning before breakfast, come back late afternoon, maybe have a coffee or tea on deck, leave again early evening and not come back until late at night. We'd exchange a few pleasantries before he retired to his cabin and this continued for the entire week of the charter. It was whilst he was renting Passing Fancy that Hervé decided to pay us a visit to discuss the events that had taken place and the ones that would be taking place. He marched up the gangplank with his suitcase, shook hands with Jill, Pierre and myself and planted a kiss on Sophie's proffered lips. It was evident from the eager look in his eyes that he was looking forward to a night of passion with her. Little did he realise then that the poor girl was probably exhausted from energetic trysts with Peter and who knew who else.

"Hello, Sophie has told me all about your week at Ile Levant and I'm shocked," he said to us. We smiled, keen to elaborate. "I'll put my suitcase in a cabin and we'll go for an ice-cream and talk about it," he said, "I'll unpack later."

Pierre went to his cabin after the initial welcome, as did Sophie, wanting to prepare herself for the trip ashore and the promised ice cream.

"I don't think that's a good idea," I told him.

"What do you mean?" he asked.

"Well, you know that the boat is chartered, so theoretically it's not yours for this week."

"I thought there was just one person aboard," he argued.

"That's right, one person but it's now his boat so we should check with him first."

"Well, where am I expected to sleep?" he pleaded.

"I don't know but you can't sleep here without the charterer's permission."

"Of course I can, I own this boat," he told me.

"That's true, you own it but not for this week, you can stay here until the charterer comes back but then you may well have to leave. He's paid in advance for the entire boat for the week and it's up to him what he decides to do with it and who he has on board," I told him.

He was not happy. His face turned red, more with embarrassment than anger. He hovered for a while. Jill and I stood looking at him waiting for his reaction.

"Right, I'll leave my case here and go to find a hotel," he said.

"OK, I'm sorry but the boat and crew are here for the charterer's benefit this week."

Exasperated by what I'd said, he called down to the cabin to Sophie.

"Sophie, come on up here Cherie, we'll go and find a hotel."

She came up and they both went ashore. So Jill, Pierre and I didn't get our ice creams.

"Oh," he cried when he staggered backwards as his head collided with the transverse bar. The flag obviously wasn't conspicuous enough. Jill and

I felt sorry for Hervé as he wandered off with his muse, dejected and rubbing his forehead. He was a likeable person but I doubted that our charterer would have been pleased to find the owner sleeping on the boat he'd hired for himself. At the end of the afternoon they came back on board.

"I can't find a room in a hotel anywhere," he said as Sophie went down to her cabin.

"What will you do?" I asked.

"I'll have to stay on here; all the hotels are fully booked, I've nowhere else to go."

"Well, you can't stay without the charterer agreeing to it," I said, "in any case, he'll be returning soon, he usually comes back about now."

"Will you ask him if I can stay here? Explain my predicament to him and he'll understand."

"Yes, of course, he's a reasonable guy; I'll see what he says."

Hervé turned and descended the gangplank. He faltered when he reached the bar. He stared at it with trepidation, placed his hand on it as if that would prevent him from crashing into it, stooped lower than was necessary just to make sure, ducked under it, and went to look for a comfortable spot on a wall opposite us to await the arrival of the American.

"Hi," said the kindly American as he boarded.

"Hi, have you had a good day?" I asked.

"Yeah, great, Cannes is an interesting place," he replied.

"I've got something to ask you. The owner of the boat has turned up and he can't find a hotel room anywhere so he's asked me to ask you if you'd be kind enough to let him stay on board for tonight."

"Where is he now?" he enquired.

"That's him sitting over there on the wall." I pointed to the forlorn little figure sitting looking pleadingly at us with his little legs dangling down unable to reach the ground and his little arms by his sides, his hands tucked under his thighs.

"Why doesn't he ask me himself?" he said.

"I don't know, he probably thought it better if I asked you."

"Well, you can tell him that if he hasn't got the decency to come and ask me himself, the answer is no, he can't sleep here."

"I understand. I'll go and tell him," and off I went. His unhappy face looked at me expectantly as I approached. It was not a pleasant thing to have to tell him.

"I'm sorry, he said the answer is no. He thinks you should have asked him yourself."

"Well, I'll go and speak to him then. There are no rooms available anywhere. I can't stay here all night."

"I don't think it's a good idea if you just march aboard; let me talk to him again, maybe he's had time to rethink." I went back aboard and called down to his cabin.

"Excuse me, Mr Roberts, may I have a word with you?" I asked.

"Yes, of course, Captain, what is it?"

"The owner would like to talk to you. He's worried about where he'll stay tonight."

"That's not my problem. I've hired this boat for privacy and my answer is still no and I don't need to see him to tell him that."

"OK, I'll let him know," and off I went to break the news to Hervé.

He was totally deflated when I told him. Slowly, he slid down from the wall. His sad eyes gazed at me as if pleading with me to help him. There was nothing I could do and one thing was certain; he wouldn't be buying Jill and me the ice cream he'd promised us when he arrived. He set off once more in pursuit of a bed for the night, dragging his feet as he slunk away. Back on board, Jill was watching.

"Where's he going now?" she asked when I got back.

"He didn't say but he wasn't very happy."

It was Sod's law. That night the American didn't go ashore until very late and to compound the matter, he invited Jill and me for a cocktail on the aft deck. As we sat there with him, a despondent Hervé came back and sat again on the wall, staring at us as we enjoyed our drink and chat. We tried not to keep peeping at him to see what he was doing but the temptation was too great. We noticed that he never once stopped glaring in our direction. When at last the American left, Hervé came and collected his case.

"Do you have anything to eat?" he begged, "I haven't been able to find

248

a restaurant to serve me; they all say they have no room, I'm starving."

"We've already eaten; I don't know what's available. What have you got Jill?" I asked her.

"Oh, I'm sure I'll be able to find something; wait here," she said.
She reappeared shortly afterwards accompanied by Sophie.

"There's not a lot because we usually prefer to shop for fresh produce each day because the fridge isn't working very well and as we've already eaten, we can only offer you a sandwich," Jill told him.

"Anything, I don't care, just feed me, I'm so hungry and still don't know where I can spend the night," he said.
With that, Sophie went down to the galley to prepare a snack for him and he started to follow her.

"You do realise that there may be trouble if the charterer comes back and finds you here, don't you?" I warned him. He stopped.

"What, are you saying that I can't go down there to eat?" he said.

"No, I'm just pointing out that he wasn't happy that you asked if you could stay on board and he said categorically no, so there could be trouble if he comes back and finds you here."
He agreed that it would be better if he stayed on deck. Sophie brought him a sandwich which he devoured in seconds. He really was very hungry. She made him another and that too disappeared in a flash. When he'd scraped up and eaten all the remaining crumbs, he sent Sophie to retrieve his case and they both wandered off into the night together in search of accommodation. We didn't see them again until two days later when he brought Sophie back to resume her crew position. Hervé explained how they eventually found accommodation outside of Cannes, and he now seemed relaxed and happy after his two-day tryst with his Sophie, who was equally happy, judging by the radiant smile on her face. He gave me a wad of money for the running of the boat and departed, wishing us well. When the American left, he thanked us and gave us a substantial tip. It was an easy charter as there had been little for us to do. He ate all his meals ashore and apart from sleeping aboard, used the boat only to shower before he went ashore for the night. What a contrast to the previous charter!

CHAPTER 11
CORSICA AND SARDINIA

I only wanted to help

Within two weeks of the American leaving we were offered and accepted a two-week charter, this time going to Corsica and Northern Sardinia. The group consisted of a charming middle-aged French couple and their daughter and her husband who were in their 20's. We were waiting on the aft deck to greet them when they arrived in two cars. They unloaded their luggage and cases of food and wine onto the quay. Sophie and Pierre brought it all aboard whilst Jill and I welcomed the four newcomers and explained the accommodation arrangements.

"Hello Captain," each of them said as they came aboard and shook my hand.

"Hello, welcome aboard," I replied.

"Hello," they said to Jill, who shook their hands and then took them to the cabins below whilst I helped Sophie and Pierre with the luggage.

"We'd like to set sail for Corsica straight away Captain, where do you suggest we start?" The patriarch said.

I didn't hesitate; Calvi on the North West coast is often the first port of call for yachts heading to Corsica, so I suggested that and he agreed. When they had unpacked and got into clothing more suitable for the hot weather, Jill prepared a lunch for everyone from the produce they had brought aboard and Sophie served it to them on the table on the aft deck. We ate ours in the saloon and as soon as everybody had finished we prepared for sea. With everything battened down and the course set, I started the engines. It was always pleasurable to hear the twin engines start up, first one and then the second so that they thumped away in concert. It was music to my ears as it heralded a trip to sea once more. We cast off and motored slowly out of the port. We, the crew and the charterers were happy.

During the twelve hour passage to Calvi, we came to realise just how hot the cabin floors became after several hours cruising at high engine revolutions. The floors had been laid over the unlagged exhaust pipes and we were aware that they became hot, but the passage to Corsica revealed just how hot they could get. We had only cruised at low revolutions through the French canals and we hadn't been at sea for any length of time with the perverts. So, in addition to the decks being too hot to stand on, now the cabin soles were the same and we wondered what else could happen. The passage to Corsica was choppy but not too uncomfortable, which was a good thing because we were towing the heavy speedboat. Four-hour watches were arranged with Jill and me taking the first and last so that we would be on watch when we arrived. Night passages, when reasonably calm, were always enjoyable when everybody else was asleep and Jill and I were alone in the wheelhouse with the comforting throbbing of the engines beneath us. That's when we were able to discuss freely and enjoy those few hours alone, appreciating the exceptional position we were in - sailing to Corsica on a moonlit night, with moonbeams lighting up the sea to fluorescent silver. Those moments were unique and precious. When we were around twenty miles from Corsica we looked for the two flashes every ten seconds of La Revellata, the lighthouse that would lead us into Calvi. Making landfall in a foreign place was always one of the best moments of navigating. To see the flashing light, or if it was daylight, to see the town and harbour entrance of a place that we'd never been to before on the horizon, was always a thrill. It appeared exactly where and when we expected it to and it was in the early hours of the morning that we dropped anchor in the bay of Calvi. We pulled the speedboat alongside, lashed it into position and went to our bunks to sleep for the few hours remaining to us. We had a peaceful sleep, rocking gently in the swell and awoke to a stunning sight. Calvi is one of the most beautiful places in Corsica. The magnificent bay is protected from the Mistral and as the sun rose and shone on the town and the majestic mediaeval citadel that is perched on a granite rock, it took our breath away. We sat in awe on the foredeck enjoying our breakfast before the charterers awoke and started demanding our services. There were other yachts anchored and many smaller ones moored to the quay.

The Genoese had taken control of Calvi, together with Bonifacio and other important Corsican towns in 1161, and it became a confederate of Genoa in 1278. Six years later the entire island of Corsica was made a Republic of Genoa. The Corsicans rebelled against Genoese domination in 1729, led by Giacinto Paoli. The Genoese withdrew into their citadels and sent for foreign assistance, first from Austria and then from France. Defeated by professional troops, the Corsicans relinquished violence but kept their organisation. After surrendering to the French in 1739, Giacinto Paoli went into exile in Naples with his then 14-year-old son, Pasquale. An older brother, Clemente, remained at home to liaise with the Revolutionary Diet, or People's Assembly.

In 1755, Pasquale was persuaded by his brother Clemente to return from Naples to lead a revolution. The people of Corsica ratified a republican constitution that proclaimed Corsica a sovereign nation, independent from the Republic of Genoa. Paoli, the new president, occupied himself with building a modern state by establishing an administration, a justice system and a currency. Genoa responded by selling the sovereignty of Corsica in perpetuity to the French by secret treaty in 1764, allowing Genoese troops to be replaced quietly by French ones. When all was ready in 1768, the French made a public announcement of the union of Corsica with France and proceeded to the re-conquest. Paoli fought a guerilla war from the mountains but in 1769 he was defeated by vastly superior forces and took refuge in England, where he was fêted and given a state pension and a residence in New

Bond Street, London. He was an inspiration for freedom fighters everywhere, including the U.S., where his ideas influenced the setting up of their constitution. Later, in 1794, he returned to take Calvi again, this time in allegiance with the British. It was during the siege of Calvi that Admiral Horatio Nelson, who was a Captain at the time, lost an eye when a shell exploded on the ramparts sending a shower of rock splinters towards him, one of which caused his injury. For two years Paoli led Corsica for a second time, supported by the British. He was finally defeated in 1796, when Corsica was definitively returned to French rule, but there is still a vibrant, and sometimes violent nationalist movement to this day. Paoli died in exile in London in 1807, aged 82, and a bust was erected that same year in Westminster Abbey to commemorate him.

The charterers awoke late. They hadn't slept well during the crossing because of the rolling of the boat in the choppy sea, but they were anxious to go ashore and explore the enticing town. Once they'd finished breakfast I told Pierre to take the family ashore in the tender and then come back for Jill and me. We had a wonderful time exploring and then at a pre-arranged time, Pierre came to take us back to Passing Fancy so that he and Sophie could then look around themselves. It was very late in the day when the charterers signalled us from the shore. Pierre went to collect them and when they boarded, they produced fresh spiny lobsters that they had bought from one of the local fishermen. They handed them to Jill to cook and then shared them with us. We had such a good time in Calvi.

Very early the next morning, we weighed anchor for a 75 nautical mile journey south to Ajaccio, the capital of Corsica. Ajaccio was ruled by the Romans from the 2nd century onwards, but by the 8th century, the city was deserted and ceased to exist. It was rebuilt by the Genoese at the end of the 15th century as they sought to assert their control over the southern part of the island. Corsicans were banned but as the city grew and prospered they gradually integrated. Napoleon Bonaparte, whose father had been a secretary to Pasquale Paoli, was born in Ajaccio in 1769, the same year as the siege of Calvi. In the 19th century, Ajaccio became a popular winter resort for the wealthy, in particular, the English. In early September 1943, the inhabitants rebelled against the Nazis and it was subsequently the first French town to be liberated from the German occupiers on the 9th September – an honour often erroneously awarded to Bayeux in Normandy, which wasn't liberated until the 7th June 1944.

We arrived there at night and moored stern to the quay, which required us to rig up the gangplank. The first person to use it to go ashore the following morning suffered a nasty crack on the head. Once again the warning flag had failed. Before they left to visit the town they informed me that one of the toilets wasn't working. These were a constant problem. The mechanisms were such that a seacock needed to be opened and then a lever at the side was pumped to bring in sea water. The next procedure was to press down on a foot pedal to open a flap valve, close the seacock for the inlet, open another seacock for the outlet and pump the lever again to empty the toilet straight into the sea. Nothing was to go into the toilet except pee, poo and paper but there were times when other objects were thrown in despite instructions to the guests not to do so. When that happened, the flap valve would not work and the excrement and paper would churn around and remain in the toilet bowl.

There were always plenty of jobs to do when we arrived in port; the salt had to be washed off the boat, stowed items brought back out, sun lounger cushions placed on the decks, flowers put on the aft deck and so on - so having to repair toilets as well was exasperating. I sent Pierre down to get it working again while Sophie and I hosed down the boat. Once I'd finished my chores I decided to see how he was progressing. Jill was busy in the galley.

"Have you seen Pierre?" I asked her.

"He's still down there cursing away," she said smiling, and I could hear strange Flemish expletives floating up from below. I smiled too and we both laughed as he grunted and blasphemed.

"He's taking a long time, I'd better see if he needs any help," I said.

"He's not happy, better make sure you don't upset him anymore," she warned.

I descended the stairs and saw him on his knees with his head over the toilet and an array of tools on the floor.

"How're you doing there Pierre?" I asked.

"Bloody thing, not good," he replied in his broken English. He looked at me, distraught.

I leant over to look in the toilet. It was full of brown water, mangled up paper and excrement and stank horribly. Pierre went back to work with his head over the foul, stinking mess and with a rod prodded at the flap valve.

"What happens when you pump it?" I asked and pumped away vigorously on the lever.

"AAAARGH, AAAARGH, AAARGH, "Pierre screamed as he shot upright as fast as lightening. He stared at me in horror. The contents of the toilet bowl had shot up with an explosive force. He had a million more brown freckles than he normally had and tiny bits of brown mangled up paper and excrement stuck to his face and hair.

"AAARGH," he screamed again as he rushed into the shower.

I collapsed on the floor in laughter. Jill heard the screams and came running down to see what horrible accident had occurred.

"What happened?" she cried. I was hysterical. I sat on the floor holding my stomach; it was hurting so much from laughing.

"I ... I," I couldn't say any more, I was laughing too much. I pointed to the toilet and made a pumping movement with my hand to try and explain what had happened.

"AAARGH," came another cry from the shower as Pierre scrubbed frenziedly at his face and then another cry "AAARGH." Jill started to laugh.

"Pierre ... Pierre," I tried to tell her what had happened but couldn't. Each time I tried to talk I just burst into laughter. I pumped my hand again at an imaginary lever as I pointed to the toilet with my other hand and then pointed to the shower, then threw both my hands up to mimic the foul, stinking mess flying up in the air. She got the message and convulsed into laughter herself, collapsing alongside me as we listened to the cursing and scrubbing taking place in the shower. We laughed so much it hurt. Pierre was in the shower for so long he must have used up a lot of our water supply. Eventually, Jill and I managed to control ourselves. Pierre came out of the shower and stood in the doorway of the toilet compartment looking at us with the most disgusted look imaginable on his face. When we saw him, we just cracked up and broke into laughter once more. "There is nothing in the world so irresistibly contagious as laughter and good humour." – Charles Dickens.

The Captain knows best

We stayed in Ajaccio for the rest of that day and Jill and I paid a brief visit to the Napoleon museum, which had originally been his home. The next day, with Pierre still rubbing his face, we set off for Propriano, 25 miles south of Ajaccio. This lovely town, located on the southern shore of the beautiful Propriano Bay in South West Corsica, is surrounded by magnificent beaches of white sand and we couldn't resist the temptation to anchor off one of them. It was perfectly calm; the breeze of the previous day had died down and there was only one other yacht there. Swathes of the beach were covered in linen laid out to dry by the local women. It was hot and Pierre took the charterers ashore to the beach, where they stayed for lunch leaving us alone. He then came back and the four of us went ashore to explore for a while. Later, back on board, we swam in the unbelievably clear water. It was sublime. The charterers returned sometime after they'd finished their lunch - and since it was such a glorious place to be, we stayed there until late afternoon and then went to Propriano for the night. This delightful town and port were developed in the early 19th century when a road was built to connect Ajaccio to Bonifacio. It was once inhabited by Romans, Greeks and Turks but very little remains of the early settlements that were subjected to frequent invasions by Vandals in the 5th century, Saracens in the 8th century and pirates in the 18th century, when it was pretty much destroyed.

The next day we did a short 30 mile run to Bonifacio on the southern tip of the island, the setting for Guy de Maupassant's story "Vendetta". When we rounded the Cape to the southern coast, the scenery changed to oddly shaped, precipitous white limestone cliffs and as we approached them we saw the gleaming white buildings of the old town perched 70 metres up on a 1600 metre long, 100 metre wide promontory. The buildings extended along the top of the cliffs and because the cliffs below had been worn away by the rough seas for which this area is renowned, it looked as if the buildings were overhanging the precipice. We rounded the promontory and followed a 200 metre wide channel leading to the port. It was then, and still is, one of the most spectacular harbours in the Mediterranean and totally protected from winds of any direction. We cruised along the fjord-like channel that was once part of a valley leading to inland Corsica. Sea levels were much lower in prehistoric times and the islands in the Bonifacio Strait were connected to each other and to the mainland. Bonifacio remains one of my favourite places. The old town was originally a fortress built in 828 by Boniface II of Tuscany to defend the Tuscany boundaries and was subsequently named after him. Over the years it was subject to numerous attacks, but the worst disaster was in 1528, when the plague killed 4,300 of the 5,000 inhabitants.

The new town extends along the length of the inlet and at the far end, we reached the crowded harbour. There are often many yachts moored here seeking protection from the wind and waiting for it to subside so that they can navigate the Bonifacio Strait. Fortunately, it was calm when we arrived. I motored in and saw an opening between two yachts. I spun Passing Fancy around 180 degrees, dropped the anchor and backed onto the quay.

The sun was blazing down as usual the next morning but the weather forecast was predicting more wind than we'd had over the previous days. The charterers went ashore to do some shopping, and Jill and I were sitting on the aft deck when they came back. They informed us that they wanted to go to Porto Cervo on the Costa Smeralda in Northern Sardinia and have lunch at sea on the way. Jill and I gave each other knowing looks.

"The idea would be reasonable if it were a calm sea, but the forecast is for more wind than usual today and the Bonifacio Strait is renowned for wind and rough seas. My advice is to have lunch here and then set off, we'll still be there well before nightfall," I said.

"Oh no, there isn't any wind at all," the Father said.

"Well, there isn't in here, we're completely protected in this inlet," I told him.

"Oh it can't be that bad, let's go, we like the idea of lunch on deck whilst we're cruising along in the sunshine," he argued.

"Well, if that's what you want but I want to point out that it may be a bit uncomfortable."

"It will be no problem, we don't mind if it's a little choppy. There's not that much wind," he insisted. Jill and I looked at each other again and I could see that she wasn't pleased. When they'd gone, I said, "This is going to be fun."

"I'm not sure what I'm going to be able to do in that tiny excuse for a galley," she said.

"Well, I'm sure you'll think of something simple and doable." Jill thought about it for a while aware of the difficulty we would face.

"There's not much because of that stupid fridge. There's a packet of chicken legs, I think I'll cook them to have with a salad."

"Sounds good. Bearing in mind that it's going to be a rough ride, I think we might as well get going before the wind gets too strong and get it over with so that at least we'll get to Porto Cervo with time to relax afterwards," I said.

"Oh, what fun we're going to have," she said and disappeared down to the galley.

Pierre and Sophie were sitting on the foredeck and I called them to tell them what the plan was. I then sent Sophie down to the galley to help Jill. Pierre and I prepared for sea in a leisurely manner to allow the girls plenty of time to fix the food. We cast off, and towing the speedboat, motored out of the protection of the inlet. I could see some white caps in the distance and it looked choppy. The Bonifacio Strait has a notorious reputation among sailors because of the many islands, shoals, strong currents and rough seas whipped up by the wind. From the West or the East, it funnels through the narrow 10 mile channel that separates Corsica from Sardinia to the South. In the summer months it is common for strong winds to blow from the west and anything above force 4 further out to sea causes an uncomfortable sea in the strait, where the wind strength can reach from force 7 to force 9. It wasn't that strong when we left but strong enough and likely to increase as the day wore on. We headed into it. The charterers were laughing; they seemed to be enjoying it as we began to roll.

That soon changed. Porto Cervo was 30 nautical miles away, not too far but far enough when being thrown around like a cork. I set a course to pass clear of the Lavezzi Islands that lie 5 nautical miles south-east of Bonifacio. The further out we motored, the worse it got and it wasn't long before the charterers began to regret their decision. Pierre stood on the aft deck for a while to keep watch on the speedboat that was careering around behind us as we rolled violently from one side to the other and I could hear the curses and the clattering of dishes from the galley. Jill had to find a way to wedge herself in to remain standing upright and at the same time prevent the dishes from flying around and spilling their contents. By the time she and Sophie had finished and it was time to set the table we were well out into the thick of it. The charterers were determined. They sat at the table on the aft deck and I called Pierre and told him to help the girls serve the meal. He set the table and the charterers held everything in place. Sophie passed up the plates of food, two at a time and Pierre performed the amazing feat of keeping himself upright as he staggered to the aft deck and put the food on the table, followed by Jill, who repeated the same precarious balancing act. Sophie was down in the galley tidying up and stowing loose items. It was never going to work. The charterers were holding everything in place on the table and unsuccessfully trying to scoop the food into their mouths with one hand whilst with the other they tried to hold onto the plates, the wine glasses and wine. They just didn't have enough hands; even a group of octopi would have had difficulty. In addition, they'd started to feel the effects of the motion. They got very annoyed and called Jill.

"We can't eat like this, can't you do something?" The patriarch said.

"How can I do anything, I can't stop the boat from rolling around," she said.

"Well this is ridiculous, look at it, everything's on the move," he said as his hands flew across the table grabbing the moving objects. The other three were doing the same. Hands and arms were going in all directions to stop things from sliding across the table. They never did manage to eat anything and started to look decidedly queasy.

"This was a stupid idea; you should have listened to the Captain," his wife yelled at him.

"Well, what do you want me to do?" he yelled back then turned to Jill.

"Jill, you've got to do something."

"Oh, just take it all away, Jill," his wife said.

"Shall I keep it for later?" asked Jill.

"No, no, just throw the bloody stuff away, I don't feel like it now," and she rushed from the table.

"That was a stupid idea, we can't eat it, it may as well be thrown away," she said as she passed me on her way to her cabin.

I called Pierre and Sophie to go and help Jill clear away and maintaining their balance, they made short shrift of it. The other three charterers rushed down below, no doubt to throw up. As Jill passed me with two plates of food, she looked and at me and giggled and I smiled back at her.

"Is that being thrown away?" I asked.

"That's what Madame said," she replied.

"Well, I'll have that," I said, grabbing the chicken leg and the rest of the crew did the same.

When everything was cleared and stowed away, Jill, Sophie and Pierre came to join me in the wheelhouse. We couldn't help but laugh about it all.

Once clear of the Lavezzi Islands, I altered course, steering east to pass to the north of the Santa Maria Islands that lie off the northern coast of Sardinia. The sea was then on our stern creating a more comfortable corkscrewing motion and not so much rolling from side to side. When we'd cleared Santa Maria and started heading south-east again to pass east of Isola Maddalena, the sea got a little calmer and by the time we reached the island of Caprera, the charterers reappeared and asked again for something to eat. Jill took no chances this time, she prepared a huge bowl of couscous which she took to them, placed on the table with four forks and left them to it.

A load of tripe

The Costa Smeralda in northeastern Sardinia is the most popular part of the island for yachtsmen. There are lots of small islands and plenty of majestic, well-sheltered bays with large, deserted beaches of pristine white sands, where yachts can anchor in crystal clear blue water. Porto Cervo (deer port) is set on the southern and eastern shore of a magnificent sheltered, natural harbour. It was a poor, isolated area until Prince Karim Aga Khan Ismaili visited and saw its potential. In 1962, together with a consortium of international industrialists and financiers, he transformed that part of the coast and built the port. It is one of the most expensive yacht harbours in the world with some of the most expensive properties, some are reputed to be worth up to 300,000€ per square metre. The sumptuous hotels and gourmet restaurants are all designed to ensure that the rich and famous who go there will want for nothing. It became an instant success. We anchored in the bay and leaving Pierre and Sophie aboard, Jill and I took the charterers ashore in the speedboat. We had a good look around then went back so that the other two could do the same. We spent a calm, comfortable night there.

Porto Rotondo is just 15 miles south of Porto Cervo and that is where we went the following morning. This port was developed in the 1960's by a Venetian consortium and is entirely dedicated to tourism. It lies between two bays, Cugagna and Marinella and is a favourite spot for the International jet set. We dropped anchor in the bay of Marinella to the east of the port and stayed there for lunch. It was a beautiful bay, totally protected from the wind; the sun beat down from a clear blue sky and we spent the time swimming in crystal clear water. Towards the end of the day, we returned to Porto Cervo for the evening and anchored. The charterers went ashore for an evening meal, leaving us four crew members to enjoy a meal on the aft deck. It had been so delightful in the bay of Marinella that we went back again the next day. Nobody was in a hurry to leave, so we weighed anchor much later than intended and set course for Porto Vecchio, 50 miles away in southern Corsica.

It was dark when we arrived at the entrance to the large, well-protected Gulf and the many resorts along the northern shore were lit up. We motored along in the Gulf for three miles, where it then turned to the south; the port was a further two miles away, tucked into the far southwestern corner. Porto Vecchio means "old port" and the name is probably derived from the remains of an old Roman port, which may well have been abandoned because of the prevalent malaria in this once marshland area. It was rebuilt by the Genoese in 1539. They preserved the Roman ruins within the city walls and established salt flats producing

1000 tons of salt a year. Most of the inhabitants died from malaria and subsequent settlers suffered the same fate in 1546. The town has been inhabited and abandoned numerous times and many unsuccessful attempts had been made to drain the marshes. It wasn't until malaria affected the Allied troops when they landed there in WWII that the marshes were finally drained and filled and the mosquitoes were destroyed with spray. Since then the population has expanded.

The fortified town is built on a steep, seventy-metre high hill overlooking the harbour and it looked very inviting when we entered and moored up. We were hungry as our food supply was very low - we'd not bought anything since we'd left Bonifacio. As soon as the gangplank was lowered, the charterers scarpered off to find a restaurant. We had to wash off the salt that covered the boat and tidy up and by the time we'd finished, it was almost ten p.m. Starving, we wasted no time dressing for a shore excursion to find somewhere to eat. Feeling tired as well as hungry, we climbed the narrow, cobbled streets, but the further we climbed the more despondent we became. Each restaurant we found was either closed or wouldn't serve us because it was too late. We were getting more and more disheartened, until finally, high up in the town, we came across a small, dark eating place. To call it a restaurant would be stretching the limits of the imagination but the lights were on, so we went in and were welcomed, more or less, by an elderly, tanned woman dressed in black and an equally elderly, unshaven male. He had a modicum of salt and pepper hair and was also dressed in dour clothing, covered with a filthy apron, which had once been white. The place was completely empty and we were about to find out why. The few tables that were there were covered in blue and white checked plastic tablecloths and the lights had low wattage bulbs. The floor was tiled with terrazzo tiles. It looked dirty but it may have just appeared so because of the poor lighting.

"Bonsoir Madame, Can we eat?" I asked.

She looked at her companion who we presumed was the cook and he nodded agreement.

"Mais oui," she replied.

"Can we see the menu please?"

"Tripe," she said. (Pronounced treep.)

"Pardon?" I enquired.

"Treep," she repeated.

"Is that all?" we asked.

"Treep," she replied. She wasn't a particularly vocal person. We looked at each other. Jill had never been a lover of offal; I, on the other hand, would eat anything and love to try anything new. Sophie and Pierre had bemused looks on their faces. We had two choices, tripe or treep, or nothing, so reluctantly we chose the tripe. A litre bottle of red wine, that we hadn't ordered, was placed on the table. We didn't complain. It was drinkable and most welcome. When the wine was half finished, Madame came from the kitchen carrying two plates, followed by the gentleman who had until then not uttered a word, carrying the other two. She placed her two plates on the table and before Monsieur could do the same she stopped him. She then took a serviette from the table nearest to ours and with brisk waves of her arm, brushed crumbs from our table in all directions, scattering them all over us. We recoiled. We hadn't expected that but found it highly amusing. The tripe looked and smelled disgusting, and it tasted exactly as it looked and smelled. In fact, to be completely accurate, it was utterly revolting. It was the first time any of us had eaten tripe and Jill and I made sure it was the last. We have never forgotten that meal but we were so hungry we ate it and with another litre of wine to accompany it we became inebriated enough to momentarily forget how awful it was.

We stayed the next day and night in Porto Vecchio. The forecast was excellent the next day and I suggested to the guests that we spend the day in a peaceful anchorage at the Lavezzi Islands, the most southerly point of Corsica and France and only a short distance away. The area can be dangerous because of the strong currents and large number of reefs. In 1855, the wooden French frigate La Semillante left Toulon with 380 sailors and 393 soldiers aboard en route to the Crimean war and got caught in a violent storm at the mouth of the Bonifacio Strait. She ran aground on the reefs, broke up and sank on the night of 15 February with the loss of every soul on board. Only 560 bodies were washed up onto the coast. The others were never recovered. An altar is dedicated to them on the island of Lavezzi where they were buried in the two naval cemeteries, one for the captain and the priest and the other for the remaining 558. That was one of the heaviest losses of life in the history of the French navy.

The uninhabited Lavezzi archipelago is made up of six small granite islands around the main one, Lavezzi, where it is possible to find an anchorage in two small, unprotected bays with rocks on either side. Prudence is paramount but the weather was set to be perfect; it was too good an opportunity to miss visiting this little piece of paradise. We left after a late breakfast in a calm sea with no wind and a clear blue sky. Studying the chart carefully to avoid the multitude of rocks in the pristine water, I motored into the inlet on the eastern side of the island where we dropped anchor and stayed for the majority of the day. The sea there is rich in aquatic fauna and flora; coral, mother of pearl, sponges, grouper, turtles and dolphins. It was a wonderful day and everybody was happy. Towards the end of the afternoon, we weighed anchor and set off for Bonifacio for the night. From there we made our way back to Calvi stopping off once more at the places we'd already visited.

On the day before the charter finished and well before any charterers were awake, we set sail from Calvi very early in the morning in a light wind that increased as we sailed on. By the afternoon, it blew fairly hard and since we were heading straight into it, Passing Fancy was pitching uncomfortably in the choppy sea. We arrived at Port Pierre-Canto in the evening, by which time, thankfully, the wind had decreased and the sea had flattened out. We'd had an amazing cruise but it was good to be back in our home port and moored to the quay. The charterers went ashore to eat in a restaurant. Pierre and I washed the salt from the boat, Sophie tidied up the cabins and the rest of the inside whilst Jill cooked a succulent meal that we ate on the aft deck in the warm evening air, discussing the good and bad points of the two weeks we'd had in Corsica and Sardinia. In the morning, after they'd placed their baggage on the quay, the charterers came back aboard to thank us and give us a large tip before they said goodbye. For the remainder of that day we just rested and in the evening, with the money they'd given us, we went to a restaurant and enjoyed a relaxing meal.

The heat in the wheelhouse had been unbearable each day in Corsica and Sardinia and I insisted that Hervé did something about it. He was reluctant to spend more time and money and it was only when Sophie told him that she would leave him if he didn't that he relented. He sent a small team of his workforce down from Belgium with two of the plastic hatches that he fitted to his fleet of coaches. They were installed within a few days but not only were they totally ineffectual, they looked ridiculous and were not items one would normally fit to what was supposed to be a luxury yacht. The constant faults and defects were becoming more and more tiresome to live with.

CHAPTER 12
ASCENDING TO THE LIGHT

Creepy Crawlies

Another one week charter was offered by the agency. It was for three French couples, a young married couple, their parents and grandparents. They too wanted to go to the ever popular Corsica, in particular, Ile Rousse, visiting Calvi first. Crouched over the small dining table in the saloon, I laid off the course. Jill, Pierre and Sophie stowed everything and closed the portholes. I started the engines. The gangplank was hauled in and stowed, the anchor heaved in and we set off late in the afternoon. The charterers weren't affected by the choppy sea but they were affected by the heat in the cabins that had the unlagged exhaust pipes running beneath them. The cabins became so hot that the charterers found it difficult to sleep as we motored through the night; standing on the floors barefoot was painful, which made it difficult when they wanted to get up in the night to use the toilet, especially for the elderly couple. Getting out of the bunks with the boat rolling around was bad enough without having the hot cabin sole to contend with as well. We heard someone cry out in shock and Jill went to investigate. She saw the grandfather dash into the companionway and hop along painfully on alternate feet to the toilet compartment. She stood at the top of the stairs to make sure he was OK. When he came back, she watched him take a flying leap from the companionway into the cabin in the hope of making it to the bunk without having to negotiate the hot floor. A loud crash and a yell told us he hadn't made it. The distance, though small, was too much for him and he'd crashed into the side of the bunk and collapsed onto the hot floor. The younger ones acquired a slick manoeuvre, jumping into the cabin and planting one foot momentarily on the floor whilst they grabbed the side of the bunk and vaulted in. They were not happy. Understandably, as the charter fee was costing them thousands of francs per day. It was surprising that during the season we didn't get more complaints, or more serious consequences as charterers were forced to leap across the cabin each time they wanted to get to their bunks.

Twelve hours after leaving Cannes we dropped anchor in Calvi Bay and managed to grab a couple of hours sleep. Come morning, the couples were anxious to get ashore after having been thrown around for most of the night because of the rough sea and suffering burnt feet from the hot cabin floors, so I told Pierre to take them in the speedboat. He thought it would be funny to play a practical joke on them. It wasn't funny and was not appreciated by them, expressly by the elderly gentleman who was the target. The outboard motor wouldn't start so Pierre removed the seat cushion and the hatch that was covering the battery compartment to check the wiring, which was okay, then went back to check the ignition switch at the fore part of the boat. Meanwhile, two other speed boats roared past us and the wash from their propellers caused our speedboat to roll around and sent grandad falling backwards onto the battery.

"Attention, that's 2000 volts!" screamed Pierre.
The terrified gentleman shot upright grabbing hold of the others to maintain his balance; his face was white with fright. Pierre found it all highly amusing and fell about laughing. Nobody else was the least bit amused and I wasn't happy when I was told about it.

Jill and Sophie kept the inside of the yacht clean. They made up the bunks each day, did the shopping and Jill cooked the meals, putting into practice all that she'd learned on her cookery course in Southampton and improved constantly. The elderly gentleman either had the shit scared out of him during the overnight passage or had a bowel problem that caused him to evacuate part of its contents whilst lying in his bunk, or maybe he couldn't get to the toilet in time, or couldn't face leaping across the hot floor. Either way, Jill had to clean up his soiled sheets, a distasteful task which occurred more than once during the charter.

The next day, we weighed anchor and headed off to Ile Rousse, a beautiful place to visit, with its very popular, long, immaculate, white sand beaches. The town is set in a natural harbour protected by six small islets, which these days are connected to the mainland by a causeway. The principle island is Ile de la Pietra, composed of red porphyry rock, hence the name, which was originally Isola Rossa (Red Island) when Corsica was under Italian administration. Earlier, under Roman rule, it was known as Rubico Rocega (Red Rock).

In 1759, when Corsica gained its short-lived independence, Pasquale Paoli decided to build a port in the north west of the island to try and intercept maritime traffic between Genoa and Calvi. Ile Rousse seemed an obvious choice, since it had already been a small fishing port for centuries. The new port and town were laid out progressively over the next hundred years and a fort was constructed to protect the town, which had in the past been prone to attacks from the sea. The port is now the most important in volume of maritime traffic after Ajaccio and Bastia. A statue of Pasquale was erected in 1864 in the Place Paoli in the centre of town. Ile Rousse and Saint Florent are the only communes in Corsica with French names, all others, which were founded by the Genoese in the middle ages, still retain their Italian names.

We went alongside the jetty constructed on Ile de la Pietra and once we'd finished mooring up the charterers asked me to take them in the speedboat to a beach they knew west of the islets, where they wanted to spend the day. When we got there, they disembarked and requested that I pick them up in time to return to Passing Fancy to prepare for an evening meal in a restaurant ashore. Jill and I spent some much appreciated time together, wandering around the town and enjoying a relaxing meal on board and Sophie and Pierre also took some time off. At

17.30 hours, dressed in swimming trunks and flip-flops, I started the outboard motor and motored slowly around the Ile de la Pietra into the open sea where I opened up the throttle. The boat leapt forward and I headed west to meet the charterers at the pre-arranged spot on the beach. It was a good feeling racing through the waves alone in the sunshine into a slight head on breeze, so I turned and headed further out to sea at a rate of knots to prolong the thrill. I shouldn't have done that!

There was a crack. The engine stopped and the bow sank down as the boat came to a sudden halt a fair distance from the Ile de la Pietra. I tried starting the engine again, and again, and again. It wouldn't start and it became obvious that no matter what I did, it wasn't going to start. I was in a very awkward predicament. The charterers were sitting on the beach in their swimwear expecting me. I was too far from the port and the shore to attract attention, in fact, I had no means of contacting anybody and the wind was increasing a little. I sat for a while weighing up the options available to me. There weren't many. I surveyed my surroundings and there was nothing but the red rock with the lighthouse at the top, otherwise open sea all around me. My glance kept returning to the lighthouse perched way up high. I guessed there had to be a road leading from it, which must ultimately lead down into the town or somewhere nearby. However, I wondered if I could scale the rock dressed in flip flops and swimming trunks.

There didn't seem to be a choice but how was I going to get there? I looked around for something to use as a paddle and the only loose items in the boat were the seat cushions. I grabbed one and holding it at one end, with my other hand in its middle I pushed it into the water. It just bent in half and floated to the surface. I found a way of holding it by placing my arm along its length to keep it under water and by submerging my arm and the cushion together I started paddling as best I could on one side, but apart from spinning the boat around in a circle, I didn't move. It clearly wasn't going to work so I discarded the cushion and looked for something else. The only other place to look was under the bow section where there were all manner of bits and pieces of rope, a bailer, a sponge and other completely useless articles. Underneath everything, I found a small paddle, barely more than half a metre in length but I was overjoyed to see it. I pulled it out and started paddling. The problem was, by paddling on one side of the boat I was again turning around in circles. The distance from one side to the other was too great for it to be practical to keep changing sides, so I crawled along to lie on the front section of the boat with the upper part of my torso suspended over the bow, which immediately sank down with my weight, causing the stern section to ride up high behind me, and sending me slithering forward at a frightening rate towards the sea. I grabbed at anything that was in reach to arrest my flight and lay for a while wondering how best to proceed. Once I'd decided on a plan of action, I used my feet to keep me in place on the slippery surface of the gelcoat so that my hands were free to use the paddle. I set off. Not very much happened but with perseverance, slowly, exceedingly slowly, worryingly slowly, the boat moved forward a little at a. time. It was uncomfortable leaning over almost in the water with my head tilted up as far as possible to see where I was heading. It took a long time, so long in fact that by the time I finally reached the rock it was dark.

There was by that time a fair swell running, which battered the boat against the rocks when I reached them, making it difficult for me to get ashore. Judging the distance and the right moment, I leapt onto the sharp, jagged rocks, carrying the boat's painter in one hand and grabbing a rock with the other to prevent myself from toppling over. Exhausted, I looked around for a place to tie the boat so that I could return for it if I ever made it back to Passing Fancy. I made it fast to a suitable rock then sat down and rested, dreading the climb up to the lighthouse in the dark. I had never liked heights, my legs would wobble just watching a film of someone high up. I stared up once more at where the lighthouse, now hidden from sight, ought to be. I gritted my teeth, mustered up the courage and set off.

I do not recommend rock climbing in the dark dressed in swimming trunks and flip-flops. I couldn't see much, so felt for hand and foot holds and pushed and pulled myself up. As I gained height I began sweating with the effort, which encouraged all manner of insects to stick to me. I didn't dare to try and brush them off for fear of falling. When I poked my fingers and toes into the tiny, sharp crevices to give me purchase they got cut and bled, which just attracted more insects to come and bite me and feed on my blood. Halfway up I thought of the three rules of mountaineering, "It's always further than it looks. It's always taller than it looks. And it's always harder than it looks". It was almost 23.00 hours when I finally made it to the top. I collapsed over the topmost part of the rock and about three metres from me was a couple of lovers sitting on a bench in each other's arms. They ignored me completely. They were so entranced with each other that they were oblivious of the arrival of a bloodied, exhausted, half-naked foreigner emerging from the sea and collapsing in front of them. I lay there drained for a while staring at them in disbelief. They looked at me but didn't move or show any sign of concern or interest in my sudden and unexpected appearance.

Once recovered, I staggered to my cut and painful feet and hobbled past them. At the very least, a "Good evening" wouldn't have gone amiss, even though it would have been extraordinary in such unusual circumstances. I shuffled wearily downhill along the road wondering where I would finish up when the most wonderful apparition appeared before me. There were Jill and Pierre walking uphill towards me. It was their last act before alerting the authorities.

On the way back to Passing Fancy I was told that the charterers had waited in vain and eventually hailed a taxi to bring them back to Ile Rousse in time for a belated meal ashore and then returned and went to their cabins, worrying about what had happened to me and how their holiday would be affected. I was ravenous and drained when we reached Passing Fancy. I had a whisky, a shower, a meal and wine and related to the crew in full technicolour all the details of my adventure. After that, I slept soundly.

The next morning I approached a local fisherman and persuaded him to take me to where I'd left the speedboat and to tow it back to the port for me. In the daylight, the rock looked a lot less steep and a lot less high than when I'd scaled it in the pitch black of the night. Surprisingly, the boat wasn't as badly damaged as I'd feared considering it had been battered against the rocks all night by the swell. It transpired that the cylinder head had cracked, which is the reason it wouldn't start. The sea around Corsica and onwards to Cannes can be very rough when the Mistral blows and it can pick up in the blink of an eye. Towing a speedboat across a hundred miles of open sea can be problematic even in calm conditions, so I hoped the weather would be kind when it came time to go back.

We stayed another day and night in Ile Rousse and the following day set course for Capraia, 18 nautical miles east of Corsica, leaving the speedboat safely moored to the quay. Capraia is a volcanic island of just 19 square kilometres, which had been a penal colony until 1986 and is the third largest of a chain of seven islands forming the National Park of the Tuscan Archipelago between the Tyrrhenian and the Ligurian Seas. Elba is the largest and Giglio the second largest. It was called Caprara in Roman times after the wild capers that grew there and was occupied by Pasquale Paoli's troops during the Corsican administration. The island has an outstanding wild, Mediterranean landscape with exceptional fauna, including mouflons that were introduced to the area during the Neolithic period. They have adapted to the mountainous interiors of the Mediterranean islands and are one of the two ancestors of all modern sheep. There are also colonies of European shags that feed mostly from the bottom of the sea and they have been recorded to dive to a depth of 45 metres.

We dropped anchor in a spectacular bay on the east coast in incredibly clear water. We could see the anchor lying on the seabed of white sand at a depth of ten metres and the swimming was fabulous. We spent a glorious, peaceful day and night in those idyllic surroundings before heading back to Ile Rousse for two more days, after which we cast off for the return passage to Cannes. Fortunately, the weather was agreeable and I was able to tow the inoperative speedboat with no difficulty. Back in Cannes, under Hervé's instruction, we left it tied to the quay so that it could be inspected by the vendor since it was still under guarantee. The charterers thanked us. They were happy with their holiday despite the mishaps and gave us a hefty tip before they left. When we'd cleaned and stowed everything, we used the tips to treat ourselves to a meal in a local restaurant.

The two hatches that had been fitted to ventilate the wheel house served no purpose. Not only did they provide no ventilation but the sun shone through the plastic, if anything making it even hotter.

CHAPTER 13
IT'S SUPPOSED TO BE SUNNY

And then we were three

B y the very nature of yachting, the boats were constantly on the move and at one stage we were moored next to a yacht owned by a music mogul who was a regular judge on the TV program Juke Box Jury. He was friendly and we came to know him and his brother quite well. It goes without saying that celebrities were a standard feature of the Cote d'Azur and Jill went weak at the knees one day when she met the handsome Tony Curtis. A film company was interested in chartering us for a TV series called the Persuaders and they arrived with Tony and his co-star Roger Moore but that's another story on another yacht and in any case, they didn't choose us, which is just as well as Jill may have been a bit uncontrollable. But back to Passing Fancy. When the music impresario left and his place was taken by a beautiful, modern yacht, the owner had noticed how conscientious we were and how hard we worked and asked us to leave Passing Fancy to take command of his yacht on a permanent basis. It would have been a well-paid job and a definite step up the ladder on a yacht that we would have been proud of. Alas, we declined. We didn't want to let Hervé down, so as tempting as it was, we stayed on the disaster-prone Passing Fancy.

Sophie often disappeared for days and nights. There were so many eager young men who called by seeking out her administrations that we never knew which one, if any, had struck lucky. Additionally, she still spent time with Peter who had moved to the old harbour of Cannes. Whatever she was participating in with all these young men was certainly energising her. She couldn't seem to get enough of it, much to the delight of her male suitors. Then, one morning after one of the rare occasions when she'd slept aboard Passing Fancy, she didn't appear for the usual routine of breakfast and boat maintenance.

"She is unwell," Pierre told Jill and me over breakfast.

"I'm not surprised after all that she's been up to," I said, "What's the matter with her?"

"I don't know," he said. "She won't open the door to her cabin." When we had no guests on board she and Pierre each had their own cabin.

"Well, you'd better go and see if she's OK. We may have to call a doctor if it's serious."

Pierre went back down to her cabin and after a while came back up looking worried.

"She's had a miscarriage," he said.

Jill and I looked at each other, wondering how we would handle the unexpected event when Hervé next made one of his regular phone calls to talk to Sophie. Fortunately for us it was Pierre who took the call; he chatted at length with Hervé and had no choice but to tell him what had happened. A few days later Hervé flew down to Cannes, by which time Sophie had moved in again with Peter. Hervé was not happy.

"Where is she?" he demanded of me when he found her cabin empty.

"I'm not certain but I believe she may be with somebody in the old harbour of Cannes," I replied truthfully since I didn't know where Peter's boat was moored; only that he was in the old harbour. Hervé sensed my reluctance to get involved in what was a domestic crisis so he turned to Pierre. They had a lengthy chat on the quay out of earshot but since they conversed in their native language I wouldn't have understood a single word anyway. Satisfied that he had as much information as he needed,

Hervé stormed off in search of Sophie.

"He won't believe that she had a miscarriage," Pierre confided in me afterwards.

"He probably does but prefers to dismiss it," I said.

We didn't see either of them again until they came aboard and Hervé told us that he and Sophie would be returning to Belgium. We weren't displeased as the situation on board had become awkward since Sophie had decided to do her own thing.

So then we were just three, Jill, Pierre and me and we had a minor celebration. No more wondering what Sophie and Hervé talked about together on the phone and no more eager suiters loitering on the quay. Pierre was beginning to feel homesick and like Jill and me was becoming increasingly disenchanted with Passing Fancy and the endless problems. I was beginning to regret not having accepted the job offer on the yacht next to us, but we'd made our decision and had to cope as best we could with all the faults of the Passing Fancy.

25. Struggling to look at a chart!

Things started looking up when Hervé called to tell us that we'd had a last minute booking for his scheduled cruise and that we were to go to Fiumicino (Rome) to meet up with six Americans. Already the impossibly tight itinerary had been changed, as the brochure stated pick up was to be at Sorrento, but it didn't matter to us if we were in Rome or Sorrento as long as it was somewhere we hadn't been to before. Hervé sent the necessary funds to cover fuel and food costs and all the harbour fees with plenty in reserve and we prepared for sea. There was a limited time schedule so we were obliged to get to Fiumicino as soon as possible, which meant cruising nonstop from Cannes, 294 nautical miles to our destination. It was by that time September and from mid-August, the weather had begun to be more unsettled, but it was still pleasant when we cast off.

A course was set from Cannes to take us clear of Cap Corse, the northern most point of Corsica, 128 nautical miles away. The first part of the trip was enjoyable with the three of us taking turns at the wheel; I set watches so that we changed every four hours through the days and night with Jill having extra free time to prepare the meals. The wind started to freshen the closer we got to Corsica, which we'd come to expect after having made the voyage already a couple of times, but for all her faults, Passing Fancy was good in a rough sea. By the time we were in sight of the Cape we were suffering from a severe pounding by the high winds and rough seas. When we'd rounded the cape and altered course to pass along the west coast of Elba, a further 42 nautical miles, the island of Corsica was offering us some protection from the weather. The new course took us into the Ligurian Sea, named after the Ligurian people who had inhabited its coastline. It is the area of the Mediterranean that runs from the French-Italian frontier to Cap Corse, covering Liguria, (the Italian Riviera) and Tuscany. The maximum depths are found northeast of Corsica in what is now an 84,000 square kilometres whale and dolphin sanctuary, established in 1999. From Elba, we altered course again into the Tyrrhenian Sea to take us on the 58-mile stretch that would enable us to pass between the rocky Argentario peninsular on the Italian mainland and the island of Giglio, lying 12 miles offshore. The Tyrrhenian Sea is named after the Tyrrhenian people, the Greek name for the Etruscans, who predate the Ligurians. This ancient civilisation has fascinated scholars and has been the subject of a great deal of controversy. It is thought that they were led by a Prince Tyrrhenus, and may have come from Lydia, now western Turkey, and settled in the central western area of Italy that is now Tuscany and Umbria. The Etruscans were explored extensively by D.H.Lawrence in 1927, after which he wrote a very comprehensive book called 'Etruscan Places'. The Tyrrhenian Sea is bordered by Corsica and Sardinia to the west, the west coast of Italy to the east and Sicily to the south. There are mountain ranges and active volcanoes beneath its surface due to its proximity to the African/Eurasian tectonic plates.

We were still feeling the effects of the north-west wind but we weren't being thrown around as much and it was lessening all the time. The final course alteration took us on the 72 nautical miles to our destination, Fiumicino. The wind started to increase in strength once more and the sky clouded over.

A very naughty boy!

It was late afternoon when we eventually reached the approaches to Fiumicino, 36 hours after leaving Cannes. We were feeling weary from the journey and the battering we'd taken; there was a big swell running and it was raining. There were a few craft entering and exiting the narrow entrance so I slowed down to assess the situation. Fiumicino means little river and there is no harbour as such. It is actually a canal linking the Tyrrhenian Sea to the River Tiber and lies north of the river mouth, 15 miles from the outskirts of Rome and 2 miles south of the Leonardo da Vinci International airport, Italy's largest. The Admiralty Pilot book said that a pilot was compulsory to enter the canal. We were tired and as I watched, it seemed straightforward enough, albeit tricky as the strong wind would be skewing us from the stern as we entered. I decided that under the circumstances I didn't want to hang around for a pilot in the increasingly bad weather and guessed that maybe the rules wouldn't be strictly applied to a yacht like ours. I couldn't see any great difficulty so motored in. It wasn't quite as easy as I'd thought. The heavy swell and strong wind made it difficult to hold the boat steady as I lined it up to keep close to the southern arm of the canal entrance. Jill and Pierre were looking a bit concerned and I didn't feel any better myself but concentrated on getting in safely. It was not a particularly attractive place. There were lots of fishing boats and other craft moored on the northern arm and I found a vacant spot on the southern arm where we moored up alongside. It was a relief when I stopped the engines and we appreciated the fact that the cubicles weren't jumping around when we took a hot shower. We needed to be refreshed for the following morning to prepare the yacht for the Americans' arrival, so once we'd eaten we were looking forward to getting a good night's sleep. It was not to be. The storm worsened. We bounced around alongside the quay all night long, and the rain lashed down creating an awful din as it splattered with tremendous force on the steel decks above our cabin. Even though we only had two tiny portholes, the cabin lit up each time there was a flash of lightening, followed by rumbles of thunder that were getting closer all the time. And then it happened. A terrifying, explosive crack so fierce that it made us both jump and our hearts pounded as our cabin lit up brilliantly from the lightning flash.

"What the heck was that," I yelled as I jumped out of my bunk.

Meanwhile, Jill had sat bolt upright, her face drained of blood, and peered out of her porthole to see a huge cloud billowing up into the black sky. A storage tank had been struck by lightning and had exploded. The remainder of the night was complete chaos with sirens howling and people shouting and screaming. We had no idea what the tank contained, but it had exploded with a mighty bang and we didn't get much sleep at all after that. We heard no more about the explosion. Nothing was mentioned to us by anybody we met and to this day we are none the wiser.

The next day, a smartly uniformed member of the port authority stood above us. The Italians seem to be very good at producing elaborate, stylish uniforms and it almost distracted my gaze from the grave expression on his tanned face as he glowered down at me from the quay. He was tall for an Italian and he had locks of black hair protruding from beneath his stylish peaked cap. The quay was quite high which made him look even more imposing as I looked up at him.

"You came-a in-a yesterday without a pilot-a," he said.

"Oh, did I need a pilot?" I said feigning ignorance. I was feeling exhausted after the rough sea crossing and a sleepless night and didn't relish more problems.

"Do you not-a have an admiralty sailing directions on board-a?" he demanded.

"Er, yes, I have," I answered, getting a little anxious.

"Well, didn't you read it-a before coming in-a here?"

"Er, we were late arriving and I didn't see anything mentioned about a pilot," I lied, feeling more nervous than before.

"You are in-a serious-a trouble-a," he threatened.

I looked up at him innocently as I gulped and felt a strange feeling in my stomach. Oh dear, I thought to myself, now I'm for it.

"Come-a to my office and-a bring-a me the book-a," he said with deadly seriousness.

"Of course," I said with a quiver, trying not to show any fear in my voice.

He marched off to his office a short distance away. I turned to Jill and gulped, then went into the saloon to collect the book. I climbed up onto the quay and with the book in my hand, slunk away to the office offering up a silent prayer.

"Entra," he bellowed when I tapped on the door. I went in and he told me to stand by his desk and open the book at the relevant page. I opened it with a slightly shaky hand.

"Show-a me," he said. I offered him the book opened up at the section for entering Fiumicino.

"Read-a this to me," he demanded. I read that it said a pilot was compulsory when entering the canal. He was clearly not in a very forgiving mood. He gave me a lengthy lecture about me being a very naughty boy, interspersing it with threats as I stood there wondering how it was all going to end. When he'd finished berating me, he sent me back to Passing Fancy warning me to never do the same thing again. I never did. I was still learning and that's one lesson that I didn't forget. I returned feeling very foolish and so relieved I could have kissed him.

We'd stocked up with everything that we'd thought we might need for the charter before leaving Cannes but the yacht still had to be prepared. It had to be cleaned inside and out, the bunks made up, the engines checked and a cruising schedule prepared.

A race against the Mistral

The Americans arrived the next day. There was no way we could consider adhering to Hervé's ridiculous schedule, particularly as they had boarded in Rome and not Sorrento. So when they had installed themselves I suggested we devise our own cruise and make Elba our first port of call, which was 126 nautical miles distant. From there we could go on to La Spezia, which was on the schedule in the brochures they had with them. They agreed straight away, partly because I don't think they knew much about either of the places or even where they were, just excited to be doing a Mediterranean cruise on a private yacht. So with that settled, we cast off and retraced our passage to the Argentario Peninsular and from there I laid off a course for Portoferraio in Elba, travelling once again through the night to arrive there the following morning. The storm had fortunately passed through and the wind had lessened but there was still a swell running, so we rolled around a fair bit. The Americans looked disappointed at first but the sky gradually cleared during the journey and they began to relax. In the morning everybody was happy when they saw the sun rising and the island of Elba on the horizon. I wasn't so happy when I noticed the altocumulus castellanus clouds forming in the distance. I remembered learning about them in my meteorology lessons and knew that when they appeared early in the morning on a sunny day, they would almost certainly develop into cumulonimbus clouds bringing thunderstorms later.

Portoferraio is situated on the north coast of Elba on a hilly promontory that is surrounded on three sides by the sea. It is a colourful, lively town and the charterers loved it there. It is Elba's largest city, founded in 1548 by Cosimo de Medici, the Grand Duke of Tuscany and was originally called Cosmopoli. England, France and Austria vied with each other for possession of the town in the 18th century because of its strategic position. The British held it until 1802 when France took possession under the Treaty of Amiens.

We set sail for La Spezia late in the evening - and the rain, thunder and lightning began. It was a miserable, uncomfortable 95 nautical mile journey through the night but at least the wind didn't blow with too much force, and it wasn't so uncomfortable that Pierre and I couldn't sleep as we changed watch every four hours; Jill relaxed as best she could for most of the time so that she would be available for any cooking or stewardess duties. However, for the unsuspecting Americans, it was awful. They didn't sleep well, some of them not at all as we rolled around in the choppy sea. They weren't expecting such a rude introduction to Mediterranean cruising and were both surprised and disappointed. When dawn broke, Jill, Pierre and I were together in the wheelhouse as we always were when making a new landfall and the headland of La Spezia came into view in the grey, murky distance. The Americans began appearing in the wheelhouse looking dishevelled. One of them was clutching the brochure advertising the cruise. He held it up to me.

"This is not what we expected," he said, gazing despondently at the grey, water laden sky and the waves crashing against us as we motored our way towards the headland.

"I'm sorry it's like this but there's nothing I can do about it," I said.

"Look at this. It says here that we would have clear blue skies and calm seas," he moaned as he pointed to the printed paragraph that had enticed them there.

"Well, mostly that's true but it can't be like that all the time," I reasoned.

"Well, that's what we paid for and so far it's not been very nice has it?"

"No, but it will be better tomorrow," I assured him, hoping that I was right. His companions started gathering around us looking upset.

"I certainly hope so," he said as he showed me the beautiful pictures in the brochure and read out the poetic prose describing the luxury cruise. "Look, that's what it's supposed to be like, look at the pictures here, look how lovely the weather is, why isn't it like it says in the brochure?"

I looked across to Jill who was grinning at the ridiculous comments from the Americans and I found it difficult not to do the same. It was unfortunate for them but brandishing the brochure in front of me couldn't change anything. I might be clever but not that clever! King Canute didn't have much success so there wasn't much prospect of me succeeding either.

We motored up to the town of La Spezia, which did not look at all inviting, there were too many commercial and military craft moored there. La Spezia is second only to Genoa in terms of population in Liguria. It is one of the main Italian military bases housing the navy's arsenal and it is also a major commercial port. During WWII, after the Italians had surrendered to the allies, their navy was ordered to sail from La Spezia to Malta and into the custody of the British. The Germans tried to prevent this happening but were too late so they took their revenge by executing the remaining Italian Captains. Following the liberation, more than 23,000 Jewish survivors of the concentration camps and other displaced Jews, sailed from La Spezia to Palestine and on Jewish geographical maps, La Spezia is called "Shàar Zion," which is Hebrew for Gateway to Zion. I slowed the engines down to idling revs whilst I decided on the best option.

"Do you want to stay here?" I asked the disgruntled Americans.

"It's not what we expected," one of them said disappointedly.

"We passed a nice little bay further back. It might be better there if you'd like to try it," I suggested.

"Yes, we saw that too, let's go there," they agreed, so I turned the boat around and headed back to the seaward end of the bay and we moored up at Le Grazie, a charming small town and harbour, one of three that comprise the municipality of Portovenere, the others being Fezzano and Portovenere itself, together with three small islands, Palmaria, Tino and Tinetto. To the west of La Spezia lies the municipality of Le Cinque Terre, a rugged portion of coast comprising five beautiful and popular villages that were made World Heritage sites in 1997.

We stayed until the following morning when at 06.00 hours we set off for the 40 nautical mile run to Portofino, passing through a small channel between the mainland and Palmaria. The storm had passed by the time we left so the passage was reasonably calm and straightforward.

26. In Porto Chervo

Portofino was another port on the schedule, so at that stage we were doing well. It is such a picturesque place we were sure that once there the Americans would start to feel better about the cruise. In fact, it has been reported that it is the most photographed village in the world and anybody who has been there would understand why. The beautiful village curves around the coast and the houses are painted a variety of different colours, with an unbroken line of restaurants, cafés and shops along the waterfront. The small harbour lies at the end of a spectacular creek that is well camouflaged by the magnificent surrounding landscape of the Tigullio Bay. The town is thought to have been founded by the Romans who named it Portus Delphini, (Port of the Dolphins) because of the huge numbers of dolphins that inhabit the bay. It was once a fishing port and became part of the Kingdom of Italy in 1815. When the British aristocracy began visiting and building expensive properties in the same century its popularity grew, attracting ever more expats. The fishing industry declined and was replaced by tourism. The town, harbour and creek of Portofino are so beautiful that there is a full-scale replica of it at the Universal Orlando Resort in Florida and it is also thought to have inspired the construction of the Italian style village of Portmeirion in Wales. The architect denies this but he did say "How should I not have fallen for Portofino. Indeed its image remained with me as an almost perfect example of the man-made adornment and use of an exquisite site". It also inspired the creation of the seaside town around the harbour at Tokyo Disney Sea in Japan. It is a much favoured destination of the rich and famous and it was a truly delightful place for us to visit.

We arrived there before midday and the Americans were overwhelmed. They rushed to get down the gangplank and look around as soon as we'd moored up.

"Shit!" We heard. In their haste to get ashore the first one down the gangplank smashed his head on the bar.

Aware that we could never visit all of the places promised in the brochure that had enticed them to book, and that they seemed to always have with them ready to produce and complain at a moment's notice, I was anxious to visit as many as possible to keep them happy. So, I suggested that we set course for Cannes after the evening meal. I also had a pretty good idea that a Mistral was on the way and wanted to get to Cannes before it arrived; otherwise we'd be storm-bound in Portofino and way behind on our schedule. It's surprising how little time people wish to spend in each harbour. Their main objective seemed to be to tick off as many places as possible after brief visits. They agreed instantly to go to Cannes.

It was a lovely, calm, moonlit night when we slipped our moorings in the evening and motored slowly out of that sublime creek. Cannes was 110 nautical miles away so I expected to arrive early the following morning. We had excellent visibility and coming after the thunderstorms, that was a sure harbinger of the Mistral. For a while, the charterers stayed on deck to enjoy the experience of sailing along the spectacular coast lit up in parts by the lights of towns and villages. The sky was breathtaking with an abundance of bright stars. They were overjoyed. I, however, knew that the crystal clear visibility was a warning of something worse to come. The night passage was a joy, but by the time we were abreast of Monaco, the wind had started to pick up and it gradually increased as we approached Cannes. Jill and I were thankful that the sea wasn't too uncomfortable and that we'd managed to moor up in Port Pierre-Canto before the Mistral struck. The Americans went ashore to explore Cannes; the leader of the pack, actually avoided banging his head on the bar, a rare occurrence indeed. They were gone for most of the day, returning to shower before going back out to a restaurant in the evening. The wind had increased throughout the day. Jill, Pierre and I were pleased to have an opportunity to relax and enjoy a peaceful meal in the saloon as we listened to the whistling of the wind and incessant rattling of sailboat rigging, which made us doubly grateful to be safely tucked up in harbour. We knew that it would be infinitely worse outside in the open sea. In the protection of the harbour, one could be forgiven for thinking that the wind wasn't too strong. We'd had trouble in the past convincing our charterers that it was a different matter altogether out at sea and they were rarely convinced until we'd left for our destination and then they'd wished that they'd believed us. The incident in the Bonifacio Strait was a good example.

A fistful of dollars

The next morning the Mistral was still in full force and the forecast was for it to continue for the next few days. Our itinerary was to visit St Tropez but I refused to take them anywhere knowing full well what the consequences would be if we left the safety of the port. They were excessively vocal in letting me know their disapproval but I told them that we would stay in harbour until the wind abated. They produced the brochures once again and pointed out the itinerary.

"Look, it says that after Cannes, we go to St. Tropez," one of them said.

"Have you seen these pictures of lovely sunshine and a calm sea?" another said, shoving the brochure under my nose.

They insisted on berating me but I was adamant that we would not leave the safety of the port and I started to get a little annoyed with their refusal to understand. Finally, they accepted the situation and sulked until they left to spend another day ashore. Jill, Pierre and I recuperated from the exhaustion of the previous days of getting to Fiumicino in the first place and the subsequent night passages. We still needed to be on call during each day, and it never occurred to the charterers that we may be tired or need to rest. Pierre was becoming more disheartened each day and was missing home. The following day the wind showed no sign of easing, if anything it was even stronger. I walked to the end of the quay and looked out to the horizon and could see that the sea was huge. Not surprising as the wind had already been howling for two days. I expected trouble from the Americans and I wasn't mistaken.

"What are we doing today?" one of them asked.

"Unfortunately the forecast is for more of the same so we have no choice. We have to wait for the weather to improve," I said.

"We've already been here for two days. We've missed going to St Tropez and we're supposed to go to Corsica next."

"I'm aware of that," I replied "but the wind is too strong, it could be dangerous. I can't do anything about it, we just have to wait and hope that the weather improves soon."

"Well, how soon?" one of them demanded.

"I don't know. As soon as it's safe to leave we'll set off for Corsica, maybe tomorrow if we're lucky," I told him.

"Well that's not good enough, we want to leave otherwise we won't have time to see all that we're supposed to see." He was getting belligerent. The others had joined him and were looking at me angrily. One of them had the brochure in his hand ready to recite the itinerary and tell me how it clearly says that they would be sailing on the calm, blue water of the Mediterranean under clear blue skies.

"Look," I said mustering up as much authority as I felt necessary to convince them "We can't leave when force eight to nine gales and high seas are forecast. I'm responsible for the safety of this vessel and the lives of everybody on it and I'm not leaving here until the weather improves. I know it's disappointing for you but it can't be helped."

"The wind isn't that bad and we want to go to Corsica," they were saying one after the other.

"It isn't in here but I can assure you that it's a totally different kettle of fish out there."

"We don't believe that the wind can be that bad, it looks perfectly alright to us and we want to go. We don't want to spend another day here; we want to go to Corsica."

They didn't give up. They continued to harangue me and they got increasingly angry. It was evident that they were going to continue battering me verbally until I succumbed. I did my best to stay calm. I looked at Jill standing beside me and could see that she was not happy. Her big brown eyes had a look of apprehension. I thought about all the implications and knew that the only way to shut them up was to give them what they wanted. I decided that no matter how bad it was I wouldn't turn back, as at that stage in my career I didn't want to lose face in front of experienced Captains by scuttling back into harbour once I'd left. In hindsight, I realise that it was foolhardy to have allowed my decision to be influenced by concerns about what other people might think of me. I calmed myself, thought carefully about what I would say, and told them what they wanted to hear but with a proviso.

"If we leave here, there will be no turning back under any circumstances. The boat can ride the rough sea and the crew can take it. It will be very rough out there and you will regret that you didn't listen to me."

"That's OK, let's go," they said cheerily. They were smiling. They'd won. But Jill and I knew what lay in store for them and for us too.

"I want you to understand that there will be no turning back. I repeat, it will be very rough and possibly dangerous. You do know that I will not come back here if you find it too rough. Do you understand and accept that? I will not turn around once I leave here. I will not stop until we get to Corsica. That's what you want isn't it?" I couldn't have put it more forcefully.

"Yes, yes, let's go," they were almost jumping with excitement.

288

I looked out to the horizon again then looked at Jill. She looked worried but not overly so and I knew that she would support me in every way and that she had total confidence in me as I had in her. In any case it couldn't be any worse than the voyage from Gibraltar to Hamble in the cutter, or so we thought. Pierre wasn't so convinced and he also looked worried but I knew he'd be OK. He was a strong, capable, adaptable guy and we'd had our share of rough weather together. We knew we could cope.

I laid off the course to Calvi whilst Jill and Pierre stowed for sea. They lashed everything down that was likely to move and closed the portholes. I started the engines. Jill and Pierre hoisted in the gangplank and lashed it securely. Pierre went into the engine room to check that nothing was likely to move and securely lashed anything that was suspect. All the cabins were checked to make sure that everything that could move was securely stowed. The galley pots and pans were stashed securely. When we were satisfied that it was safe to go, we checked and then double checked once more. The charterers watched us bemused and it was clear that they thought we were overreacting just to make a point. They smiled as they watched us. When I was finally satisfied, I went to the wheelhouse. Jill went to the foredeck. Pierre stood by on the aft deck.

"That's it, cast off," I called to them.

I put the engines into ahead and motored slowly out of the port whilst Jill and Pierre pulled in the fenders and stowed them. We were off come what may. I'd had enough of the Americans' whining ever since they'd come on board. I headed towards the Iles de Lerins. They gave us some protection but as soon as we'd cleared them and were exposed to the full force of the wind we started crashing around. The Americans looked horrified as they tried to maintain their balance and we'd only been going for about twenty minutes.

"Captain, you were right, take us back," they pleaded as they crashed from side to side of the wheelhouse.

"I told you what it would be like out here and that I would not turn around, so we're going to Corsica. That's what you insisted on doing and I'm obliging you so that you can go to Corsica," I said.

"We're sorry, we'd like you to take us back," they begged.

"I'm not going back now; we're carrying on to Corsica, that's where you insisted on going and we have to adhere to our schedule. That's what you keep telling me." Passing Fancy was being tossed around quite badly when I altered course from the islands to Calvi.

"How long will it take?" they asked, fearing the answer.

"If we're lucky, twelve hours," I said. That sent them into panic mode and they scrambled down into the saloon to settle in as best they could, chattering and gibbering among themselves like a bunch of demented chimpanzees as they tried to crawl across the floor on all fours, clinging onto whatever they could even if it was each other but mostly they were rolling from one side of the saloon to the other and bumping into the chairs and table.

It was worse than I'd feared as we crashed and rolled and pitched and shuddered our way across the hundred mile stretch of open sea. The Americans were too terrified to go down into the cabins. They huddled on the floor of the saloon swallowing seasick pills like sweets. Every now and again we would hear them calling out, screaming at each other for more Marzine.

"Who's got any more Marzine?"

"For Christ's sake, I need some more Marzine."

"Somebody get the Marzine," and so it went on until we heard somebody say "There aren't any more, we've had them all."

We'd been thrashing our way through the vicious sea for several hours and they'd swallowed their entire supply of the travel sickness pills. Two of the men crawled up the ladder into the wheel house bouncing up and down as the vessel rose up one wave to the crest, then crashed down again into the trough sending sea water sloshing along the decks and against the windscreen before rising again and plummeting back down. They crawled to me and started pulling at my legs, imploring me, begging me to take them back to Cannes.

"It's too late now. It's safer to continue as we are. It would be too dangerous to try to turn around in this sea, and anyway we're already over half way."

"Oh my God," came the reply.

"Dear God, help us," they wailed. I knew how they felt; Jill and I had offered up that prayer ourselves more than once when we were crashing our way back to Hamble from Gibraltar. This was different though. In the Atlantic, the waves roll across huge stretches of water and are longer and the vessels ride them easier. In the Mediterranean, the waves are shorter and steeper. Any mariner will want to avoid sailing in a Mistral, which often reaches force eight or more in strength, with waves from two to more than four metres high. Our voyage that day was the worst we'd experienced since sailing back across the Bay of Biscay in the cutter. At one stage, a large wave took us by surprise. The bow rose up alarmingly high then slammed back down again into the trough as the stern came up and we rolled over to one side at the same time. The noise of the engine changed dramatically as one or maybe even both of the propellers must have broken clear of the water. It happened at the same time that Pierre had scrambled up onto the area behind the wheelhouse windows to look at the chart. He was thrown back and slammed against the instrument console, then in the other direction, where he hit the windows. When he slid towards the instrument console for the second time, he managed to grab hold of it and stabilise himself. Every one of the Americans let out a terrified scream, shouting for God to save them. They finished up in a tangled mass of limbs, clawing at each other as they were thrown across the saloon floor. Jill, Pierre and I laughed it off as we were by then accustomed to the violent motion. The closer we got to Corsica, the more violent the wind became and the more savage the sea. Each time we were thrown upwards and then crashed down into the sea again, the boat shuddered along its full length as we hit the water with a mighty bang. I struggled constantly with the steering wheel in a desperate attempt to maintain the correct heading each time the waves smashed into us and threw us where we didn't want to go. Buzzy Trent, a pioneer of big wave surfing was correct when he said "Waves are not measured in feet or inches, they are measured in increments of fear."

It was far worse when it started to get dark and we couldn't see the waves approaching, but by this time we were nearing Corsica and were looking for the Calvi light. We saw the loom of a lighthouse in the distance, which was comforting as we crashed and banged our way towards it. Sometimes it was visible as we surged up to the top of the waves and then it disappeared as we plunged back down into the trough with a loud smack and the whole boat trembled as the Americans let out terrified screams. Between being carried viciously upwards and plunging back down again, when they weren't screaming they were whimpering or praying.

Calvi lighthouse has a beam that can be seen for twenty miles so we should have seen it a bit sooner than we did but at least we'd seen a light. It was such a comforting feeling. It wasn't easy trying to count the flashes whilst we tried to maintain our balance with the boat careening all over the place. In the brief instants that the glimpses of light were visible Jill and I couldn't agree on what we'd seen. It didn't make sense, the flashes were confusing. After much peering into the darkness whilst hanging on to steady ourselves from the violent motion, we finally agreed that we'd seen three flashes every twelve seconds and not the two flashes every ten seconds that we'd expected to see. Wherever we were going to finish up it wasn't going to be Calvi.

I gave the wheel to Jill to continue on the course whilst I studied the chart to try to make sense of what we'd seen. Wedging myself against the side of the wheelhouse, I searched for a lighthouse with three flashes every twelve seconds and discovered that the gale had blown us nine miles off course and we were headed for my nemesis, Ile Rousse. The lighthouse that I had scaled the cliff to reach, had beckoned me once more. Psychologically it was consoling once we'd seen the light and ascertained where we were but we still had another twelve miles of being thrown around all over the place to cope with. The saying "Any port in a storm" had never been truer for us and our terrified guests.

The Americans were still rolling around whimpering and groaning on the saloon floor as we rounded the pier and went alongside the ferry berth. When we'd made fast and switched off the engines they were overcome with relief. They staggered slowly up into the wheelhouse one at a time and shook my hand, apologising profusely for not listening to me and thanking me so much for getting them to Corsica alive. They looked absolutely dreadful from the thrashing they'd just had. When they'd recovered sufficiently, they went down into their cabins and came back up with fistfuls of dollars that they were stuffing into my hands in appreciation as they stood next to me wobbling on their still unsteady legs.

"Thank you so much, Captain, thank you so much," they repeated several times. "You were wonderful, thank you." Thank you seemed a rather inappropriate response to what I'd just put them through but hey, we'd made it. They were in Corsica, which is what they'd demanded. Ok, they weren't in Calvi but they were alive and safe and in the beautiful island of Corsica. Jill, Pierre and I were exhausted. We all slept well after that crossing and in the morning as soon as our guests woke they prepared themselves and hastily went ashore. They didn't wait for breakfast; they just wanted to feel the comfort of the stable quay beneath their feet. We didn't see them again until after lunch time.

"We've decided that we don't want to continue. It's not how we thought it was going to be," one of them said.

"We're leaving. We've arranged to go back to Rome and then we're going home," another one said.

They wasted no time in packing. They'd apparently already pre-ordered a taxi before coming back to the boat because at virtually the same moment that their cases were placed on deck a car pulled up and the driver started piling their luggage into the boot. They couldn't wait to get off the boat. They each came up to the three of us in turn and shook our hands and said goodbye. They thanked me over and over again and gave me more fistfuls of dollars, reiterating how wonderful they thought I was and then they climbed into the taxi and disappeared into the distance. I doubt very much that they ever booked another cruise or even went anywhere near a boat again. It was the last time that I ever did such a foolhardy thing, but in those days I was young, courageous, confident and loved danger and the adrenaline rush it gave me. I had in Jill the best crew and companion I could have hoped for, somebody I could confide in and trust implicitly. She was always by my side supporting me and was capable of accomplishing whatever needed to be done. We had started our adventure together and learned together so that we thought as one, but I still had a lot to learn and I never again allowed myself to be bullied into making a rash decision.

To stay or not to stay

I called Hervé and told him what had happened and he understood and took it very well. We were storm bound in Ile Rousse for a further three days until the Mistral abated, then we cast off and left for Cannes. On the voyage home we were slowed down because although the wind was much less, we were beating into the heavy swell that remained from the gale. It was still rough but was nothing compared to what it had been and we had a pleasant enough crossing back to mainland France. The wind lessened and the sea became more comfortable the further we got away from Corsica.

Back in Cannes, Pierre informed us that he'd had enough and wanted to leave. His decision had nothing to do with the crossing to Corsica; in fact, he'd seemed to rather enjoy it. He'd been threatening to leave for some time as he wanted to return to Belgium and be with his family. We were sad to be losing him as we all got along so well and he had a similar sense of humour to Jill and me, but we understood his reasons for leaving; we were also getting fed up with the constant problems. On top of everything else, the fridge had stopped working completely, making it impossible to keep food cool. In spite of being told about it many times, Hervé was reluctant to spend any money on it. I wasn't happy not having a tender to replace the speedboat and the wheelhouse was still far too hot. It was unbearable most of the time and the ugly thick black rubber seals around the windows were peeling off. We still had the unachievable cruise schedule that we knew we could never adhere to, which would be even more difficult as the seasons changed and the Mistral started to blow more often; if there was another booking there was bound to be as much trouble from the charterers as we'd just had, maybe even more.

Jill and I sat down and discussed whether we wanted to continue under those circumstances. It was a tough decision to make. We didn't want to let Hervé down; we were both loyal people and felt we had a responsibility. In the end though, we decided that we would do as Pierre had done and inform Hervé that regrettably, we'd decided to leave as well. We didn't feel good about it. Even to this day we feel guilt and sadness but we felt that there were just too many problems. The season had virtually come to an end anyway as we were by that time well into September and in any case there were no more bookings that we knew of. When I called him to tell him our decision he told me that he'd had another booking and the charterers needed to be picked up once again in Fiumicino; Passing Fancy had to be there in two weeks' time. I asked if he could find a replacement Captain and somebody to replace Jill. He said he would try. I told him that we would get Passing Fancy to Fiumicino for him in time for the charter and that would give him the time he needed to find our replacements. If he managed to do that then we would prefer to leave in Fiumicino.

One week later, Pierre's replacement arrived. He was a stocky, dark-haired Greek, called Nico. A replacement Captain had also been hired and he would take the command from me in Fiumicino so all was working out well for everybody concerned. We enjoyed the rest of our time in Cannes and when the time was ready to leave I called Hervé to let him know when to expect us in Fiumicino. His attitude had changed and he wasn't as friendly as he usually was. I understood his annoyance that we were leaving. Jill and I felt uncomfortable about it ourselves but there was no way that his planned itinerary could be carried out and he still refused to believe that we could only cruise at eight knots and not the sixteen he'd hoped for.

We hadn't been paid for two months, which wasn't that unusual in the yachting business. However, I wondered if Hervé was thinking of not paying us as his attitude towards us had changed. To be prepared, I called the Panamanian Embassy to discuss the possibilities and was assured by them that if that was the case the yacht would not be allowed to leave harbour until we had received all that was due to us. The Panamanian Embassy had an excellent reputation among yacht Captains for protecting them against unscrupulous yacht owners. The more we associated with or were told about wealthy individuals the more we realised just how unprincipled and ruthless some of them could be. They would think nothing of allowing the Captain and Crew to work for the entire season and then at the end, refuse to pay them. The usual recourse was to slap a writ on the mast to prevent the vessel from moving until the matter had been resolved. We were told that such occurrences were not unusual. One Skipper I know removed both starter motors from the engines and hid them until he got paid. I suppose the wealthy do not get rich by giving money away! The Dalai Lama said "People were created to be loved. Things were created to be used. The reason that the world is in chaos is because people love things and use people." I wonder if he said that after talking to yacht skippers! Probably not. But I should also point out that the majority of yacht owners were very good to their Captains and Crews. Jill and I were fortunate because everyone we had worked for was principled, courteous and very generous.

When the time and the weather was favourable, we cast off from Port Pierre-Canto for the final time with the courses set to take us directly to Portoferraio in Elba, where we intended to spend some time to rest before continuing on to Fiumicino. It was a treat to have plenty of time to make the journey and enjoy exploring Elba a bit more when we arrived there. I'd calculated that if we did eight knots, we'd be there after 20 hours motoring depending on the wind and sea conditions and with luck, it wouldn't take that long. The voyage went well. There was a strong wind blowing as we neared Corsica and especially as we rounded Cap Corse. The wind strength often increases at the Cape but we rode it out and compared to the last crossing it was straightforward. We arrived in Portoferraio in good time and decided to stay there for a couple of days as we were ahead of schedule for the handover in Fiumicino. We reconnoitered as much as possible in the time available to us and visited the house where Napoleon had lived after his exile to Elba following his defeat by the allied forces during numerous battles, including the battle of Leipzig, known as the battle of the nations. It was the largest battle in European history until WWI, comprising the armies of Great Britain, Portugal, Spain, Prussia, Russia, Sweden, Austria and some small German states, together known as the sixth coalition, which vastly outnumbered Napoleon's French Army that also included Poles, Italians and some Germans. When Napoleon's senior officers refused to fight anymore and large numbers of his troops deserted, he was left with no alternative other than to sign the Treaty of Fontainebleau. In 1814, Napoleon was sent into exile in Elba and the French gave him sovereignty over the island allowing him to retain his title of Emperor. During the three hundred days of his reign, he established a small army, a navy, built new roads, overhauled the legal and education systems, modernised the agriculture industry and developed the iron mines. The town grew quickly and when new iron mills were constructed in Rio Marina, Portoferraio became the main shipping port for transporting the iron ore to the Italian mainland, hence its current name, Italian for Iron Port. When Napoleon escaped from Elba to invade France, the island was returned to Italy and became part of the Kingdom of Italy in 1860. Elba's iron deposits are among the oldest in the world and have attracted Mediterranean powers since the beginning of history. The Etruscans called it "The Island of a thousand fires" and it is thought to be the reason that they extended their reign as far as Elba. The iron mining industry began to decline in the 1950's due to industrial action and the arrival of tourism. The last mine closed down in 1981.

It was in Elba that Jill and I first tasted prickly pears whilst walking on the island with Nico. He stripped some from the cactus plants, brushed off the spikes and opened them up for us explaining how it was done in Greece. Prickly pear is reputed to have antiviral and anti-inflammatory properties and contain useful minerals and vitamins. I suppose it has to have something going for it, and it certainly isn't the taste!

We weren't in any hurry to leave for Fiumicino as we still had plenty of time to get there; when we did leave, the passage went well with reasonable sea conditions. With vivid memories of my last time at Fiumicino, I radioed ahead to order the pilot. When we arrived I slowed the engines down to tick over and we wallowed around waiting for him in the swell outside the entrance. Hervé and Sophie had arrived a couple of days earlier and I'd radioed ahead giving them our time of arrival, so they were waiting for us on the quay and boarded as soon as we'd moored up. Sophie had altered her attitude towards us as well. She was still pleasant but made a deliberate attempt to clean the interior of the boat in front of Jill, the implication being that Jill hadn't been caring for the interior as well as she had. I went ashore to complete the reams of paperwork in the port office and when I returned, Hervé paid us everything that was due and I handed over the command to the replacement Captain. We packed our bags, said our goodbyes and caught the train to the centre of Rome. We stayed in that fabulous city for a few days and had an amazing time relaxing and visiting as many of the amazing tourist attractions as we could before we booked our flights back home to London and then onwards to the Hamble once more. The thought of staying in a cold, wet, grey United Kingdom and living a mundane life was not an attractive one, so we decided that as soon as we got home we'd start looking for a new command.

CHAPTER 14
THE DAY THE LIGHT WENT OUT

For whom the bell tolls

W e'd given up our accommodation in the village of Hamble before we left to join Passing Fancy and what little belongings we had were in storage. When we arrived back in the U.K., we expected to be setting off again in the not so distant future, so stayed alternately with Jill's Aunt and Grandmother in Shirley, Southampton and with her cousin Simon and his wife Linda, who lived in Lower Swanwick. Whilst waiting for another command to materialise, I started work in the warehouse of W.H. Smith in Southampton, stacking the books, magazines and stationery after they were delivered. This gave me the perfect opportunity to scour the situations vacant columns of the yachting magazines before they went on display and became available to the public. I left shortly afterwards when I found something else which required a bit more use of my brain and started work in an office at Regents Park, Southampton. It was terribly boring and miserable. The office manager was a control freak and wouldn't allow any talking in the office, consequently nobody was happy there and I was amazed how the other staff members whispered to each other hoping they wouldn't attract the attention of the tyrant. I rebelled and disobeyed. There was no way I would permit him to control me that way. In any case, I knew it was purely a temporary situation and that I would soon be sailing away again to a fabulous life in the Mediterranean. Jill applied for a position of telesales girl for United Poultry Marketing in Hedge End, a town to the east of Southampton. When they discovered how talented she was and how many GCE's she had, she was offered the job of ledger clerk. We were staying with her Aunt and Grandma in Shirley at the time so I cycled into Southampton each day and Jill took our car for the journeys to Hedge End.

Jill's Father, Harold, and his wife Claire, had sold the pub in Shaftesbury and with Claire's daughter Diane, moved to a rented house in Milford on Sea, a scenic village on the shore of the Solent that had become a resort and a desirable place for retirees after WWII. We visited them and all the other members of her family as often as possible. There was so much love and compassion among them and everybody loved Harold, or as he was affectionately called by the family, Pop. I can't help but wonder whether that overwhelming love throughout the family influenced my decision when I asked Jill to marry me. Pop was a gentle, popular, loving and much loved soul who had a perpetual smile whenever I met him and I never heard him raise his voice. He didn't judge people, in fact I only ever heard him say nice things about them. Music was a leveler - whether a high court judge or a bin man, they were all equal when they played their instruments. He had a brilliant mind, which was so preoccupied with ideas that he was prone to absent mindedness, often turning up late for appointments or even forgetting them completely, which the rest of the family accepted with goodhearted humour. Jill remembers as a small child, waiting for him to collect her from school one day and he'd completely forgotten. He did arrive eventually, at night, and Jill was so pleased when she saw the headlights of the car approaching. His ex-wife, Jill's Mum however, although amused by it after the divorce no doubt found it exasperating when she was married to him. He played piano, alto and tenor saxophone, clarinet and cello and for many years was one of Southampton's prominent musicians.

In November Pop developed a swollen left leg that his doctor had no explanation for.

"I want to know why I have one leg bigger than the other; I asked the doctor and he just shrugged his shoulders," he told us when he came to visit one day. He was sitting, slouched in an armchair smiling but obviously concerned. His clothes were a bit rumpled, his tie was twisted and we noticed that he hadn't shaved. He always had far more important things on his mind.

"Have you shaved today?" Jill asked him. He rubbed a hand over his chin and smiled.

"Oh, I forgot all about it," he replied. Jill and I looked at each other and smiled. It was those little absent minded things that gave him his unique, lovable personality.

He stayed with us for the rest of the afternoon and in his typical accepting way never mentioned the swollen leg again. The next time we saw him, although the swelling in his leg had lessened, the leg hadn't returned completely to its original size, but he made no further mention of it.

Three weeks later Claire called us and told us that Pop was in bed, suffering from an excruciating, persistent headache that he'd had for a few days and nothing would relieve it. Claire had called the doctor who didn't visit but prescribed Codeine in hot milk, which did nothing to ease the pain and only made him nauseous as Pop disliked milk. She was worried and said he was in great pain, so Jill and I drove to Milford on Sea to visit and see if there was anything we could do to help. When we arrived and went to his bedside we were shaken to see him so racked with pain. He looked as though he had shrunk to a shadow of his former self and it was heart-breaking to see this wonderful man suffer so. The amazing thing was that he didn't complain. The pain was so intense that his head visibly throbbed on the pillow. Orthodox medicine had nothing to offer other than the hot milk and Codeine and the doctor hadn't even taken Pop's blood pressure, so Claire, who was a vegetarian and open minded to alternative treatments, searched for an alternative practitioner in a book that she had. She called a Naturopath who mercifully visited that same day. After examining the agonised Harold, he advised us to soak a sheet in ice cold water, strip him, wrap him in the sheet and place hot water bottles on his feet; then cover him with blankets. It was mid-winter and the house had no central heating so it must have been an awful treatment to endure but anything had to be better than the terrible torment of the headache. Pop didn't resist and said nothing. He just allowed the three of us to carry out the Naturopaths instructions. What transpired had a profound impact on me and influenced the rest of my life. Jill and I stayed the night and the following morning the headache had gone. We removed the sheet and saw that it was stained brown and had a disgusting smell. The treatment had drawn the toxins from his body. Overnight, the Naturopath, with his simple, natural treatment had accomplished what the doctor had been incapable of doing.

When I was 16 years old I visited a doctor for a minor health problem and the more I questioned him about it, the more I came to realise how limited his knowledge was. I had been taught that we were created in God's image. If that were true, then how come I was unwell because God presumably doesn't get ill. I wanted to know why I was unwell so that I could prevent it happening again. Of course, my questions went unanswered; in fact, the doctor became irritated that I was questioning him. On the way home I was deep in thought and decided at that young age that I would do my best to stay in good health and to avoid the medical profession as much as possible. The miraculous transformation in Jill's Dad after the naturopathic treatment convinced me that I was on the right track. Just like the Bloodhound effect, it was a Eureka moment for me and set me on a lifelong study of alternative methods of healing. Over the past 40 years I've trained in many modalities of natural healing and one day a third Eureka moment happened when I read a small paperback book on Applied Kinesiology. I decided without any hesitation that I would be a Kinesiologist. I trained with the Academy of Systematic Kinesiology in London and went on to have my own successful practice and to train others.

It tolls for thee

On the afternoon of 14th of January, whilst at work having a surreptitious, whispered conversation with a fellow worker, the office manager's door flew open and my fellow worker's face changed colour to a deathly white.

A reprimand or maybe even dismissal was a possibility. However, the tyrant's gaze was fixed on me.

"You have a phone call," he called to me in a voice that conveyed his displeasure that the office routine had been disrupted. I went to his office and picked up the phone lying on his desk.

"Hello," I said into the receiver. There was silence for a while and then Jill spoke in a faltering, tearful voice and I knew something serious had happened.

"Dad's collapsed at work and he's been taken to hospital," she sobbed. I was stunned, unable to speak for a while.

"Oh my God," I said.

"We have to go to Lymington Hospital right away," she said and explained that she'd received a phone call from her Aunt Marie telling her that Pop had suffered a massive cerebral hemorrhage and was not expected to survive for long.

"Of course, can you come and collect me,' I said. I explained what had happened to the disagreeable office manager and told him that I was leaving for the day and maybe longer. He looked daggers at me and reluctantly agreed that I should go.

Jill wasted no time driving from Hedge end to Southampton and when she arrived at the gate I was waiting for her. I opened the car door and got in. She was crying so I put my arm around her, held her tight and did my best to console her. We changed seats so that I could drive us to Lymington as fast as was safe in our little car. For hundreds of years, some of the greatest scholars have struggled to define time. They haven't succeeded because it doesn't exist. It is purely a construct of our minds that we each perceive differently and during that journey, each minute of clock time seemed like ten to us as we raced to our destination. When we arrived we were taken directly to where Pop lay unconscious. Claire was by his bedside weeping. She and Jill hugged and wept together and then we sat and watched and waited and hoped and wept as that kind, wonderful man who was so full of life and ideas and music and light, lay before us silently slipping away.

We stayed with him until five o'clock that afternoon when the brilliant and much loved musician breathed his last breath and the light that emanated from him was extinguished. Never again would we hear his sweet music. His soul departed to join the spirit world that is everywhere and nowhere, so maybe he is now at one with the divine music of the spheres, unable to be heard by human ears but eternally emitting its ethereal sound across the infinite expanse of the universe.

Pop had departed this life the day after his 55th birthday from the same cause that had claimed the life of his twin brother five years before. With anguished hearts, we returned to Milford on Sea and in the evening the police called and came to take Jill to the hospital to identify he body as the heartbroken Claire was far too traumatised to go. She wept and wept and I stayed with her and her daughter Diane to offer what little comfort I could and to make and answer any phone calls. The question arises, that has no answer: How would Pop have fared had he sought help from the Naturopath for his leg instead of relying solely on orthodox medicine, which offered no treatment or explanation? We stayed with Claire and daughter Diane until we felt it appropriate to return to Southampton. The funeral had been planned to take place at West End Crematorium in Southampton the following week. So popular was Pop, that there was a huge crowd of tearful mourners waiting with us on the cold, dark day and the rain beat down as if the heavens wept with us, joining us in our untold grief. Jill was standing with her mother, both of them sobbing. The cars and the coffin hadn't arrived on schedule, in fact they were very late and we began to wonder what could have caused such a delay.

"He's even late for his own funeral," her Mother said, shuffling her feet in agitation, which lightened the atmosphere temporarily for them both.

When the coffin eventually arrived we learned that the ferocious storm of the previous day had brought a tree down, blocking the road and the cars had to wait until it had been cleared. I was awestruck by the overwhelming number of people who came to pay their respects. The church was filled to capacity. Those who couldn't find an available seat, stood, and those who couldn't squeeze into the church remained outside in the rain. When the moment came, the curtains opened, the coffin slowly disappeared from view and Pop was gone from this physical world forever but would always remain in our hearts. His ashes were brought to the family and were placed around a rose bush in the gardens. The unfathomable void that was left by his unexpected death left the family distraught. Jill was so devastated by the loss of her beloved father that she cried for a whole week and one of her brothers didn't speak throughout the same week, the other grieved in his own way, keeping his grief inside, which may well have contributed to his own premature death. The Grandmother and Aunt were heartbroken and I was saddened to see them all suffer so. Although all that remained of Pop's body was the ashes around the rose bush, his consciousness remains, is eternal and with the universal consciousness resides in all things animate and inanimate.

"Do not stand at my grave and weep,
I am not there, I do not sleep.
I am in a thousand winds that blow,
I am the softly falling snow.
I am the gentle showers of rain,
I am the fields of ripening grain.
I am in the morning hush,
I am in the graceful rush
Of beautiful birds in circling flight,
I am the starshine of the night.
I am in the flowers that bloom,
I am in a quiet room.
I am in the birds that sing,
I am in each lovely thing.
Do not stand at my grave bereft
I am not there. I have not left."
— Mary Elizabeth Frye

CHAPTER 15
AS GOOD AS IT GETS

The job that nearly wasn't

We replied to an advertisement for Captain and Cook that we'd seen in 'Yachting World' and were invited to London for an interview. The owner of the boat was a courteous, pleasant merchant banker. It so happened that one of his business contacts was a director of Ship Towage Ltd., so after I told him of my six plus years on the Thames tugs, he naturally sought his opinion.

"If he's managed to last more than six years on our tugs then you can't go wrong with him," was his reply.

Shortly after the interview, he wrote to offer us the command of his forty seven foot motor yacht based in Juan-les-Pins. The salary was generous and in addition we were to receive a daily food allowance which virtually doubled our salary. The yacht was fitted with twin General Motor's V8 turbocharged diesel engines and he arranged for me to attend a week's training course at the factory in Manchester. The hotel had been pre-booked and he sent me more than sufficient money to last me the week. I travelled up to Manchester on the train and on the first day after the introductions and formalities, I was taken to the workshop and placed before one of the engines on a stand.

"I want you to dismantle the engine completely and then rebuild it," my instructor said. "You have everything you need here."

And so, under his expert tuition, I set to work. There were astonishing rows of tools of every description available on the bench in front of me.

After a few days, our new boss called to ask if I needed any more money for expenses. He'd already given me more than enough. If he was that generous, I thought to myself, then I'm going to enjoy working for him. I missed being away from Jill terribly. We'd lived together in close confinement without being apart from each other for many, many

months and it felt like I'd lost a part of myself. At the end of the week, clutching my certificate in my hand, and feeling confident that I no longer had need of an engineer in our future ventures, I packed my bag and returned to Southampton.

27. With my instructor at G.M. Motors.

....

The sky was heavily overcast. It was a typical British cold, grey, wet and windy day and the rain seemed to be pelting down with a vengeance as Jill and I left the hotel that the owner of the yacht had booked for us to spend the night before flying out to Nice. Before we left, we'd been given a big fat wad of cash to buy everything we needed, with plenty left over to arrange hotel accommodation in Cannes and to pay any expenses incurred once we'd taken command of the yacht. We ordered a taxi to take us to the airport. When the time came for us to board the aircraft it seemed as if the heavens wanted to convince us that we were doing the right thing in leaving our friends and family behind once more. The rain was relentless. We took the seats that had been reserved for us and beamed with pleasure. We didn't have long to wait before the powerful jet engines roared and we were thrust forward along the runway. Elated, we held hands and looked at each other. Jill's eyes registered a mixture of emotions as the plane climbed steeply, whisking us off to Nice. Once more we were headed for a new adventure.

When we arrived we took a taxi to Cannes and checked into a hotel to wait for the yacht to be launched. She had been stored for the winter in a hangar at La Bocca, a town west of Cannes and was to be brought to Cannes by road transport and chocked up ashore until the launching cradle became available. We made use of the free time to buy a couple of sets of summer and winter uniforms for each of us. No expense was spared.

Our job was very nearly over before it had begun. On the day of the launch, we sat waiting in Le Vol à Voile, a bar on the quay Saint Pierre that was a regular haunt for yacht crews. We were having a good time, spinning salty yarns and getting to know fellow mariners, including the Englishman, Kevin, who worked at the shipyard and who was in charge of the launching procedure. The moment came when he was called for duty and we went with him to watch as the vessel was placed into the slings and wheeled to the launching bay. She was lowered down into the water and the mooring ropes were attached and made fast. We weren't able to get aboard as the distance between the boat and the side of the launching bay was too great, but we wouldn't have been able to do much anyway as by then it was early evening and Kevin had decided to put off the rest of the work till the morning.

"She'll be OK here for the night," said Kevin.

"Are you sure, because I'd be happier if we could get her moored to the quay so that we can move our gear aboard. It would save us time tomorrow," I said.

"It's late now and everybody's knocking off, so I recommend you wait until morning. The boat will be perfectly safe here, nobody can get aboard at the moment anyway. We often leave craft moored here like this because we need time to check everything. If the batteries are flat the engine won't start anyway," he added.

"OK, you know better than me what the routine is," I answered.

There was an easterly wind picking up but Kevin convinced us that there was no cause for alarm, so we left and went back to the bar for a final drink before returning to the hotel. When the time came for us to leave it was dark and the wind had increased in strength.

"Let's just go and check that everything's OK before we go to bed," I said to Jill and we strolled back to the launching bay.

When we got there I was alarmed to see the boat careering around in the confined space, with the mooring ropes being stretched to maximum capacity. She was surging backwards and forwards at speed. The forward ropes would slacken as the stern ropes twanged bar tight and then the next moment, the reverse would happen as she surged in the opposite direction. I watched for a while wondering what to do. I couldn't get aboard. I was very worried. There was no question of leaving the boat like that. Somebody that I didn't know came up to us.

"The forecast is bad, the east wind is supposed to be increasing a lot during the night," he informed me.

That was not a comforting thing to be told. The old harbour of Cannes was not well protected from the east wind and the launching bay was directly opposite the entrance so that the swell rolled straight in. Already the situation looked dire and it was going to get much worse. I rushed back to the bar and asked our new found acquaintances if there was anybody who could help tow the boat to a mooring on the quay otherwise she could get badly damaged.

"Come with me," said Fred, one of the Skippers that we'd met previously. We went over to a group of French men seated in one corner of the bar. Fred explained our predicament to them. They grumbled and discussed among themselves for a while. It didn't look hopeful and I was extremely anxious. I hadn't even boarded the boat yet and it looked like I was going to be partly, if not totally responsible for her demise.

"D'accord," one of them finally agreed. They stood up.

"We'll be there as soon as possible, you go to the boat and we'll meet you there."

310

I could have hugged him I was so grateful. Sure enough, they arrived in a powerful launch and came alongside so that Jill and I could get in with them and then they motored into the launching bay. With difficulty in the uncomfortable swell, Jill and I scrambled up the sides and onto the deck of the yacht. It was a miracle that the mooring ropes hadn't already parted with the intense strain on them. By this time other helpers had arrived. A tow rope was attached and the launch was put into gear to take up the slack. Our mooring ropes were cast off and Jill and I pulled them in as quickly as possible as we were towed out into the safety of the port. I tried to start the engines without success. It was late, 11.30 at night and the wind was howling as we were towed to an appropriate distance from the Jetée Albert Edouard for Jill to drop the anchor. She then cast off the tow rope so that the launch could come to our stern and pull us closer to the quay. I threw a rope to somebody waiting on the foredeck of one of the yachts already moored there. When it was made fast, I hauled us astern as Jill payed out the anchor chain and eventually, with much-appreciated assistance from others, we were safely moored stern to the quay and protected from the easterly wind. The gangplank was placed in position and resisting the now ingrained urge to duck under the non existant head banging bar, we were able to return to the hotel for a good night's sleep.

Kevin came to the boat the next morning with his colleagues to check that everything was functioning as it should. He made no apologies for his bad advice of the previous evening. They carried out their inspection and got the engines started and said their goodbyes. Jill and I cast off, motored to the fuel jetty, filled the tanks and set course for Port Gallice where the owner had his own mooring. From that moment on there were no further major problems, apart from the first trip with the owner on board. We'd had an enjoyable day anchored in the bay of Garoupe, a splendid, curved stretch of white sand on the eastern side of Cap d'Antibes, which is protected from the afternoon southwesterly sea breeze that can be quite strong at times. As we approached the port entrance on our return at the end of the day, the owner decided that he would like to take over from there on and into the berth. He took the helm and I watched. The breeze was fairly strong and was blowing the vessel where he didn't want it to be. He pulled and pushed the single lever controls, engaging astern and ahead positions and increased and decreased the speed in all manner of combinations until he'd somehow managed to end up beam onto the bows of one of the moored yachts, with its mooring ropes passing directly beneath our propellers. He realised that whatever he did from then on could only end in disaster.

"Here, you'd better take over," he said and handed me the controls. So there I was, in a difficult situation not of my own making. I didn't dare turn the propellors for fear of getting the mooring rope tangled around them and we were stuck firmly against the other yacht's bow with the wind blowing our stern around 180°, which meant that very soon it would collide with another yacht. However, with much jiggery-pokery, I accomplished the feat, extricated us from our embarrassing predicament and backed safely into our berth. How could my new boss not be immensely impressed and eternally grateful that he'd chosen me as his future Captain! He didn't try out many more manoeuvres himself after that.

The new boat could not have been more different to Passing Fancy. She had been constructed by Chris Craft, a renowned and respected American shipyard based in Sarasota, Florida. Christopher Columbus Smith was just 15 years old when he built his first wooden boat in 1874 and seven years later, together with his brother Henry, he began to manufacture them full time. They produced upmarket boats for the likes of Henry Ford and William Hearst. Chris Smith died in 1939 but the company continues to exist. During WWII, they focused on producing military craft and in the 1950's sold high-end vessels to celebrities such as Katherine Hepburn, Frank Sinatra, Dean Martin and Elvis Presley. It was in 1964 when they introduced the striking new all fibreglass Chris Craft Commander. It had impressed our new boss so much that he'd ordered one and had it sent across to the Mediterranean as deck cargo on a merchant ship. The accommodation and everything about her had been well thought out. Our wood panelled cabin in the fore part of the vessel was nicely furnished with a good sized shower room on one side of the cabin and an electrically operated toilet on the other. From there we walked into the well-equipped galley and the crew dining area that extended the full width of the boat. There was a large fridge, a dishwasher and an array of electrical gadgets that automatically started the generator when they were switched on. Some hinged steps lifted up to give access to the engine room beneath the saloon floor and led up into the saloon where there were excellent seating arrangements and a dining area. At the aft end of the saloon, steps led up into the well-ventilated wheelhouse that had a large chart table and excellent navigation aids like radar, radio direction finder, automatic pilot, VHF set, ship to shore radiotelephone, searchlight and an intercom system to all cabins. More steps led from the saloon down to the guest cabin and the owner's stateroom. Air conditioning and central heating were fitted throughout and we had a flying bridge, which was a luxury for me but perfectly normal for motor yachts that cruised the Mediterranean, except, of course, the appropriately named Passing Fancy. All future steering could be done in the open air. There was a small motorbike provided for transport, which could easily be stowed on deck when we went to sea and an inflatable tender on davits with a stowage area on the aft deck for the outboard motor. Jill and I had grown so close having been with each other virtually 24/7 since we married that we were also pleased that we wouldn't require any additional crew. We didn't need any convincing that we'd made the right decision in leaving the Passing Fancy.

The owner was exceedingly generous. Each time he left us after he'd visited; he gave us a wad of money and instructed us to have a good meal in the very expensive restaurant in the harbour. He would do the same whenever Jill or I had a birthday, and on our wedding anniversary he provided us with a car and sent us to a high-class restaurant in Cannes. For Christmas, we were given gifts from Harrods. In January he flew us to the U.K. to visit the Earl's Court boat show and spend time with our families. He had his Rolls Royce waiting outside his house so that he could take us to a restaurant in London when we arrived.

With the owner and his charming wife aboard, we cruised along the coasts of the French and Italian Rivieras and the west coast of Italy as far as the Island of Elba, stopping in such places as Monaco, Sanremo, Genoa, Portofino, Portovenere and Viareggio among others. In the other direction, we cruised as far as the Iles de Hyeres visiting all ports on the way. Both the owner and his wife were kind and considerate and unlike many yacht owners never at any time made any attempt to exploit us; quite the reverse. He loaned the yacht free of charge to an influential friend who owned a well-known publishing company and told him to tip Jill and me £15 for each day he used the boat, a considerable sum in 1970 when the average weekly wage was £30. We also had two charters; the first was a French politician who chartered the boat for a month. He owned a villa in Sainte Maxime and only used the boat for a few hours on an occasional day so that he could swim in the sea. When we first arrived there, a van came and parked at the end of the gangplank and the politician's valet brought crates of food and wine aboard which we stowed away. After that, we saw nobody for over a week so I became concerned and called the charter agency.

"Oh, don't worry, he'll come to the boat when he's ready," I was told. Two days later his valet arrived.

"We'll want to go out tomorrow for a couple of hours, do you need any more food and drinks?" he asked.

"We still have everything that you brought because nobody has been here," I replied.

"Oh no, that was for you two," he said. How very different to the days of Passing Fancy when we were almost running out of money on the canal trip and were sometimes hungry because we had to economise. During the month that we were there at Sainte Maxime, the boat was hardly used at all and we ate and drank the finest food and wines. On the few days when we went out for a couple of hours, the valet did everything that was required other than seamanship duties. He produced some excellent meals and even waited on Jill and me. When the charter ended, we were given a very large tip and the owner gave us a percentage of the charter fee. Additionally, we were left with a large quantity of expensive wines and all manner of luxury foods.

The second charterer was a wealthy French socialite accompanied by a famous author. They were equally generous and just like the politician, hardly used the boat at all; they merely wanted to be able to swim in the sea occasionally in a quiet bay away from everybody else. We were living the high life and getting paid handsomely into the bargain. The socialite bought Jill an exclusive perfume that she liked so much that she still buys the same one to this day, almost fifty years later.

Too hasty, too soon

Whilst we were in Juan-les-Pins, we had a pleasant surprise when we learned that our old friends Bob and Tina were due to arrive in the same harbour to take command of a motor yacht that was being delivered from Malta. We wasted no time in getting together and swapping yarns about our adventures and invited them aboard our boat for a get together the night before our boss was expected to arrive. We had so much to talk about over a few bottles of wine and the reunion was lively, to say the least. Jill prepared a meal for us and when the dessert arrived, Tina squirted some Chantilly cream on hers, or would have done if the nozzle hadn't been pointing towards Bob instead. His cream covered arm snatched the canister from her and squirted her back and then a Chantilly cream battle took place between the two of them. Much of it found its way into various areas of the saloon which we'd just prepared and cleaned for the owner's arrival, so after they'd staggered down the gangplank in an inebriated state, Jill and I had to clean the inside all over again. We were satisfied that we'd removed all traces of it when we fell into bed exhausted, but at the same time invigorated by the evening's exchanges.

"I can smell cream," the owner said the next day as he came into the saloon.

Juan-les-Pins, situated on the now famous Cap d'Antibes, was a delightful place to be based. When the Duke of Albany, the son of Queen Victoria, came across it in 1880, it was a forest of parasol pines frequented by the locals where they picnicked and collected firewood and pine cones. Parasol pines have been cultivated for at least six thousand years for their edible pine nuts and have now become native to the area, hence the name Juan-les-Pins. There were lovely beaches on both sides and it soon became a popular place for the wealthy and privileged to visit. In the 1920's, it was regularly frequented by American celebrities such as Scott Fitzgerald and Douglas Fairbanks, who initiated the "The Crazy

Years" of boisterous fun and jazz. After WWII, it once again became an exuberant, exciting place of jazz and became known as the European New Orleans, now its sister city. Local and New Orleans jazz bands would parade through the streets creating a carnival atmosphere. Sidney Bechet, the renowned American jazz saxophonist, clarinetist and composer, married there in 1951 after relocating from America to France in 1950. There were orchestras playing in the streets and celebrities came from far and wide for the occasion. One of Sidney Bechet's famous hits was called, "In The Streets of Antibes" and each July there is a jazz festival, "Jazz à Juan", featuring world-renowned jazz artists performing on a stage set in a pine grove next to the seafront. Behind the stage, 50 ceramic tiles containing the hand prints of famous musicians have been set into the pavement.

We had plenty of free time there and made friends with other crews who introduced us to ex-pats and we were invited to parties and other events. Our social life at times became quite hectic. One of our friends, a

nurse who worked at Sunny Banks, the English hospital in Cannes, was a cat lover, as was Jill and when her cat gifted her with a number of kittens, it took Jill a whole two seconds to decide that she wanted to adopt one. I opposed this on the grounds that it would be impractical to have a cat on board and in any case it wasn't our boat and the owner might not like cats. Ninety minutes later after we'd left our friend and returned to Juan-les-Pins, I acquiesced and we turned around and drove all the way back to Cannes to become the honoured guardians

28. Twinkle relaxing.

of an adorable, playful little tortoiseshell and white kitten that we named Twinkle. We took her back to our cabin and placed her gently on the floor. To our surprise, she immediately leapt into the air and flew directly at another identical cat. She smashed into it headfirst and fell to the floor in a crumpled heap, stunned. It was the first time she'd seen a full length mirror. Fortunately, when I told the owner that we had another crew member who was furry, mischievous and useless in all aspects of seamanship, he readily accepted her. She became accustomed to the motion of the boat and from that moment on accompanied us on all of the future cruises.

Winter gave us the opportunity to explore more of the surrounding area and towns in the battered old Simca Aronde that we'd bought for 250 French Francs, approximately £25. In November the rains came, and behind us, in the Alps, it fell as snow. We'd never skied before, so were eager to give it a go. We went to Valberg, a village in the Southern Alps that was first established as a resort in 1936. It is at an altitude of 1700 metres with 90 kilometers of runs. On the first day, Jill negotiated the nursery slope reasonably well, as did I, but after a while, instead of traversing I decided to be more ambitious and pointed my skis straight downhill, taking off at great speed. I should have mastered the art of stopping first. I was out of control and called for everybody in my path to get out of the way as I zoomed downhill, gaining momentum as I went. Crowds had gathered near the bottom of the slope, so to avoid crashing into them I veered off piste to my left and towards the heated, outdoor swimming pool. The snow around the pool was piled higher than the level of the pool itself and at the end of my run I hit the pile of snow and carried on upwards until I took off and flew through the air, smashing into the wire netting fence around the pool. My skis went straight through the mesh and I only stopped when my boots hit the fence and my body kept going until it too slammed to a halt. I grabbed hold of the wire mesh and there I stayed firmly embedded, unable to move. I couldn't get back to ground level because my skis were jammed solid and I couldn't remove them because I was hanging onto the wire fence. At that stage nobody was swimming. All activity had stopped as a crowd collected at the poolside, captivated by the antics of the lunatic hanging on the fence a few feet from the ground. Jill wasn't much help because she was in another of her uncontrollable I laughing fits along with what seemed to me to be the entire population of the ski resort. I called her to come and unclip me. Asking Jill to do anything at all when she was laughing only made her laugh all the more. She did at least make some attempt to reach me, not an easy task for her with the long skis on her feet and other skiers whizzing around her. She stopped and looked at me and tried to stop laughing. I got cross with her. I was stuck in a humiliating position and I so wanted her to release me from my boots before the amused crowd of onlookers grew any larger.

"Come on, hurry up," I shouted. I shouldn't have done that. She almost collapsed with laughter. She struggled on and between intractable bouts of laughter, with me clinging impatiently to the mesh fence she mercifully arrived and helped me unclip my skis so that I could drop to the ground. Once that was accomplished I had to add to my humiliation by trying to extricate the skis from the fence that had gripped them tightly when the mesh had expanded. I had to pull so hard I feared that I would bring the whole lot down on top of me. All this was under the fascinated gaze of the poolside watchers who were probably hoping for the worst.

In time we became accomplished skiers. The resorts were just a ninety-minute drive away so it would have been possible if we chose to, to ski in the morning and spend the afternoon sunbathing on the beach or vice versa but we enjoyed our time in the Alps too much to do that. We were living an idyllic lifestyle marred by just one thing – we were crewing a motor yacht and I wanted to sail; it was the goal I'd set myself after watching the film clip about the Bloodhound. We hadn't sailed much in the cutter, the winds had been either too light or too strong. I longed to sail again and appreciate the joy of switching off the engine and feel the power of the wind propelling us through the water. I didn't have long to wait.

Realising the dream

We were becoming well known to the various yacht agencies and in February 1971, we were recommended by one of them to a Dutchman who was looking for a Captain and wife team to take command of his seventy-foot ketch. He liked what he saw and heard about us, so he offered us the job, which was difficult to refuse. The boat was everything I'd ever dreamed of. For the second time, Jill and I had to seriously consider the effects of us quitting a yacht. We agonised over it deep into the nights and days until we were exhausted discussing the pros and cons.

I was disappointed that we hadn't ventured very far on the Commander. With the exception of the cruise around Elba, we'd mostly spent days anchored either one side or the other of Cap d'Antibes or Cap Ferrat. If the wind was from a westerly direction, we'd anchor in Garoupe Bay on the east of Cap d'Antibes or in the bay close to St-Jean-Cap-Ferrat, which has been a sought after area for royalty and wealthy aristocrats since the 19th century and where some of the most expensive property in the world is found. If the wind was from the east, we'd anchor in the bay close to the famous Hotel Eden Roc on Cap d'Antibes or in the bay of Villefranche, one of the deepest natural harbours in the Mediterranean with depths of up to 95 metres in the outer parts, which extends a mile to the south and forms a 500-metre abyss known as the undersea Canyon of Villefranche. If we weren't in one of those bays then we'd be between the two islands offshore from Cannes. Ultimately we decided that the ketch was too good an opportunity to pass by so we left the Chris Craft and what we didn't

29. The ketch in Menton harbour.

realise then, the best boss we'd ever have.

We were sent to Menton where the ketch was moored for the winter. Menton is situated on the French-Italian border and is known as the Pearl of France. It was there that we spent the latter part of the winter and the spring, in the old harbour. Our time there was a delight; we regularly nipped across the border for the Friday market in Ventimiglia, the first town in Italy and once a week we'd go to see the latest English language film in Monaco and of course, there was the skiing. Menton had once been a part of the Republic of Genoa and was ruled by the Princes of Monaco when it was acquired by Charles Grimaldi in 1346. When the principality of Monaco was reconstituted in 1814, Menton was placed under the protectorate of the King of Sardinia. Forty-six years later, a treaty was signed between the Kingdom of Sardinia and Napoleon III, when the county of Nice was annexed to France as a reward for the assistance France gave to Italy during its war with Austria. Under French rule, Menton became a popular tourist resort and British and Russian aristocrats built luxurious villas and palaces there that still remain. The warm microclimate makes it ideal for the cultivation of tangerines, oranges and especially lemons. A lemon tree is on the town's coat of arms, and every year a citrus festival that was first created in 1928, is held around February - March.

When the summer season began we sailed to the old harbour of Cannes where we remained for the duration of our time aboard this beautiful yacht. The old harbour is located at the opposite end of the Croisette to Port Pierre-Canto and lies at the foot of the old quarter of Le Suquet. For a hundred years, the fisherman of Cannes had demanded a quay to protect the boats from the violent South West wind and Lord Brougham, through his contact with King Louis Philippe, eventually initiated the building of the port in 1838. It was also due to his influence that the promenade in Nice came to be called the Promenade des Anglais. There is now a statue of Lord Brougham on Cannes waterfront in recognition of all that he had achieved for the city. The principle quay is the vibrant Quai Saint-Pierre with its many restaurants, bars and shops and we were fortunate to have a mooring there, close to the market. The son of Queen Victoria, the Prince of Wales and future King Edward VII, was an instigator of the yachting activity in Cannes and in 1898 he laid the first stone for the quay that now bears his name, Jetée Albert Edouard. It was during our time there that we were interviewed by a prospective purchaser of the Bloodhound. As he explained his ideas to us it became obvious to me that he fancied Jill and from time to time he offered her forkfuls of his lobster thermidor. I quietly fumed inside each time he did so and I was particularly annoyed that I wasn't offered any. We were to have been given the job but ultimately we were told that the contract for the purchase was never completed; either that or he changed his mind because of the disapproving looks I gave him each time he gazed salaciously into Jill's eyes; or it could even have been because of my look of resentment each time he gave Jill another bite of his lobster. I managed to resist the urge to just plunge my fork into his plate and help myself.

If a vision of a dream is held for long enough and you have faith in your ability to achieve it and remain positive and unafraid to take a risk, that dream will become a reality. The yacht was magnificent. She was a

traditional vessel built in 1952 at Bangor in Wales by A.M. Dickie and Sons Ltd. She had a hull of African mahogany that had been painted a gleaming white and the decks were of teak planking. She had a long counter stern and a small bowsprit. She had a draught of seven and a half feet and her gross tonnage was 42. The shining, varnished teak wheelhouse, the varnished wooden spars, the shrouds filled with tallow and painted white and the 1270 sq. ft. of red sails were a romantic memory of a bygone age. The centrally heated accommodation was excellent. There were three double cabins with two shower rooms, a good sized saloon and a large galley with two refrigerators.

30. Making the most of the sun.

The sizeable engine room had ample space to walk around the engine. It housed a 1.5 kw Coventy Victor generator and a Glennifer DC six in line cylinder diesel engine with a decompression lever on each cylinder. This meant that the engine couldn't be started from the wheelhouse; I had to go into the engine room to decompress some of the cylinders and start it and stop it from there. This was an unusual arrangement, as on every other boat I had been on all I had to do was turn the ignition key in the wheelhouse.

She had a good sized wheelhouse with a large wooden varnished steering wheel and unlike the motor yachts with their single lever engine controls; she had a gear lever on the port side of the wheel and a throttle lever on the starboard side. There was an additional steering wheel on

321

the aft deck, giving good visibility of the length of the boat and the set of the sails. The traditional design made for harder physical work in sailing her, using blocks and tackles in places. The anchor was the old fisherman type, much heavier and more difficult to handle than the plough or flat anchors whose shanks would simply retract into a hawse pipe, leaving the flukes firmly pulled up against the hull. We had to attach a trip rope to it when we dropped anchor to help us manhandle it and haul it back up. When we weighed anchor, it would be hauled up using the winch until it was almost out of the water, then I would pull on the trip rope that was attached to the anchor crown to swing it horizontal, enabling Jill to hook a block and tackle to its balancing band. It was an awkward process at the best of times. Then we'd haul it up on a davit where it was firmly lashed in position for short voyages. If we set off on a long sea passage, the anchor stock would be folded alongside the shank so that we could bring it aboard and lash it to chocks on the foredeck. It was quite a procedure. Fisherman anchors are not as efficient as some other anchors in sand and mud bottoms and when a strong wind blew, we often had problems with the anchor dragging, especially in the old harbour of Cannes where the Quai St Pierre was exposed to the east. We had a few sleepless nights worrying that we'd drag and hit the quay and on more than one occasion I had to start the engine and turn the propeller at tick over speed to prevent our stern from smashing into the quay when a strong easterly blew.

We didn't have the luxury of an echo sounder but instead had a lead line. These had been used since Greek and Roman times. It consisted of a tapered cylinder shaped lead weight with a hollowed out section at the base, which was filled with tallow that allowed samples of the seabed to be obtained. The lead was attached to a line that was marked at one fathom sections with a mark of leather. When I eased the boat in to an unknown anchorage, Jill would swing the line and throw the lead ahead of us, feeling for the markers as the line flew through her fingers. When I reached the spot where the line was perpendicular, Jill would call out the depth. In the past it was customary to call out "By the mark...," followed by the depth if the marker was at water level or "By the deep..." if the water level was between the markers; for instance, "By the mark two" or

"By the deep two and a half". In the 1850's, Mississippi river men used old fashioned words for numbers and instead of two, they would say twain. It is believed that a Mississippi river pilot named Samuel Langhorne Clemens, who became a famous writer, probably took his pen name from the Mississippi river men when he heard them call out "By the mark twain".

When we first set sail it was magical. With the foresail, mainsail and mizzen hoisted and the engine switched off, it was pure bliss. Twinkle the cat sat in the wheelhouse looking out. We heeled over to port when the red sails filled with wind. The luffs were tight, the foot of both main and mizzen had been hauled tight along the booms and the leeches were fluttering gently. The port backstay was released and the starboard one tightened up. From my position on the aft deck, I gazed up at the red sails and turned the wheel slightly more to port. Jill stood on the starboard deck looking forward, grasping the shrouds to help maintain her balance. I looked at her with tremendous admiration. She had matured from my lovely eighteen-year-old bride in 1967 to a lovely young woman and a seasoned and very capable sailor, as well as a superb cook. I looked at her lithe, bronzed body clad in a bikini and toned to perfection from the demanding physical work. Her long chestnut coloured hair had been bleached by the fierce and relentless sun into a more golden shade. It was tied in a ponytail and flying in the breeze. She looked over her shoulder at me with her big brown eyes registering the thrills of sailing this beautiful yacht. We had been working together for long enough to know how the other one thought. Holding the spokes of the varnished wooden steering wheel, I cast my eyes along the length of the yacht under full sail. It was such a joyful sight and such a joyful feeling. The wind whipped the salt spray onto us, cooling us from the blistering heat of the sun blazing down from a cloudless blue sky. A strong gust of wind blew. We heeled over more to port and beneath my feet, I felt the yacht tremble slightly as she sliced her way effortlessly and silently through the waves. Off to starboard, the blue-hued Esterel Mountains receded into the distance and the old harbour of Cannes was barely visible as we headed out to sea following a course that would take us to another adventure. It had been quite a journey from my unhappy childhood to this euphoric moment. It was Morgan Freeman who said, "If you live a life of make believe, your life isn't worth anything until you do something that does challenge your reality. And to me, sailing the open ocean is a real challenge, because it's life or death."

....

Ever since I'd seen that film clip of the Bloodhound, a sea change had taken place. I'd achieved my goal of racing and with Jill, had sailed from the UK to Majorca and back, navigated the canals of Belgium and the length of France on the inland waterways. We'd cruised the Western Mediterranean and learned to ski and all the while we had been paid a handsome salary. Since the yachts were rarely used for more than eight weeks during the summer, we'd spent several months living aboard with everything paid for. We'd had far more pleasure from the yachts than the owners had and after having had the boat to ourselves throughout the winter, it was inconvenient when they wanted to use it themselves! We'd learned an awful lot, seen some awe-inspiring places and despite some of the hardships we'd suffered, the primary memories we had were of the hilarious times. I had also been surprised to learn that a lot of what I'd been taught at school was biased and untrue. Britain did not have the best of everything and the British were not the best at everything. It was a real shock to discover that the British were not liked by everybody, and even despised by some. The history I'd been taught didn't take into account the history of other countries. I also detested the British class system.

The first four years of our unconventional marriage had been a dream come true for both of us. We'd grown closer together working as a team, relying on and supporting each other as we confronted the challenges that we came up against. Jills big brown eyes had been opened wider than ever since we'd met and made our first voyage together on the cutter and I had accomplished my dream. I could allow myself a little recognition, so what could be better than to use the words of my instructor at navigation school when he shook my hand after I'd passed my exams. "Congratulations Captain."

If you have five minutes, you'd make me very happy if you could write a short Amazon review. Reviews are a huge help to authors, and I am no exception!

Thank you.

SO, WHAT HAPPENED NEXT?

I've been asked that many times, and all will be revealed in the next book, 'MOVING ON'.

New boats, new places and new adventures.

Available on Amazon.

Type Moving On Anthony Edwards (not case sensitive)
into 'Books' on Amazon's search bar

Meanwhile, here is a short extract from the new book. We are cruising off the west coast of Italy, bound for the island of Ponza, but the weather is deteriorating:

"There's a small island called Ventotene not far away, it's a prison island, we can go there if you want'" I said.

"Go there, go there, we've had enough," he said. There was a great sigh of relief from everybody and they suddenly found it possible to smile, even get excited at the prospect of some peace and quiet and for the motion to stop.

Ventotene is the remains of an ancient volcano. It is just 3 kilometres long, a mere 800 metres wide and it's territory includes the small ancillary island of Santo Stefano, two kilometres to the east. The other islands are Palmarola, Zannoni, Gazi and Ponza, which is the largest and from which they get the their collective name, the Pontine Islands, lying off the west coast of Italy. Ventotene was uninhabited for centuries due to its susceptability to attacks. It was used as a prison island by the Romans, where the unfortunate souls that were sent there, mostly starved to death. A prison camp had also been created on the nearby island of Santo Stefano by the French, and it was later rebuilt by the leader of the Italian Fascist Party, Benito Mussolini. It was there that a former Italian communist, Altiero Spinelli, was incarcerated after having been sentenced to 16 years in prison in 1927. Whilst there, he wrote the "Ventotene Manifesto," promoting the idea of a federal Europe after the war. In it, he denounces the responsibility of nation states for the horrors of war and calls for the creation of a federal Europe, the guarantor of lasting peace. He became a European Commissioner between 1970 and 1976 and a Member of the European Parliament between 1976 and 1986, the year of his death. He is buried on Ventotene and in August 2016, the Italian Prime Minister Matteo Renzi, together with German Chancellor Angela Merkel and French President François Hollande, laid a wreath at his tomb. They had met there to discuss European Union policy after the Brexit vote.

Despite the foul weather, the small island looked appealing to our passengers as it came into view in the grey mist but it was to yield unpleasant memories.

"There's a tiny port that the Romans built, we should be able to get in there and get some protection," I said. Well, technically it wasn't the Romans who did the building, they'd used slaves to dig it out of the Tufa rock.

"I don't care who built it, I'm just glad they put it there," he replied.

As we approached the entrance, I realised that it wasn't going to be easy. I saw the gap in the rock, but the port itself was completely hidden. The heavy sea and the strong wind on our stern made it difficult to hold the course steady and I began to question my judgement in continuing through the very narrow passage. The waves were picking us up, raising us to the crests, which we surfed along for a while before we plummeted down, veering sideways as the next wave arrived. There was very little room to manoeuvre a boat of our size when we entered the narrow cutting.

"Turn around, let's get out of here!" the owner said with fear in his voice.

"It's too late, I can't, we're committed now," I told him. We were heading straight for the rocks at the end of the small, cutting – and then, to starboard, I saw the passageway to the small port. It was at a right angle to where we were headed – I would never have made it simply by swinging the wheel hard to starboard, which I did anyway - I pulled the starboard single lever control to maximum revolutions astern and pushed the port one to maximum ahead."

ABOUT THE AUTHOR

Anthony Edwards was born in Gravesend, but since 1975 has lived mostly in the South of France. In 1980 He bought a ruin on three acres of land near a Provençal hill village. Together with his wife he renovated it and turned it into a self-sufficient organic smallholding. He went on to study complementary medicine and established a successful practice as a Kinesiologist, Hypnotist and Psychotherapist, and has made guest appearances on several radio programs in France and the U.K. He later moved to his present house, where he now lives with his wife and thoroughly spoilt, self-opinionated cat.

Printed in Great Britain
by Amazon

51708773R00200